Daniel Steele

Half-Hours with St. Paul, and Other Bible Readings

Daniel Steele

Half-Hours with St. Paul, and Other Bible Readings

ISBN/EAN: 9783337171834

Printed in Europe, USA, Canada, Australia, Japan

Cover: Foto ©Lupo / pixelio.de

More available books at **www.hansebooks.com**

HALF-HOURS WITH ST. PAUL

AND

OTHER BIBLE READINGS

DANIEL STEELE, S.T.D.

RECENT PROFESSOR OF NEW TESTAMENT GREEK IN BOSTON UNIVERSITY.
AUTHOR OF "LOVE ENTHRONED," "MILE-STONE PAPERS," "ANTINOMIANISM REVIVED," "COMMENTARIES ON LEVITICUS, NUMBERS, AND JOSHUA," AND CO-AUTHOR OF "PEOPLE'S NEW TESTAMENT COMMENTARY," AND REVISER OF "BINNEY'S THEOLOGICAL COMPEND IMPROVED."

BOSTON
THE CHRISTIAN WITNESS COMPANY
1895

Dedicatory

To My Two Sons in the Ministry of the Gospel,
To My Pupils in Three Universities,
To My People in Fifteen Pastorates,
AND
To All Saints who Hunger After Righteousness,

THIS VOLUME,

In a Consciousness of Its Defects,
Is Prayerfully Inscribed,
AS A TOKEN
OF RESPECT AND IMPERISHABLE LOVE.

PREFACE.

In our studies in the New Testament, we have found two grounds for special thanksgiving.

The first is that this precious volume is not limited to the four Gospels. It is true that these contain in germ form every truth of Christianity. But it is also true that they do not comprise, except in promise, any account of the marvellous completion of the system in the gift of the Paraclete, and that enlargement of privilege, deepening of experience, and perfection of spiritual life, which accompanied that crowning endowment of believers in Jesus Christ as the revelation of God. If there had been after his ascension no inspired and accredited record of the communication of God in the Holy Spirit, and of doctrines authoritatively unfolded and applied to human needs, the glorious gospel would have gone forth on its conquering career weighted with disabilities fatal to its success. It would have been like the angel of the Apocalypse trying to fly in the midst of heaven with clipped wings. But the Head of the church, in giving Christianity a good start, extended its inspired record beyond the earthly life of its Divine Founder. In fact, the pentecostal dispensation occupies more than half of the New Testament. A second topic of gratitude is found in the capacity and character of the man providentially called to lift the gospel out of the entanglements of Judaism, to cut the umbilical cord of the infant evangel, and send it forth on its universal mission.

Paul, called to be an apostle of Jesus Christ, was not only qualified to state the gospel clearly and defend it heroically, but to exemplify perfectly the full extent of its saving power. More than this, he was not, through a false modesty, ashamed to disclose and record his own interior experiences; first of conscious child-innocence (Rom. vii. 9), then of an irksome and worthless legalism (Rom. vii. 10-25), then of justification (Tim. i. 13), then the witness of the Spirit (Rom. viii. 15), followed by the inward revelation of Christ, — spiritual crucifixion and holy living. (Gal. i. 16; ii. 20; 1 Thess. ii. 10.)

After the four Gospels, two-thirds of the residue of the New Testament are made up of the history of St. Paul's ministry and his epistles, including the letter to the Hebrews. More than a third of the entire volume relates to the Apostle to the Gentiles. This is a sufficient reason for ranking next to the life of Christ in the education of the Christian minister, the "Portrait of St. Paul," especially that of which John Fletcher is the limner. I take this opportunity to acknowledge publicly that this book — now in the course of study for local preachers in the Methodist Episcopal Church — has had a large place among the influences which have moulded my religious character. A sense of indebtedness to this great apostle has prompted me to prepare this series of Bible Readings, founded so largely on his epistles, "wherein are some things hard to be understood, which the ignorant and the unsteadfast wrest, as they do also the other Scriptures, unto their own destruction." I have endeavored to expose this wresting and perversion of the truth in the interest of those who deny the possibility of holiness in this life. It is one of my aims in this book to present in popular form those results of modern scholarship which clear away misinterpretations alleged to lie against that perfection of the believer which he is commanded to seek and to obtain in the present life.

We shall not finish our expression of special thanksgiving, till we have mentioned the longevity of the beloved apostle, the latest surviving eye-witness of the incarnate Son of God, and to lift up his voice against errors which were corrupting the doctrines and ethics of the gospel of purity.

It is our purpose to rescue a text in John's first epistle from the strange work to which it has been put, a work repugnant to John's character, and contradictory to the tenor of his teaching, — the doctrine that sin as a conscious inward experience must be constantly confessed.

Finally, we purpose to show, from both the Old Testament and the New, that not a word has been inspired by the Holy Spirit which excuses or extenuates sin, and that the salvation which God has provided in the mediation of his Son, and the gift of his Spirit, reaches man's deepest need, delivering the persevering believer from the guilt of sin, the love of sin, and the pollution of sin.

CONTENTS.

CHAPTER		PAGE
I.	Did St. Paul profess Holiness or Sin?	1
II.	St. Paul's Use of Terms implying His Entire Sanctification	6
III.	St. Paul's First Prayer the Keynote of His Life	12
IV.	St. Paul's Prayer for the Fulness of God	17
V.	St. Paul a Pendulum between Praise and Prayer	26
VI.	St. Paul's Prayer and God's Fatherhood	31
VII.	For what did St. Paul ask Prayers for Himself?	36
VIII.	St. Paul, the Model Christian	41
IX.	St. Paul's Love to His Enemies Perfect in Kind	46
X.	St. Paul crucified with Christ	52
XI.	St. Paul's Perfect Faith	57
XII.	Perverted Pauline Texts quoted against Holiness	63
XIII.	Stumbling-Blocks removed	70
XIV.	St. Paul's Classification of the Corinthian Church in Two Classes	77
XV.	Prayers for the Sanctification of Believers	82
XVI.	St. Paul invents Stronger Words for Complete Deliverance from Sin	87
XVII.	St. Paul's New Words for Superabounding Grace	93
XVIII.	St. Paul's New Phrases, — Without Sin, Without Stumbling, Without Spot, Without Offence	99
XIX.	St. Paul's "Election" is unto Sanctification	105
XX.	St. Paul magnifies the Meaning of Perfection	111

CONTENTS.

CHAPTER		PAGE
XXI.	St. Paul's Doctrine of the Anointing	118
XXII.	St. Paul arranges a Bouquet of Christian Graces,	123
XXIII.	St. Paul shows the Certainty of Spiritual Knowledge	128
XXIV.	Some of the Different Meanings of the Word "Flesh"	146
XXV.	Old Testament Stumbling-Blocks removed	151
XXVI.	Enlargement of Heart	156
XXVII.	Spiritual Circumcision	160
XXVIII.	The "Overcometh" in the Revelation	168
XXIX.	Why did Moses veil His Face?	176
XXX.	An Expository Sermon	180
XXXI.	Spiritual Darkness	192
XXXII.	Conscript Christians	197
XXXIII.	Semi-Spiritual Christians	202
XXXIV.	The Ten Spies — An Evil Report	209
XXXV.	Faith Healing	243
XXXVI.	St. John interpreted and vindicated	255
XXXVII.	Holiness and Humanity	271
XXXVIII.	The Qualities of a Successful Ministry	278
XXXIX.	The Full Assurance of Faith	307

PROLOGUE.

THE sub-title of this book is a sufficient notification that it is not restricted to St. Paul's life and epistles. Moreover, it should be noted that this volume is in no sense an exhaustive treatise on the many-sided character of the apostle to the Gentiles. The incidents in his remarkable life, the historic setting and purpose of his epistles, have been omitted. Our attention has been directed to only one aspect of his character, — his personal relation to evangelical perfection, and his instructions respecting holiness of heart and life. In clearing away erroneous interpretations, and in vindicating Paul's right to the title of saint in its highest sense, a holy man without consciousness of sin, we have necessarily been polemical and iterative. The frequency with which we have, in a few instances, reverted to the same topic, has a Pauline precedent in the so-called "joyful epistle" to the Philippians, where the theme of joy occurs nine times, and occasionally with double repetition as "the result of the apostle's special love for his readers." — MEYER. We may add that this repetition of vital themes has also a sufficient Pauline apology : " Finally, my brethren, rejoice in the Lord." "To write the same things to you, to me indeed is not grievous, but for you it is safe."

The sermons not included in the title will be found to be supportive of the subject of the Bible Readings.

The Reading on Faith Healing is designed to counteract a mischievous error into which some excellent Christians are falling.

D. S.

MILTON, MASS., Dec. 1, 1894.

HALF-HOURS WITH ST. PAUL.

I.

DID ST. PAUL PROFESS HOLINESS OR SIN?

THE importance of a correct answer to this question cannot be overestimated. St. Paul was chosen by our Lord Jesus, the sole author of the New Testament, to unfold in doctrinal form, after the gift of the Paraclete, those seed truths which Christ sowed in person.

Those facts in the future work of the Holy Comforter and Sanctifier which could not have been intelligibly described before the effusion of the Spirit, were reserved to be taught by our ascended and glorified Teacher, chiefly through the Apostle to the Gentiles. If he was not an example and witness of perfect deliverance from indwelling sin, there is little encouragement for an ordinary believer to hope for such a deliverance in this life. While it is true that Jesus Christ in the Gospels teaches perfect holiness as a duty, the argument to prove that it was held up as an unattainable ideal would be immensely strengthened if his own apostles failed to actualize that ideal through the incoming and abiding of the Holy Spirit as the Sanctifier.

To prove that St. Paul was a possessor and professor of perfected holiness, we must scrutinize every word of his Epistles, the great seed-bed of Christian theology. Then we must candidly weigh every utterance in seeming contradiction to this high profession. We must study his prayers for others, and ascertain whether entire sanctification by the Spirit is not the burden of those petitions. We must then examine his requests for the prayers of the different churches in his own behalf, to ascertain whether he ever implies his own spiritual imperfection, or the existence of inbred sin in his own heart.

The scope of the question in this series of Bible Readings is so broad that it will require us to sweep over nearly one-half of the New Testament.

Another preliminary to our Biblical discussion of this question we note in the fact, that Paul's professions of holiness are, in their form, modelled after those of his Lord and Master. There are two ways of professing holiness — the wise and the proper way, and the ostentatious and distasteful way. Christ did not say in a bold and offensive style, "I am perfectly holy." He might with truth have used these words; but he would have been needlessly beclouding his own humility, and laying stumbling-blocks in the way of his hearers. At this point some modern advocates of Christian perfection are at fault. In set phrase they profess more holiness in half an hour than Jesus Christ did in all his life. His profession was by a great variety of phrases, and almost always by implication: "Which of you convicteth me of sin?" "I always do those things that are pleasing to my Father." "He that seeketh the glory of him that sent him, the same is true, and no unrighteousness is in him. For the prince of this world cometh, and hath nothing in me. I and my Father are one." These are samples of Christ's implied declaration of his sinlessness. Many expressions of Paul imply the complete extinction of sin as a principle in him. One of his modes of confessing indirectly perfect salvation through Christ, was to profess the possession of some one grace of Christian perfection. For these graces grow in clusters on one stem. The declared presence of one is proof of the presence of all. Olshausen, in his note on *Matt. v.* 48, "Be ye therefore perfect," etc., says, "For the observance of one of these commandments in the Sermon on the Mount, nothing short of perfection is sufficient. Neither pure love nor mercy can be conceived alone in the human soul without the other qualities involved in perfection." What are the graces which always imply pure love? Let John Fletcher answer: "Christian perfection is a spiritual constellation made up of these gracious stars, — perfect repentance, perfect faith, perfect humility, perfect meekness, perfect self-denial, perfect resignation, perfect hope, perfect charity for our visible enemies as well as for our earthly relations, and, above all, perfect love for our invisible God, through the explicit knowledge of our Mediator, Jesus Christ; and as this last star, love, is always accompanied by all the others, as Jupiter is by his satellites, we frequently use, as St. John, the phrase perfect love instead of the word perfection; understanding by it the pure love of God shed abroad in the hearts of established believers by the Holy Ghost."

Another observation is that St. Paul, in numerous instances in detailing his own experience, modestly uses the plural "we," instead of the singular "I." He frequently begins with the plural, but in the intensity of his feeling changes to the singular; for the emotions when stirred to their depths always say "I," as in all lyric poetry. Father E. T. Taylor used to say that he could tell a true Methodist as soon as he opened his mouth; for he always says, "I feel." Says Alford, "The attributes which especially characterize the originality of Paul as an author are *power*, *fulness*, and *warmth*." These beget informality of expression, rhetorical and grammatical inaccuracy, and an appearance of egotism. Every one to whom Jesus Christ fulfils his promise, "I will manifest myself unto him," has an individuality of experience which, springing from a peculiar sense of proprietorship in him, justifies the use of the first person singular. He is mine. Mary Magdalene had so appropriated Christ that she thought she owned him. "They have taken away my Lord." "Tell me where thou hast laid him, and I will take him away." Appropriating faith underscores the "me" and "my" in the Bible. Hence it must always appear to unbelieving reason both mystic and egotistic. But Paul always puts Christ first, not self, except when self is nailed to the cross. Then "I" stands first: "I have been crucified with Christ; and it is no longer I that live." — (*Gal. ii.* 20, *R. V. margin.*)

Tholuck calls attention to the frequency and force of Paul's self-witness, as in *Acts xx.* 19, 20, "Serving the Lord with all (possible — MEYER) humility and with many tears and temptations, which befell me by the lying in wait of the Jews: and I kept back nothing that was profitable for you." Here are several grapes which are found only in the cluster of Christian perfection, notably, "all possible humility," and perfect freedom from the fear of man, which fear prompts the prophecy of smooth things, rather than unpalatable and unpopular, yet profitable truths.

Paul's fearlessness is a token of perfect love, that love which casts out all fear that hath torment (1 *John* iv. 18). These two graces will be more extendedly discussed farther on in this series of Pauline Readings.

II.

ST. PAUL'S USE OF TERMS IMPLYING HIS ENTIRE SANCTIFICATION.

St. Paul uses many figurative expressions which manifestly imply entire sanctification. One of these is found in *Rom. vi.* 2, *R. V.*, "We who died to sin, how shall we any longer live therein." We note, in the first place, that the Pauline use of sin in the singular number designates rather a state than an act, or as Cremer says, "Sin is not merely the quality of an action, but a principle, manifesting itself in the conduct of the subject." Now, what is implied in dying or being dead to anything? "To become indifferent, to cease to be subject," says Webster, "as to die to pleasure or to sin." Chrysostom's note on this point is as truthful as it is terse, "To remain motionless as a corpse." To the same intent, yet more extended, is Alford's annotation, "Became as separate from and as apathetic towards sin as the dead corpse is separate from and apathetic towards the functions and stir of life." There can be no higher kind of sanctification on the earth. "The dying to sin," says Meyer, "is the abandonment of all life communion with it, experienced in himself by the convert. This moral change, which has taken place in him, has put an end to the determining influence of sin over him; in relation to it *he has ceased to be still in life.* This change," says Meyer "took place by baptism." To this we assent, if by baptism is meant not the bare symbol, but the thing signified thereby, the inward cleansing by the fulness of the Holy Ghost.

There has been a vain attempt to weaken Paul's declaration that he was dead to sin, by quoting his subsequent exhortation, " Reckon ye also yourselves to be dead unto sin;" as if this implied that sin was still living and active, but that we must, as the children say, " play that it is dead." This is paralleled by a new style of curing disease, "think that the leprosy is dead, and it will no longer disfigure your body." But genuine cures of leprosy under this treatment are as rare as cures of leprous souls by reckoning them freed from the terrible disease of sin before the Holy Spirit has entirely sanctified them.

What Paul means by reckoning ourselves dead to sin, is to treat ourselves, after the Holy Spirit has cleansed us from all sin by slaying the carnal nature, as we treat all dead persons; make no provision for them, give them no food, nor house-room in our homes, exclude them from our society as offensive, cutting them off forever from all bodily communion. We are to be really dead to sin, and to live and act accordingly. Colonel Hadley of New York City, who was converted in the evening of the day following that in which he had swallowed sixty-three dram-shop drinks, was so mightily converted that he became in a moment dead to alcohol, his burning appetite being instantaneously removed. Ever since July 26, 1886, he has reckoned himself dead to the bottle, by keeping away from the saloon and by frequenting the house of prayer; by giving diligent heed to make his own and others election to eternal life sure, instead of, as before his conversion, canvassing the ten thousand groggeries of the American metropolis for the election of some knavish politician to a place where he can plunder the public treasury.

God never commands us to reckon a falsehood as truth. If we are required to reckon ourselves dead unto sin, it is because such a death is a fact in our past history. Moreover, in the same verse we are exhorted to reckon ourselves alive unto God, not when we are dead in trespasses and sins, but when we have been made alive by the Holy Ghost, the Lord and giver of life. We are to reckon a reality in both clauses of the injunction,—death unto sin, and life unto God. In *Gal. ii.* 19, St. Paul tells how this death and life are related to the law of God, "For I through the law died unto the law, that I might live unto God."

In what sense did Paul die unto the law, so that he could aver that he was not under the law? In the interest of clear thought, practical ethics, and sound theology we answer, that every evangelical believer died to the law, (1) as the ground of his acceptance with God. He ceased to rely on his conformity to the law through all his past history, confessed himself guilty, and entered a new plea in the court of divine justice, "Jesus Christ the Son of God died for me—I receive him as both my Saviour and Lord, and through his mediation I beg for pardon." Paul was not under the law, and was dead to the law as the ground of justification for past sins. (2) Paul was dead to the law as a motive impelling to service. Love to the Lawgiver shed abroad in his heart had taken the place of fear of the penalty of the law. In this change there is nothing strange or revolutionary, since the interior essence of the divine law is love.

(3) Paul died to the law as the instrument of sanctification. He had discovered that it could not cleanse the impurity which it revealed within. He had found in the gospel a personal purifier, procured through the atonement, the Holy Ghost sent down from heaven in pentecostal power. He can do what neither "the blood of goats and calves," nor the most scrupulous conformity to the moral law, can do for a sin-stained soul.

(4) But Paul was not antinomian; he did not "make void the moral law through faith, but rather he established the law; for he was not dead to the law as THE RULE OF LIFE.

The iron rails can communicate no power to impel the train; but they are indispensable to direct whatever force may be applied, whether gravity, steam, or electricity. The absence of the rails at any given point of the track is ruin. Thus it is with the law of God. It has no power to impel or to attract the soul Godward; but its perpetual office is to guide the chariot-wheels of the divine love, impelling souls upward along the heavenly way.

But Paul was not merely dead to sin constructively, as some teach, sin being under the sentence of death, yet really alive. He was really dead, because he was crucified. The cross was a certain, if not a summary, way of inflicting death. (*Gal. ii.* 20, *R. V., Am. Com-*

mittee), " I have been crucified with Christ, and it is no longer I that live." This is a distinct confession of the extinction of the sin principle in him. It is not the old man tortured on the cross through scores of years, as some teach, till physical death ends the wretched life. More explicitly is this announced in *Rom. vi.* 6, " Knowing this, that our old man is crucified with him, that the body of sin might be destroyed." The Greek for destroy is never used by Paul in the sense of rendering inactive, as those assert who insist that the root of sin is not killed till it is plucked up by old Mortality himself. Says Cremer, who had no doctrinal partiality to warp his definition, " Elsewhere it signifies a putting out of activity, out of power, or effect; but with St. Paul it is *to annihilate, to put an end to, to bring to naught.*" If any expression could be stronger than this, it is found in the reciprocal crucifixion found in *Gal. vi.* 14, " By whom the world is crucified unto me, and I unto the world." "This," says Bishop Ellicott, "is a forcible mode of expressing the utter cessation of all communion between the apostle and the world." Paul and the world, the sum total of all that is opposed to the spiritual reign of Christ, regard each other as dead. There is a reciprocal crucifixion. The crucified world has no power to awaken crucified cupidity. Hence no surprise is awakened by Paul's declaration that he is made free from the law of (the uniform tendency to) sin and (spiritual) death (*Rom. viii.* 2). The proclivity toward sin is not only removed, but an upward gravitation is substituted. As the cork set free at the bottom of the sea rapidly rises to the surface, so the soul that is "risen with Christ seeks those things which are above [the higher life], where Christ sitteth on the right hand of God." — *Col. iii.* 1. This is the way men dead to sin act; for Paul proceeds to say, "For ye are dead, and your life is hid with Christ in God."

III.

ST. PAUL'S FIRST PRAYER THE KEYNOTE OF HIS LIFE.

STAND near the closet door ajar of this eminent saint, and you will learn the secret of that heroic courage, that inexhaustible patience, and that wonderful career of toil, peril, and self-sacrifice, which have made him the greatest human factor in the establishment of the Christian Church.

> "When one that holds communion with the skies
> Has filled his urn where these pure waters rise,
> And once more mingles with us meaner things,
> It is as though an angel shook his wings;
> Celestial fragrance fills the circuit wide,
> That tells us whence these odors are supplied."

It is a means of grace to study the prayers of those who — to use the phrase of Father Taylor — "were on speaking terms with God." We imbibe their spirit. We begin to climb this ladder from the top of which they have stepped to a throne alongside the archangels.

If the epistles of Paul are glorious, the prayers which abound in them are more glorious. All these recorded spiritual inspirations are pervaded by praises. They begin and end with thanksgivings. Praise paves the way for prayer, and prayer casts up a highway for praise. In some churches they have praise-meetings on one day and prayer-meetings on another. Better mix them as did Paul. Praise will light up sombre prayer, and prayer will tone down jubilant praise.

In all of Paul's prayers, there is no impracticable petition. He did not chase after unattainable ideals. When he prayed for the entire sanctification and perfection of the regenerate, he asked for blessings which believers might realize, through the power of the Holy Ghost, long before they reached their dying hour.

Paul's first recorded prayer, *Acts xxii.* 10, "What shall I do, Lord?" is the keynote of his whole Christian life — activity and not a selfish quietism. It indicates that he did not have that conception of the new birth in which the sinner is passive, or rather, passive in fulfilling its conditions. That form of piety in which the Christian devotes himself exclusively to coddling himself, to constant morbid introspections of frames and feelings, will not be found in the writings of St. Paul. We are not so much inclined to this error as were many mediæval Christians, who were taught that a soul which desires supreme good must remove, not only all sensual pleasures, but also all material things, silence every impulse of its mind and will, and be concentrated and absorbed in God; and that the monastery was most favorable for this result. Self-surrender to God is requisite to "the stature of the fulness of Christ;" but it must always be accompanied by perfect self-sacrifice for the salvation of our fellow-men. Love must be made perfect in both its Godward and manward aspects. It is a good omen when people are converted with the idea that salvation means vigorous, ceaseless work for others, and joining the church is enlisting in an army in front of an appalling rebellion.

It has not pleased the Holy Spirit to record the prayers of Saul during his three days of blindness in Damascus, alluded to in *Acts ix.* 11, " Behold, he prayeth." They were doubtless entreaties for forgiveness.

That he found pardon, and the joy that attends it, may be seen by reading *Rom. xv.* 13 : " Now the God of hope fill you with all joy and peace in believing, that ye may abound in hope, through the power of the Holy Ghost." It occurred to Paul to use the phrase " God of hope," because the word " hope " (*R. V.*) as the privilege of the Gentiles, had just been written at the end of verse 12. God is thus called because he is the object of all hope. He who is without God is without hope in the world. His future is a dark cloud in which no rainbow is set. The prayer is for fulness of joy and peace through believing. There are no happy doubters, no jubilant unbelievers. The highest joy grows on the topmost bough of faith. The seed of joylessness is unbelief.

Paul speaks of the " joy of faith " (*Phil. i.* 25) as its natural and necessary sequent. Hence, the antidote for a lack of joy, " that fruit of the Spirit," is " a little more faith in Jesus," in the words of that seraph in ebony, Amanda Smith. Faith is the only doorway for God to enter the soul, leading the blessed procession of beatitudes, — love, joy, and peace. How many try to admit them through the door of reason and fail. While his truth enters in through this door, he himself can enter only through the door of faith. He is too large for our logic, but not for our faith. So there is a good chance to experience "unspeakable joy" in the case of the countless multitudes who know nothing of the structure of a syllogism. "All joy and peace in believing" is for the ploughboy just spelling out the meaning of his New Testament, and for his sable mother who cannot even read at all, slavery having robbed her of the alphabet; for the Hindu peasant toiling for seven cents a day; and for the naked Congo African crushed by centuries of the darkest paganism. All they need to do is to hear the joyful sound of Jesus' name and believe. All the rest will follow in due season, — the spelling-book, the printing-press, clothing, the steam-engine, the post-office, the church, the college, and the hospital. Paul cannot speak of the blessedness of salvation by faith without the cumulation of phrases. The believer is to be filled with all joy and peace, and then to abound or overflow in hope, capping the climax with the introduction of the almighty power of the Holy Ghost as pledged to secure these blissful results of "believing."

"Now I pray God that ye do no evil." — (2 *Cor. xiii.* 7-9.)

Paul does not pray for things impracticable and impossible. Hence, against the dictum of the Westminster Catechism, he expects this prayer to be answered, "that ye do no evil." The pardoned are saved from sinning. In verse 9 he goes a step farther: This also we pray for, even your perfecting." (*R. V.*) What does the much debated word "perfecting" mean in this text? "Your complete furnishing, perfection in Christian morality." — MEYER. "Complete symmetry of Christian character." — WHEDON. "Perfection generally in all good things." — ALFORD. "In the faith that worketh by love." — WESLEY.

Either the prayer is for the merely ideal and unattainable, and is thus an aggravation of the deepest spiritual needs of the Corinthians, or it was possible for divine grace, through their faith, to achieve this desirable result in their characters.

IV.

ST. PAUL'S PRAYER FOR THE FULNESS OF GOD.

NOWHERE in the Scripture is the wonderfully elevating effect of the spirit of inspiration more evident than in the Epistle to the Ephesians. The writer is manifestly lifted above his natural plane of thought to height above height, making this Epistle by far the most difficult of all the writings of the Apostle to the Gentiles. Hence, it is a sealed book to the unspiritual man, however high his mere power of reason. He who with spirit-anointed vision pierces to the foundation of this Epistle will find that it rests upon a threefold basis — (1) *the will of the Father* as the origin of the church; (2) *the atonement of the Son* as the ground of our adoption; and (3) *life in the Holy Spirit* as the scope and end of the gospel.

The prayer in the third chapter of this Epistle relates to the last of these foundation-stones. It presupposes repentance, justification, regeneration, and entire sanctification. Hence it is a model prayer for those in whom sin has been destroyed. The threefold aim of such a prayer is, (1) the strengthening of the inner man for a clearer intellectual knowledge of Christ, the revelation of God; (2) the abiding of the Spirit, the communication of God; and (3) the fulness of divine glory, or all the fulness of God.

Chap. iii. 14-21. The cause for which he bows his knees is a repetition of the first verse. Hence it refers to the last words of chapter ii., the true temple of the Father, built in the Son, inhabited by the Spirit. Paul prays that each believer, and the aggregate of all the believers in Ephesus, may become such a holy temple. The first petition is that they might be strengthened with might by his Spirit in the inner man. The vessel is too weak and too small to contain all that God desires to pour into it. It must be enlarged and strengthened. The Spirit is the agent for this work. The measure is according to the riches of his glory. A king gives like a king, a God works like a God. He wants to do his most glorious work in every believing soul. This he accomplishes when the human conditions are fulfilled. The chief condition is faith as expressed in verse 17.

"That Christ may take up his abode in your hearts." This rendering gives the force of the aorist tense, "that Christ may take up his lasting abode."—ALFORD and ELLICOTT. This implies, not a destitution of the Spirit who represents Christ, but rather that the soul has not yet become his permanent abode.

Meyer says that opposed to this taking up of the lasting abode of Christ, is a transient reception of the Holy Spirit, as in *Gal. iii.* 3, "Having begun in the Spirit, are ye now made perfect by the flesh?" This is a searching question which many modern believers of the Galatian type would do well seriously to ponder. Their eager pursuit of worldly pleasures, their dallying with temptation, their inquiry, What harm in the dance, the drama, and the card-party?—

all too painfully prove that the Holy Comforter, the artesian well of water, is not in them springing up into everlasting life. They could not answer as did Ignatius when, on his trial, he was asked by the emperor, "What is the meaning of your name?"—"Theophorus" (God-bearer)—he promptly replied, "he who has Christ in his breast." Oh that there were more of these conscious Christophers bearing Christ about in the street, the car, the shop, the field, and the mart!

Men and women of this sort are never at a discount in God's reckoning. They are the salt of the earth, —yea, of the church too.

It is instructive to note that Christ dwells only in the vital centre of our being, not in the tongue, which would produce only a mouth religion, not in the hand, which would make a lifeless routine of works, but in the heart, which rules the tongue, the hands, and the feet, making them the instruments of a glad and willing service. He never takes up his abode in the brain alone; but it is his purpose, after taking possession of the heart, to extend his conquest to the head. To reverse this order would reduce Christianity to a theory instead of a joyful experience. Alas, too many have proved the truth of this declaration. A Christ flitting through the intellect now and then, gives no such repose of soul as the Christ who becomes a permanent resident of the heart, year after year, and decade after decade. The beauty of this is, that he who carries him through life will have his presence in death. A good lady in a love-feast once said, "I mean to carry heaven with me through life, then I shall be sure of it at the end of my journey."

The door through which Christ comes in and takes up his abode in the heart is faith. Faith widens the soul so that more and more can be grasped. It has been said that "more depends upon taking in faith than upon giving and doing in love. For the more we take of the fulness of God, the more we can give." Faith is the inner man's vision, his reason, and his light. Such faith is possible when the heart is purged of sin. Then the eye is purged of film. The pure in heart see God. Only they have a spiritual perception which makes him real.

"Ye having been rooted and grounded in love," rooted like a tree and grounded like a building. Those for whom Paul prays are to become established in love through the strengthening of their inner man by means of the Spirit, and through Christ's taking up his permanent abode in their hearts. Being established in love, they are able to have some realization of the greatness of the love of Christ. Love has eyes for the perception of spiritual realities. In Christianity he that loveth not knoweth not. The reverse is true in respect to things of this world. They must be known before they can be loved.

"In order that ye may be fully able [ALFORD] to apprehend [R. V.] with all saints." The tense of the verb "apprehend," Ellicott suggests, implies the singleness of the act, as if through the instantaneous perfecting of love, there comes a sudden revelation of God to the soul, in the face of his adorable Son revealed by the Holy Spirit.

This is the highest and most precious knowledge, for the excellency of which Paul counts all things to be loss, prefacing his declaration with a "yea, verily," as if he thought he had made a splendid bargain. This knowledge, which is so personal that Paul seems in the words, "My Lord," to be its exclusive possessor, he now desires only as the common property of "all saints," because he has found out that Christ can give himself entire and undivided to every perfect believer. Blessed paradox! I do not wonder that an old saint in Wales declared that "Jesus Christ was a Welshman, because he always speaks Welsh to me."

When he prays that the believers in Ephesus may be fully able to apprehend (*R. V.*) with all saints, he hints at the idea of the equal privilege of all, ascribing to the humblest Christian the highest and most precious knowledge (*Phil. iii.* 8.). Thus men at the top of their transfigured natures stand on a level in the democracy of saintship, rather of kingship; for "He made us to be a kingdom, to be priests unto his God and Father." — (*Rev. i.* 6, *R. V.*) The distinguishing privilege of the priest is access to God.

The four dimensions borrowed from the relations of space — though there are properly but three — are intended to express that comprehensive knowledge of all essential truths which St. John includes in the anointing of the Spirit, which teaches all things necessary to life and godliness. "And to know the knowledge-surpassing love of Christ." Here we have acutely conjoined contraries purposely devised by the great apostle to show the immense superiority of heart knowledge to head knowledge. Indeed, mental science has no place for the former in its enumeration of man's cognitive faculties. It recognizes only the intellect.

This is correct so far as the unregenerate man is concerned, for "spiritual things are spiritually discerned." The love of Christ is a spiritual thing. By these words we do not understand our love to Christ, but a vivid realization of his boundless love to us who evangelically believe.

Paul reaches the climax when he prays, "That ye may be filled unto all the fulness of God." (*R. V.*)

> "Love strong as death, nay, stronger;
> Love mightier than the grave;
> Broad as the earth, and longer
> Than ocean's widest wave.
>
> This is the love that sought us,
> This is the love that bought us,
> This is the love that brought us
> To gladdest days from saddest night,
> From deepest shame to glory bright,
> From depths of death to life's fair height,
> From darkness to the joy of light."
>
> BONAR.

It becomes us not to dogmatize with confidence, but to speak with modesty on a theme so high and difficult. We would suggest that the petition is that ye may be so filled with the Holy Spirit and with all his gifts and graces, as God is filled. This is expressed in a mandatory form by Christ (*Matt. v.* 48), "Be ye also perfect, as your heavenly Father is perfect." Something more than initial Christian life is here prayed for by Paul in behalf of the church in Ephesus. The new birth begins with the love of God in the heart, shed abroad by the Holy Spirit. But such a heart is narrow and needs enlargement; it has remaining defilements which need cleansing. So there are steps and intervals between spiritual infancy and manhood. The crowning act of this process of development is here denoted by the being filled with all the fulness of God. Elsewhere it is expressed by the prayer, "The God of peace himself sanctify you wholly."—(1 *Thess. v.* 23, *R. V.*) Both the filling and the sanctifying are in grammatical forms which imply singleness of action, however long the preparation may have been.

Who can adequately unfold the wealth of meaning in the magnificent ascription with which this inspired prayer concludes? Paul, having prayed for surpassingly excellent blessings for the Ephesians, with a wisdom more than human, lays in their minds a foundation for faith, by his striking portrayal of the almighty power of him who hears and answers all true prayer offered in the name of his Son. This thought, left as the last impression on the mind of the reader, is the very seed out of which faith will spring up. Let the Christian who is praying, "Lord, increase my faith," help the Lord answer this prayer by an analysis and a minute study of this wonderful doxology. Note the strength of the terms indicating the ability of God to impart all the petitions of this comprehensive prayer. He is able to do not only all we ask or even think, but "above" this; and not only above, but "abundantly," overflowingly "above." When Paul had written this, the thought of how much God had done for him caused him to strengthen the expression by the word "exceeding," interlined, perhaps, before "abundantly." Thus, the original idea of ability is, as the mathematicians would say, raised to the third power by being thus twice multiplied into itself. We are then invited to contemplate the measure, the yardstick if you please, by which God works "according to the power that worketh in us." All the past manifestations of his omnipotence in creation, providence, and redemption, are only specimens of that power which stands ready to do the bidding of human faith, pleading the infinite merit of the adorable Son of God, repeating the miracle of the creation of the sun in the heavens with glories more transcendent ; "For God, who commanded light to shine out of darkness, hath shined in our hearts, to give the light of the knowledge of the glory of God in the face of Jesus Christ."

"To him," God the Father, "be the glory," the whole glory accruing from all his gracious dealings, "in the church, the sphere of God's glory before men and angels too." *Eph. iii.* 10, *R. V.*, "To the intent that now unto the principalities and the powers in the heavenly places might be made known through the church, the manifold wisdom of God." Thanks to the Revision for bringing out to English readers the astonishing idea that archangels, Cherubim and Seraphim, are pupils studying the manifold wisdom of God, and using the Christian Church as their lesson-book. All of his moral attributes — love, holiness, justice, wisdom, and truth — are most clearly revealed in the heavenly places when they are seen in the mirror of a sanctified church on the earth. From this conception in the mind of Paul, the sublime prayer in this chapter is a natural sequence. Let every believer who aspires after the highest spirituality daily repeat it. Let every pastor teach his church to pray this prayer in concert in the prayer-meetings, and every leader teach his class to repeat it in every class-meeting, for their own good, and for the instruction of the archangels on their thrones above.

> " Yes, measure LOVE when thou canst tell
> The lands where seraphs have not trod,
> The heights of heaven, the depths of hell,
> And lay thy finite measuring-rod
> On the infinitude of God."
>
> T. C. UPHAM.

V.

ST. PAUL A PENDULUM BETWEEN PRAISE AND PRAYER.

IN the higher states of Christian experience, there is a blending of prayer and praise. This is noticeable in St. Paul. If he begins with thanksgiving, he ends in prayer; if he begins with prayer, he ends with praise. *Phil. i.* 3, 4, "I thank my God upon every remembrance of you, always in every prayer of mine for you all making request with joy." There is no drudgery in true prayer. He to whom communion with God the Father is a task has not advanced far in grace. It is very evident that the fulness of the spirit of grace and supplication has not been poured upon him. All who through faith in Christ have boldness and access or introduction to God "make requests with joy." All who come in their own name approach the throne of grace with fear and servility. To them prayer is a sad necessity, and not a delight transcending all the pleasures of sense. Bishop Janes had full sympathy with St. Paul in the joyfulness of prayer. To his room-mate who had slept an hour, and awakening saw the bishop still on his knees breathing out his silent supplications, and asked why he prayed so long, he replied, "I delight in prayer." It was the recreation of his soul and body after a day of toil in conference and cabinet. How far in the opposite extreme is the practice of the Papal priests to prescribe prayer as a penance and a penalty, imposing so many Pater Nosters and Ava Marias after the confession of sins.

There cannot be a more sad departure from the true spirit of prayer than to treat it as a punishment. We often feel like weeping over the millions of benighted souls to whom the gladness of prayer is perverted into sadness through sacerdotal despotism.

Yet young Christians to whom prayer is not a delight should be encouraged to persevere in the use of this means of grace, and to pray for such a baptism of the spirit and fulness of love as will change its irksomeness into an unspeakable joy. Thousands can attest the possibility of such a sudden transformation. They have lived months and years in a state of communion with God so intimate and delicious that, whenever they bow the knee to pray, hallelujahs spontaneously burst from their lips. This shows that in the quality of their piety they are approaching the heavenly state where prayer will be completely lost in praise.

In verse 9 Paul says, "And this I pray, that your love may abound yet more in knowledge and in all discernment (*R. V.*). There is one element of Christian character which can never exist in excess, yea, there can never be enough to satisfy its possessor. This is love. It may be perfect in kind, that is, free from all impurities, but it can never be perfect in degree.

> "Insatiate to this spring I fly,
> I drink and yet am ever dry:
> Ah, who against his charms is proof?
> Ah, who that loves can love enough?"

This capacity for growth in love will continue through life, leap over the grave, and unfold itself through the ceaseless cycles of eternity. Growth is one of the elements of heavenly bliss.

Yet it is not for an increase of their love absolutely as an end in itself that the apostle prayed, for love alone might become the sport of every impulse; but it was for its increase as the means to two important yet subordinate ends — first a sound, certain and full knowledge (*epignosis*) of the truth, and secondly a keen spiritual discernment to distinguish between things that are different, either between right and wrong, or between different degrees of good and their contraries. The whole force of temptation consists in the skill of the tempter to make evil appear in the guise of good. Triumph over temptation lies largely in the ability to pierce through the disguise, to discover the cloven foot in the patent-leather shoe. Beyond all price is a thorough knowledge of theoretical and practical truth. It is a coat of mail amid the arrows of temptation. Hence the most extended definition of Christian perfection is found in *Heb.* v. 14, " But solid food is for perfect men, even those who by reason of use [habit] have their [spiritual] perceptions exercised to discern good and evil."

Love is the medium through which the spiritual eye clearly discerns, if it be not that eye itself, as St. John intimates, " He that loveth not, knoweth not God." Ever-increasing love is ever-increasing spiritual discernment of the true nature, good or bad, of each circumstance, case, or object which experience may present. A sensitively correct moral perception cannot be too highly prized. It is the gift of the Holy Spirit improved and intensified by use. It is the opinion of Mr. Whewell, a distinguished English moral philosopher, that our power of moral discrimination may become so acute as to discern a moral element in acts now considered morally indifferent, such as the question shall I ride to town or walk; shall I wear boots or shoes, gloves or mittens; take an umbrella or run the risk of rain. If there is a moral element at the bottom of all these apparently trivial choices, it is evident that it is the design of God that we should acquire a spiritual perspicacity sharp enough to discern it.

But spiritual perception is not an end in itself, but only a means to an ultimate end, right conduct and holy character, "that ye may be sincere and without offence against the day of Christ." The common explanation of the original word for "sincere" is pure and unsullied to such a degree as to bear examination in the full splendor of the solar rays. The same idea occurs in St. Jude's striking description, "Now unto him that is able to keep you from stumbling [*sine peccato, without sin* — the *Vulgate Version*], and to present you faultless," not in some twilight region, "but before the presence of his glory." This is the aim of the gospel of Christ, to present us without defect or fault, spot or fleck, under the intense splendors of God's holiness; and it is the office of the Holy Spirit to complete such characters in this life, not in the hour of death, nor in purgatorial fires after death, as Dr. Briggs hints when he suggests that the believer's sanctification may be completed in the intermediate state. This intimates a slur upon the Pentecostal dispensation. "Being filled with the fruits of righteousness," the words "sincere and without offence" are a negative description of the workmanship of the Sanctifier. The positive side is now presented in its fullest and completest development. Righteousness is the originating cause of the fruits which richly adorn the character of the mature believer. They are essentially the same as the fruit of the Spirit, enumerated in *Gal. v.* 22, and the fruit of the light, *Eph. v.* 9, *R. V.* We are wild and worthless olive-trees, until we are engrafted into Christ, who by means of his living root renders us fruitful trees "unto the praise and glory of God." As the fruitless orchard is the shame and poverty of its owner, who has suffered the palmer-worm to devour it, so a fruitful orchard is the honor and wealth of its proprietor, attesting his patient care and toil. How ennobling and inspiring the thought that the declarative glory of the great God may be enhanced by us dwellers in houses of clay. With what dignity God has clothed us, that we should be reflectors on the earth of the glory of God that fills the heavens. Looking down upon sin from the summit of this great thought, how despicable it appears, —

"A thing most unsightly, most forlorn, most sad."

This revenue of praise which flows upward to heaven from sanctified character on earth is "by Jesus Christ," by the indwelling and working of the Holy Spirit whom he sends from the Father. "Glory be to the Father, and to the Son, and to the Holy Ghost, as it was in the beginning, is now, and ever shall be, Amen."

VI.

ST. PAUL'S PRAYER AND GOD'S FATHERHOOD.

IF there were fluctuations in the emotional experiences of St. Paul, so that he was more joyful at one time than at another, it is natural for us to expect to find traces of them in his Epistles. When he wrote to the Ephesians he must have been in a very exalted and ecstatic mood. He sees how broad and boundless is the ocean of God's love, as Faber sees it:—

> "Angelic spirits, countless souls,
> Of Thee have drunk their fill;
> And to eternity will drink
> Thy joy and glory still."

St. Paul's prayers are the outpourings of a full soul. The vast volume of water in the mouth of the Orinoco River led its discoverer, Columbus, to infer that it must be the outflow of a continent, not of a small island. So these prayers, so deep and broad, must flow from a continent of grace.

Let us dip our goblet into one of these rivers, (*Eph.* i. 16-19). The terms in which God is spoken of as "the God of our Lord Jesus Christ, the Father of Glory," are helps to our faith; they help us to conceive of him by removing the vagueness and unthinkableness of an infinite spirit. When a little boy, the writer recalls the prayer of a young circuit rider for the conversion of seekers at the altar. His address to God did not help their faith to lay hold of him, "O thou whose centre is everywhere and circumference is nowhere, save these penitent sinners." How different were the great apostle's ascriptions. When God is spoken of as the Father of Jesus Christ, he is brought near, so that we may touch him with the hand of faith. "The Father" to whom the "glory" belongs is the Father of all regenerate souls. Thus St. Paul, our prayer-leader, gives us a good fulcrum for the lever of supplication. Let us now look at the things for which he prays: "The Spirit of wisdom and revelation," that is, the Spirit who works wisdom and reveals spiritual realities, especially giving saving efficacy to divine truths. This is not merely a momentary glimpse at the time of the new birth, but a *continued* bestowal of the same spiritual intuition for the ever-*increasing* enlightenment of Christians. "In the full knowledge of him" is Alford's rendering of the strengthened word for knowledge. Our knowledge of God cannot be full in the sense of exhaustive, but it can be full in the sense of assurance and certainty. We cannot comprehend God, but we may apprehend him. "We cannot," says Gladstone, "embrace the mountain with our arms, but we can touch it with our hands." This is his common-sense answer to the agnostics who insist that God is unknown and unknowable, because we are finite and he is infinite. There is nothing of which we have exhaustive knowledge. There are questions about the smallest sand-grain which the wisest philosophers cannot answer.

The knowledge here spoken of is not philosophical, but experimental and intuitive; "penetrating and exact"—(MEYER). Hence it is satisfactory. *Eph. i.* 18, "The eyes of your heart [*R. V.*] being enlightened," is a phrase of the same import with "full knowledge." This is the effect of the incoming and abiding of the Comforter in pentecostal fulness. This kind of spiritual eyesight, this knowledge far superior to all other, may be possessed by the most obscure and illiterate chattel slave (chapter vi. 5) in Ephesus. For St. Paul does not show respect of persons when he bows before the impartial God in supplication for the brethren. "That ye may know what," or rather, how great "is the hope of his calling;" i.e., what a great and glorious hope is given to the believer. Hope always grasps future good.

The citizenship of Christians is in heaven (*Phil. iii.* 20.), whither all their thoughts and desires flow as the impetuous torrents seek the sea, to use a figure from Madame Guyon. The object of hope is also expressed by the word "glory," the essential characteristic of gospel salvation, the foregleams of which in scattered rays fall on us here, while the full-orbed splendor is reserved for us when we shall see King Jesus in his majesty descending from heaven in his personal second coming.

But what is meant by "his inheritance in the saints"? Christ is to receive from the Father the riches or transcendent excellence of glory among the saints; i.e., the community of believers will be the subjects of this bliss, and they will be the sphere outside of which the riches of glory will not be found, not even among the angels.

The last clause of the prayer is, "And what is the exceeding greatness of his power to us-ward who believe." Here is a Pauline accumulation of terms, magnifying power. It is not only greatness, but exceeding greatness of his power for which Paul prays that the believer may have an experimental knowledge. The power of God over matter has no limit but his wisdom. But the power of God in the realm of spiritual intelligences endowed with freedom is limited by the perverse use of that freedom. The grace of God which would transfigure willing souls from all sinfulness to the beauty of all holiness, stands powerless before the stubborn will. Says Jesus to the city over which he wept (*Matt. xxiii.* 37), "I would, but ye would not." No sinner can be saved without the concurrence of two wills. It is the same with the different degrees of salvation. Each uplift is by a faith which carries the will into deeper and deeper subjection to the divine will. Then there will be greater and greater revelations of the transforming power of God, from grace to grace here, and from glory to glory hereafter.

Paul does not conclude his prayer without indicating the measure of that power by citing a historical instance of its exercise in that greatest event in the annals of time,— the resurrection of Christ. The same power that lifted Christ from the tomb, and set him at the right hand of his Father as the sharer of his throne, is now available to lift every willing soul from the grave of sin, and to enthrone him with the archangels, yea, even to seat him by the side of Jesus Christ on his throne, if he will, by the use of grace divine, overcome, as the Son of God overcame (*Rev. iii.* 21). What an encouragement to faith is found in this recorded prayer.

Reader, if you wish to learn the art of believing, study this prayer on your knees. A Quaker woman of my acquaintance, seeking God's full salvation, once said to that eminent Christian lady,[1] "I wish thou wouldst believe out loud so that I, kneeling by thy side, may hear thee, and imitate thee, and learn to believe." Such a favor could not be given. But it is the office of the Holy Spirit to help us by revealing Christ to the interior eye, and guiding the hand stretched out to touch the hem of his garment. This is better than hearing another believe.

[1] Mrs. Inskip.

VII.

FOR WHAT DID ST. PAUL ASK PRAYERS FOR HIMSELF?

THE inner life of every person is inscrutable. We do not see the real self of our most intimate friend. But there are orifices through which the hidden man gleams forth. The mouth is one of these. "Out of the abundance of the heart the mouth speaketh." The requests for prayer for themselves which Christians make, reveal their spiritual condition. In our social meetings the usual requests indicate the reverse of evangelical perfection. These are fair specimens: "Pray that I may overcome the evil of my heart;" "Pray that my besetting sin may not conquer me, and that I may be faithful and reach heaven at last;" "Pray that I may be victorious over inbred sin;" "Pray that I may be willing to do or to suffer God's will;" "I sin every day; pray that I may be kept from sinning, and that I may be sanctified wholly." These requests are proof positive that the blood of Jesus Christ has not cleansed them from all sin — actual and original. They indicate that the regenerate life has not reached the point where the last touch of the new creation has purged away sin, and brought out completely the lost moral image of God.

Let us now see what the Apostle to the Gentiles invariably wishes the churches should ask for him, for he goes forward for prayers in every epistle. Turn to

Rom. xv. 30-32, "Now I beseech you, brethren, for the Lord Jesus Christ's sake, and for the love of the Spirit [the love inspired by the Spirit — Rom. v. 5], that ye strive together with me in your prayers to God for me; that I may be delivered [not from inward foes lurking in my heart] from them which do not believe in Judea; and that my service which I have for Jerusalem may be accepted of the saints, and that I may come unto you with joy by the will of God." He prays, as one on a perilous mission to persons hostile to him would pray, for deliverance from the hands that had only a few years before nailed his Master to the cross. We cannot infer from these words any imperfection in Paul's spiritual life.

In 2 *Cor. i.* 11 he again hints his desire for the prayers of believers in Corinth, "Ye also helping together by prayer for us that . . . thanks may be given by many on our behalf." Here the context shows that deliverance from persecutors is the burden of his desire, and when delivered, that all who had prayed for him might be blessed in offering thanksgivings to God.

Eph. vi. 18, 19, "Praying always with all prayer . . . for me, that utterance may be given unto me, that I may open my mouth boldly, to make known the mystery of the gospel." He wishes for persuasive utterance to enable him to fasten saving truth upon the hearts of wicked men. The burden of his desire is not for himself, but for others. He has what every preacher should have, a heart at leisure from itself through full salvation, and only anxious for the success of the word preached.

Col. iv. 3, "Withal praying for us, that God would open unto us a door of utterance, to speak the mystery of Christ." Through all his epistles up to the day of his death, this cry of Paul's heart sounds out, not "who shall deliver me from this dead body of carnality," but "utterance, effectual utterance, that I may save some of the multitudes who are thronging the downward road."

2. *Thess. iii.* 1, "Finally, brethren, pray for us, that the word of the Lord may have free course, and be glorified." In the next verse he prays for deliverance, not from the plague of an unsanctified heart, but "from unreasonable and wicked men" — fanatical Jews, who thought they would be doing acceptable service to the God of Abraham, if they should kill Paul, the supposed enemy of the religion of his own nation.

In *Philemon* 22 he invites Philemon to pray for providential protection in his journey to him, "For I trust that through your prayers I shall be given unto you." Much the same style of request occurs in Heb. xiii. 18, 19, "Pray for us . . . that I may be restored unto you the sooner." So Pauline is this request and the prayer, "The God of peace . . . make you perfect," that I have no doubt of its authorship.

Phil. i. 19, "My salvation through your prayer." It is declared by some that spiritual salvation is here spoken of, a deliverance from the love of sin, if not from the guilt of sin. But what say the great scholars and exegetes? "Deliverance from present custody," say

Chrysostom and Theodoret, "sustenance in life and bodily health," says Œcumenius; while Michaelis insists that it is "victory over foes," and Grotius suggests "the salvation of others," and Alford, "his own fruitfulness for Christ and glorification of him, whether by life or death, and so eventually his own salvation, in degree of blessedness, not in relation to the absolute fact." No one of these suggests entire sanctification from indwelling sin. If, as a school of expositors assert, Paul's spiritual life is mirrored in Rom. vii., ending with the despairing cry, "O wretched man," we should expect to find him frequently begging the churches to pray for his spiritual emancipation from this distressing bondage, called by Delitzsch "The unabolished antinomy." But the Christian world is saddened by no such doleful wail from him who said, "I am crucified with Christ; it is no longer I that live, but Christ liveth in me."

We conclude this half-hour with Paul with the following general remarks on all of Paul's requests for prayer:—

1. They are for things external and not internal; for providential protection, not for spiritual perfection. There is not the first hint of an inward warfare between the flesh and the spirit.

2. They are for greater impressiveness and success in preaching, and for the removal of obstacles to the advance of the gospel.

3. There is no intimation of doubts respecting his present and full salvation; no confession of daily sins, nor of the root of sin existing in him.

4. He never entreats the churches to intercede for his forgiveness and spiritual cleansing.

5. He evinces no uncertainty about his present and future salvation.

6. He shows that he is a man of like passions with ourselves, in his fear that evil men may obstruct the message by wounding, imprisoning, or killing the messenger. Hence we infer:—

1. That Paul enjoyed the grace of Christian perfection, being delivered both from sinning and from sin — having been saved from the first by regeneration and from the second by entire sanctification.

2. That he had a clear, satisfactory, and joyful knowledge of his sonship to God, through faith in Christ, by the abiding witness of the Holy Spirit.

3. That the self-condemning and self-loathing type of piety is not the highest style. St. Paul says nothing depreciative of the self on which the image of Christ is clearly enstamped. He is a stranger to a spiritual crucifixion in which he is forever dying on the cross and never dead.

VIII.

ST. PAUL, THE MODEL CHRISTIAN.

THE confession is painfully common in many of the churches, "I make many crooked paths." But we look in vain for anything like this in the frequent allusions of St. Paul to his own personal experience. He never intimates that his Christian course was a zigzag of sinning and repenting. The seventh chapter of Romans may be a photograph of the unregenerate Saul, while a devout Pharisee, endeavoring to realize in his own life his high ethical ideals without the aid of divine grace, and perpetually failing because of the domination of the flesh, or depraved inclination, not yet conquered by the new birth. It was never a portrait of Paul, the saint, regenerated by the Holy Ghost.

If you wish to see this latter portrait you will find it in *Phil. iii.* 14, *R. V.*, "I press on toward the goal unto the prize of the high calling of God in Christ Jesus." There is no crooked path here. For a racer with his eyes fixed upon the prize in the umpire's extended hand, practically demonstrates the geometrical theorem that the shortest distance between two points is a straight line. He "presses on," turning neither to the right nor to the left to gratify curiosity or appetite. The old crooked self which clamored for indulgence, which sowed not to the spirit, has been crucified (Rom. vi. 6; Gal. ii. 20, and vi. 14), and the new self bears the image of him who never deviated a hair's breadth from a straight line in all his earthly life.

St. Paul's rectitude, or straightness of moral character, is involved in his repeated exhortation in the form of a command, to imitate his own example, never qualifying it by any such weakening limitation as "so far as I follow Christ." Let us study the proof-texts. Immediately after the above-quoted text implying Paul's straightforwardness as a racer, in verse 14, — a perfect racer as in verse 15, — he says in verse 17, "Be ye imitators together of me." — *R. V.* He then intimates that there were at Philippi successful copyists of his own example, which was in turn a reproduction of that of Christ. "Mark them which so walk as ye have us [me] for an example." He then tearfully declares that many were making very crooked paths, alluding not to those outside of the church, but to "many" professors of faith in our adorable Saviour, whose sensual lives evinced that they were enemies of the cross of Christ, the symbol of the highest self-sacrifice. They did not imitate the purity and self-conquest of the great apostle, the founder of their church, amid tumult, imprisonment, and stripes (Acts xvi. 23). If in those days, when persecution is supposed greatly to have winnowed the church, Paul found many names on the communion roll whose sensuality was a god, rivalling the sinless Jesus, and wringing tears from the eyes of the pastor who had once rejoiced over their espousals to Christ, how abundant would be his weeping were he in pastoral contact with the many pleasure-loving members of our modern churches!

In *Phil. iv.* 9 Paul says with mandatory authority, "The things which you have both learned and received and heard and seen in me, these things do." What they learned and received related to Christian doctrine, but what they heard and saw in Paul involved his personal conduct and character. They heard his conversation, the index of the inner life; for out of the abundance of the heart the mouth speaketh. They saw his manner of life, and they are required to fashion theirs after the model of his own. St. Paul could not have given such a precept if he had been conscious of a blemished life, of trifling or impatient words, and of acts showing the serpent-trail of sin. It is a moral impossibility, except upon the hypothesis of studied hypocrisy.

The same command is reiterated with the added intensity of entreaty in 1 *Cor. iv.* 16, "I beseech you, therefore, be ye imitators of me," your spiritual father. The loving father, who is conscious of "making crooked paths," beseeches his boy not to follow his example. If the father burns incense to the vile god, tobacco, he usually entreats his son not to bend the knee to that polluting idol. The inference is irresistible that St. Paul was conscious of both inward and outward holiness.

1 *Cor. xi.* 1. The chapter division at the close of 1 Cor. x. is very unfortunate, since it separates the exhortation from the preceding argument. The *R. V.* puts that exhortation, "Be ye imitators of me, even as I also am of Christ," in the paragraph where it be-

longs. This shows in what particulars Paul wishes the Corinthians to imitate him; namely, (1) in not seeking his own profit of ease, or fame, or gain, but only the salvation of the many. This is the disposition which Christ manifested, as described by Paul in that sublime passage found in Phil. ii. 3-11, discussed by theologians as involving the doctrine of the "kenosis," the Son of God emptying himself. (2) We do not strain the text if we also make it include the imitation of the great apostle's singleness of eye in doing all things to the glory of God, and of giving "offence to neither the Jews, nor to the Gentiles, nor to the church of God." This life of perfect self-abnegation for the salvation of his fellow-men and for the glory of God, is at once the characteristic and proof of perfected holiness.

In 2 *Cor. iv.* 2 there is an unmistakable confession of this grace, not in set phrase, but in terms which necessarily imply it. "We have renounced the hidden things of shame, not walking in craftiness, nor handling the word of God deceitfully, commending ourselves [myself] to every man's conscience in the sight of God." Here is a twofold appeal in proof of Paul's rectitude of life, the human conscience, and the eye of the Omniscient, who sees through all disguises as in the splendors of noon. Another and more striking double appeal of the same kind is found in 1 *Thess. ii.* 10, "Ye are witnesses, and God also, how holily and justly and unblamably we behaved ourselves," etc. The three adverbs express the three aspects of his character as viewed by God, by men, and by his own conscience. The Son of man excepted, no man in the Holy Scriptures professes moral and spiritual perfection in terms as strong as these. For both God and man are called to attest it. Hence, it must be an inward reality, and not a mere outward seeming.

IX.

ST. PAUL'S LOVE TO HIS ENEMIES PERFECT IN KIND.

We shall use the phrases entire sanctification and evangelical or Christian perfection as synonymous, though strictly speaking, the former is an act of the Holy Spirit, and the latter, called by St. John perfect love, is a state following that act. — *Deut. xxx.* 6.

We are told by the great Teacher in *Matt. v.* 43-48, that love to one's enemies is the essence and evidence of Christian perfection. Man's love becomes, not in degree, but in kind, like God's love, when it pours itself out in benefactions upon the thankless and thankful alike, as he sends sunshine and rain on the evil and the good. Did Paul love his enemies in this Godlike style? His bitterest foes were his Hebrew brethren. Christ's prediction, "A man's foes shall be they of his own household," was fulfilled in the case of Paul. The Jews thirsted for his blood. They bound themselves with an oath of starvation that they would kill the great Hebrew heretic. They mobbed him in Jerusalem, and stoned him in Gentile cities. They hounded his footsteps wherever he journeyed. Hence he ran the risk of "dying daily," of being "killed all the day long." He was "in deaths oft." It was not the Romans, but "the Jews," who five times waled his bare back with "forty stripes save one." — 2 *Cor. xi.* 24.

Could Paul love men so full of malice and cruelty? I do not wonder that he prefaces and fortifies his almost incredible answer with four solemn asseverations, bespeaking credence to a statement so contrary to human nature: "I say the truth in Christ, I lie not, my conscience also bearing me witness in the Holy Ghost, that I have great heaviness and continual sorrow in my heart." Then he astounds the world with the declaration of love to his malignant and venomous fellow-countrymen, so strong as to prompt him to surrender up his life upon the accursed tree, making an atonement for them, in addition to that already made by the Son of God, if it were possible for a creature to make an acceptable propitiation for sin. "For I could wish myself accursed from Christ for my brethren, my kinsmen according to the flesh." — *Rom. ix.* 1-3.

Here angels and men saw divine love walking the earth a second time, incarnated in human form, and uttering from the same cross the same prayer for murderous enemies: "Father, forgive them; for they know not what they do." Does Christ prove "his love toward us, in that, while we were sinners, he died for us"? St. Paul asserts his willingness to do the same for his foes. If this is not love of the purest kind possible in men, in angels, and even in God himself, then we know not what perfect love is. Here Paul professes perfect love, excluding all that is antagonistic to it, and hence cleansing from all inward sin. Indirectly he declares that the Holy Spirit has sanctified him wholly. The same divinely implanted, unselfish love, which is attended by sacrifice, and seeks no earthly recompense, is found in his declaration — (2 *Cor. xii.* 15), "I will very gladly spend, and be spent for you; though the more abundantly I love you, the less I be loved." No taint of selfishness can be justly predicated of such love. It is as pure as that which glows in the heart of a seraph.

Let us look at Paul amid the perplexities of his administration of church discipline. He had ordered the trial and expulsion of an immoral member of the Corinthian church. His anxiety to hear what effect this excision had upon the rest of the church, and the love of the apostle's heart, which prompted this disciplinary act, are graphically portrayed in 2 *Cor. ii.* 4, "For out of much affliction and anguish of heart I wrote unto you with many tears; not that ye should be made sorry, but that ye might know the love which I have more abundantly unto you." Here we are assured that "more abundant" love grasped the pruning-knife, and cut off the diseased branch. *Query.* Is the absence of strict discipline in the modern Christian church not a proof of deficient love on the part of the administrative officers, since abundant love is manifested by Paul in purging the church of an unworthy member? The boundless breadth of Paul's love shows that like that of God it is perfect in quality. Hear his exhortation, which must reflect his own practice, unless he was a hypocrite, not a guide, but a guide-post pointing out to others the way, but not walking in it himself (1 *Tim. ii.* 1): "I exhort therefore, that supplications, prayers, intercessions, and giving of thanks, be made for all men; for this is good and acceptable in the sight of God."

The same universal love crops out in this statement, "I am made all things to *all men*, that I might by all means save some." —1 Cor. ix. 22. "I please all men in all things, not seeking mine own profit, but the profit of many, that they may be saved." — 1 Cor. x. 33. Such self-abnegation in the interest of all unsaved men indicates that Paul had reached the final step " in the long road to the end of self." His love for the church is like that of Christ, who loved the church, and as an indisputable proof "gave himself up for it." Eph. v. 25. —*R. V.* Paul was always on the stretch to be filling up "that which is behind of the afflictions of Christ in my flesh for his body's sake, which is the church." — *Col. i.* 24. For her sanctification and salvation, he shrank not from crucifixion with his Lord, "being made conformable to his death." Here is an entirety of self-surrender to Christ, a wholeness of devotion, a perfectness of love, utterly inconsistent with the least remaining carnality, which, in the regenerate, always causes a divided heart.

We cannot leave this subject without bringing forth a few of the manifold proofs of the intense ardor of Paul's love. His heart was a furnace heated sevenfold, not to burn up his enemies, but to consume their sins. Let those who conceive of Paul as a man stern and austere, study the following texts : —

1 *Thess. ii.* 7, 8, 11. "You know how we exhorted and comforted and charged every one of you, as a father doth his children : we were gentle among you, even as a nurse cherisheth her children. So being affectionately desirous of you, we were willing to have imparted unto you, not the gospel of God only, but also

our [my] own souls, because ye were dear unto us [me]." Here is a scene for a historical painting : Paul, the great theological polemic, raised up to run a dividing line between Judaism and Christianity, in such a way as to include in the latter every permanent ethical principle, and to exclude everything national and transitory in the former, with slippered feet moving noiselessly about in the nursery among the cradles, tenderly ministering to the puniest infant in whom is the breath of spiritual life. This is a photograph of perfect love.

Phil. i. 8, "God is my record, how greatly I long after you all in the bowels of Jesus Christ." This text implies an identity with Christ, so intimate that his heart beats in the apostle's bosom with an unspeakable intensity of yearning love. Surely Paul fulfilled the second table of the law ; he loved his neighbor as himself. This was possible only when he was obeying the first great commandment, "Thou shalt love the Lord thy God with all thy heart." We have educed proofs that are absolutely unanswerable, that the Apostle to the Gentiles was fulfilling both tables of the law.

If Paul is the only one who has measured up to Christ's command, "Be ye therefore perfect, even as your Father in heaven is perfect," it is sufficient to prove that the command is not an unattainable ideal, but a practicable requirement which all believers in Christ have the gracious ability to perform, if they have received their heritage in Christ, the fulness of the Holy Spirit.

Paul's love was universal, embracing every character and condition of mankind. We have noted his intense affection for his enemies, his abundant love toward the disorderly Corinthian church and its offending member, as well as his tenderness toward spiritual babehood.

It remains for us to speak of two other classes, who were the objects of his melting love: First, the Galatian converts on the spiritual retrograde. Hear his tender expostulation, " My little children, of whom I travail in birth again until Christ be formed in you. Where is the blessedness ye spake of? Am I to become your enemy, because I tell you the truth?"—*Gal. iv.* 15-19; and secondly, his love for Christian strangers whom he knew only by report. For such he is ready to lay down his life. "As much as in me lies, I am ready to preach the gospel to you that are at Rome"—implacable, relentless, cruel Rome, fattening on the spoils of nations, and thirsting for the blood of the Apostle to the Gentiles. Why did Paul thrust himself into this cage of ravenous beasts? *Rom. i.* 9–12, "God is my witness, whom I serve with my spirit in the gospel of his Son, that without ceasing I make mention of you in my prayers . . . For I long to see you, that I may impart unto you some spiritual gift, to the end ye may be established."

We have heard of preachers who daily bear on their hearts in prayer the churches to which they have proclaimed the unsearchable riches of Christ, but how many can be found in the whole course of history, who, "without ceasing," pray for the churches in which they may be stationed in the future?

X.

ST. PAUL CRUCIFIED WITH CHRIST.

MANY people are perplexed to understand the exhortation to give up self to Christ and to have no will of their own. We are so created that we must regard our own welfare. Self-love is implanted in our natures. If it would be destroyed, there would be nothing to which God or man could appeal. Neither threatening nor promise would move such a soul. Moreover, self-love has the approval of Christ in his epitome of the moral law. He makes it the measure of our love to our neighbor — "Love thy neighbor as thyself." But selfishness differs from self-love in this, that self is exalted into the supreme law of action. The well-being of others, and the will of God, are not regarded. This is the self that is to be crucified. Says St. Paul, "I am crucified with Christ, but it is no longer *I* that live, but Christ liveth in me " —

Gal. ii. 20 — as punctuated by Alford. The former *ego* of selfishness has met with a violent death, having been nailed to the cross, and Christ has taken the supreme place in the soul. The very fact that this death was violent implies that it was instantaneous, a very sharply defined transition in St. Paul's consciousness. There is some one last rallying point of selfishness, a last ditch in which the evil *ego* intrenches itself. It may be some very trifling thing that is to be exempted from the dominion of Christ, some preference, some indulgence, some humiliating duty, some association to be broken, some adornment to be discarded. "Reign, Jesus, over all but this," is the real language of that unyielding heart. This trifle, held fast, has been the bar which has kept thousands out of that harmony with the divine will which precedes the fulness of the Spirit.

But when this last intrenchment of self-will has been surrendered to Christ, he is not long in taking possession. The fulness, as well as the immediateness, depends on the faith of the soul in the divine promise. For there is a difference between the subjugation of the rebel and his reconstruction in loyal citizenship, between the death of sin and the fulness of the Christ-life. But the great distinctive and god-like feature of man is his free will. The memorable event, the pivotal point on which destiny, heaven, or hell hinges, is the hour of intense spiritual illumination, conviction of sin, when sin is deliberately chosen — "evil, be thou my good" — or voluntarily rejected. Submission to Christ is an act of faith. It could not be possible without confidence in his veracity and goodness. Hence, justification and emergence into "the higher life" frequently take place when the only preceding act which impressed itself on the memory was not an act of faith, but of surrender, which is grounded on trust as its indispensable condition.

Some writers on advanced Christian experience magnify the will, and say to inquirers, Yield, bow, submit, to the law of Christ. While the evangelist of the Wesleyan type says, Believe, believe Christ's every word. Both are right. Perfect trust cannot exist without perfect consecration. Nor can we make over all our interests into Christ's hands without the utmost confidence in his word. Hence, crucifixion with Christ implies perfect faith in him, not only when he is riding in triumph into Jerusalem amid the huzzas of enthusiastic men and the hosannas of willing children, but when the fickle multitude are crying, "Crucify him." From the beginning Jesus intimated that discipleship must be grounded on an acceptance of himself, stripped of all the attractions of riches or honor. To know him after the flesh, from some selfish and worldly motive, is to fail to know him in that way which insures eternal life. To an enthusiastic scribe who had just seen the glorious display of power in the healing of Peter's wife's mother and the casting out of demons, and who was taking only a romantic, rose-colored view of discipleship prompting the thoughtless promise, "I will follow thee whithersoever thou goest," Jesus replied, "The foxes have holes, and the birds of the air have nests; but the Son of man hath not where to lay his head." "Let him who follows me know that he is following a pauper, fed at the tables of friends, and soon to be buried as a beggar at their expense." "If any man will be my disciple, let him deny himself, take up his cross daily, and follow me." Here, over the very gateway of the kingdom of Christ, stands chiselled the stony words "Crucifixion of self." Hence, it is no stern requirement of the so-called higher Christian life; it is the condition of the lowest degree of spiritual life.

The higher the degree of life the higher the required consecration.

Hence, love made perfect requires as its antecedent that perfect surrender which, in the strong language of St. Paul, is crucifixion with Christ. The difficulty with average Christians is, that they faint beneath the cross on the *via dolorosa*, the way of grief, and never reach their Calvary. They do not by faith gird on strength for the hour when they must be stretched upon the cross. They shrink from the torturing spike, and from the spear aimed at the heart of their self-life. This betokens weakness of faith. But when the promise is grasped with the grip of a giant, no terrors, no agonies, can daunt the soul. In confidence that there will be after the crucifixion a glorious resurrection to spiritual life and blessedness, the believer yields his hand to the nail, and his head to the thorn crown. That flinty centre of the personality, the will, which has up to this hour stood forth in resistance to the complete will of God, suddenly flows down, a molten stream under the furnace blast of divine love, melted into oneness with "the sweet will of God." After such a death there is always a resurrection unto life. An interval of hours or even of days may take place before the angels shall descend and roll away the stone from the sepulchre of the crucified soul, and the pulsations of a new and blissful life be felt through every fibre and atom of the being. It is not the old life that rises, but a new life is breathed forth by the Holy Ghost. "I am crucified with Christ, it is no longer I that live, but Christ that liveth in me." (*R. V. Am. Committee.*) "Dead indeed unto sin," "but alive unto God through Jesus Christ."

"He walks in glorious liberty,
  To sin entirely dead:
The Truth, the Son, hath made him free,
  And he is free indeed.

Throughout his soul Thy glories shine;
  His soul is all renewed,
And deck'd in righteousness divine,
  And clothed and filled with God."

He who enjoys this repose is brought so intimately into sympathy with Jesus Christ that he is all aflame with zeal, and aroused to the utmost activity to save lost men. As a venerable preacher, widely known, quaintly expressed it, "I enjoy the *rest* of faith that keeps me in perpetual *motion*."

XI.

ST. PAUL'S PERFECT FAITH.

WE continue our proof that St. Paul enjoyed and professed entire sanctification. This grace is implied in that perfect faith which never lapses into doubt. Such a faith gives perfect victory over the world, which is a comprehensive term for all moral evil or sin. This faith is confessed in

Phil. iv. 13, "I can do all things through Christ which strengtheneth me." One of the highest tests of faith to a man of taste and culture like Paul, who seems to have been brought up in the lap of plenty, is that extreme and pinching poverty that knows the keen cravings of hunger. The devil was cunning enough to assail Jesus when he was hungry. Hear what Paul says in the preceding verse, "I know how to be abased, and I know also how to abound: in everything and in all things have I learned the secret both to be filled and to be hungry, both to abound and to be in want." (*R. V.*) Then follows the sublime confession of the great apostle that in such distressing circumstances he has a faith in Christ which keeps him from sinful repinings and charging God foolishly. His is not the surly philosophic stoicism of Dr. Samuel Johnson in Grub Street, who, when in destitution, once closed a letter with "yours *impransus*" (without breakfast); but it was a cheerful, yea, even joyful, suffering of privations, because of his intense love to him who had not where to lay his head, was fed at other men's tables, and buried in a borrowed tomb. This perfect faith gleams out in

2 *Tim. i.* 12, "I know whom I have believed." Here faith is perfect because it has merged into knowledge. Faith is the only door through which a knowledge of God comes into the soul, the only path which leads to a clear apprehension of spiritual realities. Paul well understood, from his own experience, this relation of faith to knowledge, and to evangelical perfection.

In stating the purpose of the Christian ministry to be "for the perfecting of the saints," he adds, "till we all attain unto the unity of the faith and of the knowledge [perfect knowledge — ALFORD] of the Son of God." Here are not two unities, but one, made up of faith swallowed up in the full blaze of knowledge. He then intimates that this is a necessary element of a perfect man who receives "the fulness of Christ," or of that plenitude of grace which he communicates. See Eph. iv. 11–14.

Paul makes his present knowledge of Christ the basis of faith that he will keep him from sin in the future — "And I am persuaded that he is able to keep [or guard] that which I have committed unto him [my deposit — *Greek*] against — that day." If Paul's experience in the past had been one of sinful stumblings and sad falls, he could not have had so strong a trust in Christ to uphold him in the future.

In 2 *Tim. iv.* 18, there is another outflashing of this

perfect faith, "And the Lord shall deliver me from every evil work, and will preserve me unto his heavenly kingdom." "Every evil work" must include moral evil or sin. In answer to the question, What evil work? Dean Alford answers, "The *falling into the power of the tempter;* the giving way, in his own weakness and the desertion of all, and betraying the gospel for which he was sent as a witness." If he had complete confidence in the power of grace to keep him in the future, he certainly had faith to be cleansed from all present sinfulness.

The texts quoted in proof of Paul's perfect faith are only samples of many of the same kind.

If we can educe from Paul's epistles proofs of his entire self-abnegation in the interest of Christ, we shall demonstrate his holiness of heart and life. Turn to

Phil. iii. 4-8. After enumerating the successive steps of vantage which he enjoyed as an ambitious Hebrew eager for ecclesiastical promotion, Paul says, "Howbeit what things were gain to me, these have I counted loss for Christ. Yea, verily, and I count all things to be loss for the excellency of the knowledge of Christ Jesus my Lord." Such language is not a characteristic of the consciousness of inbred sin, in which there is always a coddling of self and a "provision for the flesh to fulfil the lusts thereof." The Edwardian theology made selfishness the root of all sin. On this theory, perfect self-abnegation is entire sanctification, at least on its human side. Where this entire abandonment of self unto God exists, He will not be backward in performing the divine part of this work.

Rom. xiv. 7, 8. "For none of us liveth to himself,

and none dieth to himself. For whether we live, we live unto the Lord."

This may by some people be considered as Paul's unattainable ideal of a true Christian. But who can prove that this ideal was not realized in Paul's experience? If there is nothing in his life and character contradictory to it, then it should be regarded as a reflection of his own spiritual visage sanctified by divine grace. That there is nothing of this kind we shall show, when we examine misinterpreted passages in Paul's epistles.

Acts xxi. 13. "For I am ready not to be bound only, but also to die at Jerusalem for the name of the Lord Jesus."

This is a veritable man, having flesh and blood, not an imaginary ideal. The statement is intensely personal and realistic, "I am ready to die." He does not say, "We are ready;" he could not speak for another in such a positive manner. People conscious of a sin-ward bent are not perfectly ready to go to the judgment. Such a consciousness makes cowards of many Christians. All their days they are in bondage to the fear of death. Not so Paul. "I am ready to be offered." Such language proves two facts, (1) a total and irreversible self-surrender to Christ as both Saviour and Lord, and (2) a conscious meetness for standing in the presence of the Holy God, surrounded by the holy angels and "the spirits of just men made perfect" (the spirits of perfected just men — *Greek*). The dominion of the fear of death is broken when love is first inspired in the penitent believer; but fear itself is cast out when love is made perfect. This is why Paul was ready to die.

> "His love, surpassing far
> The love of all beneath,
> We find within our hearts, and dare
> The pointless darts of death."
>
> C. WESLEY.

St. Paul's spirit of self-sacrifice glows in every epistle, "Even as I please all men in all things, not seeking mine own profit, but the profit of many, that they may be saved"—

1 *Cor.* x. 33. It was not spasmodic, but habitual and characteristic. A niggard can once in a while painfully screw himself up to a generous contribution, to fall back again into his dominant penuriousness. But Paul, by the grace of God, was so thoroughly transformed that self-abnegation for the good of others had become second nature. He was even happy in self-sacrifice. Hear him, "and I will very gladly spend and be spent for you,"—not to win your favor,—"though the more abundantly I love you, the less I be loved." If perfectly disinterested love ever dwelt in one human bosom, besides that of Jesus Christ, it dwelt in the Apostle to the Gentiles. Covetousness is usually the last of the brood of vipers to be utterly destroyed in the heart of man. In Paul the serpent was more than scotched, he was killed outright. Proof—

Acts xx. 33. "I have coveted no man's silver, or gold, or apparel." Wishing to have a free pulpit, perfectly independent of the pews, he adds, "Yea, these hands have ministered unto my necessities, and to them that were with me." This witness cannot be impeached. The proof is complete. Paul was wholly saved from covetousness, which salvation is not only a long way toward entire sanctification, it is entire sanctification.

We will arrive at the same conclusion if we demonstrate that he was completely delivered from a love of human applause.

Gal. i. 10, *R. V.,* "Am I seeking to please men? If I were still pleasing men, I should not be a servant of Christ." Man-pleasing was not his ultimate aim. He employed it as a means to his lofty Christian end, "Even as I also please all men in all things, not seeking my own profit, but the profit of the many, that they may be saved." This deliverance from a love of popular applause is a very great salvation of which Paul speaks again in

1 *Thess. ii.* 4, "So we speak; not as pleasing men, but God, which proveth our hearts." Paul's conquest of this evil propensity is seen in his style of preaching, "not with enticing words, but in demonstration of the Spirit and of power." The Holy Ghost has very little use for fine writing. A florid style muffles his sword. It is impossible to tickle the fancy and pierce the heart at the same time.

XII.

PERVERTED PAULINE TEXTS QUOTED AGAINST HOLINESS.

ST. PAUL is the great logician of the New Testament. He has long and intricate arguments expressed in an involved style, frequently branching off from the main line of thought and returning to it again further on, making his meaning obscure. Hence, even St. Peter, a brother apostle, and, as the Romanists aver, infallible in all theological and ethical questions, asserts that there "are some things hard to be understood" in all our beloved brother Paul's epistles, which the "ignorant and unlearned," and he might have added, the designing, "wrest, as they do the other Scriptures, unto their own destruction." Thanking Peter for his frank confession that he had to sweat over Paul's epistles, and for freely according to them a rank with the Old Testament Scriptures, we proceed to an examination of texts quoted against Christian perfection, or inward and outward holiness in this life.

It is confidently asserted that St. Paul, in *Phil. iii.* 12, disclaims the completeness of his spiritual life, and professes moral and spiritual imperfection. The *R. V.* represents him as saying, "Not that I have already obtained, or am already made perfect."

The verb "obtained" is here absolute; i.e., it has no object after it. What object must we supply? It is natural to supply it from something before uttered. The last preceding noun, "resurrection from the dead," makes good sense as the object of obtained. But why should St. Paul assert a fact so manifest as this, that he had not risen from the dead? Did any one assert that he had risen? Yes. Some were spiritualizing the resurrection, perverting St. Paul's own words in Eph. ii. 6, and Col. iii. 1, into an argument against the resurrection of the body, while others were boldly declaring, "that the resurrection is past already." — (2 Tim. ii. 18.)

Under this state of the facts, it was not the declaration of a mere truism, for Paul to aver that his resurrection was future, not past.

Let us now see what he means when he denies that he is "already made perfect." The *R. V.* "made perfect," or perfected, is a more accurate translation of the original than the adjective "perfect" of the *A. V.* All the Greek lexicons and annotators insist that this verb "made perfect" here signifies "complete my course," just as the same verb is used by our Lord Jesus Christ in

Luke xiii. 32, "The third day I shall be perfected." Does Jesus here disclaim moral wholeness and spiritual completeness and perfection? Certainly not. Neither does St. Paul. Both speak of finishing their earthly course without the most distant hint of any spiritual imperfection in themselves. In fact, St. Paul in the fifteenth of this chapter classifies himself among the perfect in these words, "Let us therefore, as many as be perfect, be thus minded." This can mean nothing less than a state of moral completeness and undoubted loyalty to Christ, the love of God being so fully shed abroad in his heart as to exclude all that is antagonistic thereto. He means what St. John calls "the love of God perfected, casting out all fear that hath torment." The twelfth verse is beautifully harmonized with the fifteenth. In the twelfth St. Paul disclaims perfection as a victor, since he has not finished his race and touched the goal; in the fifteenth he claims perfection as a racer, "having laid aside every weight, and the sin which doth so easily beset."

The prince of exegetes, Meyer, thinks that the prize which Paul had not grasped is expressed in 2 *Tim. iv.* 8, "a crown of righteousness, which the Lord, the righteous judge, shall give me at that day." As this refers to the time of the second coming of Christ, which is followed by the resurrection in which the saints are raised with bodies like unto his glorious body, it follows that our exposition is essentially the same. There is an agreement that the object not yet attained is in verse 12, the reward of the righteous judge, not moral perfection, and that the perfection professed in verse 15 refers to moral completeness.

If any one of my readers still doubts the correctness of our exposition, I refer him to Dr. A. Clarke's Commentary for a full statement of the meaning of the Greek verb *teleiöo,* in connection with the Olympic games, also to all the Greek lexicons, which, without any exception at all, define its secondary meaning "to finish one's course." Paul could well say, when midway in his career, I have not yet received the prize; I am not glorified, for I have not finished my course; I have a conflict with the powers of darkness still to maintain, and the issue will prove whether I should be crowned. But a few years after this Paul sees that the end of the race is near. He is a prisoner in Rome, shut up in the Mamertine prison. Looking backwards he says, "I have finished my course." No more conflicts with Satan and his human allies await me; my hand touches the prize in the hand of the judge, — the crown of righteousness. Up to this hour when the block and the headsman's axe are in full view, he knew that there was a possibility of failure, that he was in an enemy's land. Hence he was "temperate in all things."

This brings us to another misunderstood text —

1 *Cor. ix.* 27, "I keep under my body, and bring it into subjection." This is often quoted to prove that depravity, the root of sin, was still in Paul, and that in these words he disclaims holiness of heart. But mark the terms used. He speaks of the body, and not of the flesh as depravity. He speaks only of appetites, in themselves innocent, and not of sinful passions and tempers. Adam and Eve in Eden had natural appetites needing moral control and receiving it up to the sad hour when through unbelief sin came into our world. Were our first parents in the least unholy because they had appetites requiring repression? By no means. We argue that subjection of the body to the highest moral ends is a proof of holiness. Natural appetites in men are no more sinful than they are in horses. But they are the gateway through which sin enters when indulgence is granted against the moral law, written or un-

written. Paul set a strong guard at that gate. In so doing he declares his hatred of sin, and not his proneness to sin.

But did not Paul say "I die daily" in 1 *Cor. xv.* 31? And does not this imply, if he was dying to sin daily, the continued existence of sin in him? Yes; if he thus died to sin. But there is no hint of sin in the text. The dying daily is a vivid statement of his peril of a martyr's death every day. See the context. If the dead rise not, and if Jesus Christ has not put the seal of truth upon his gospel by his resurrection, why do I stand in jeopardy every hour, daily running the risk of a violent death? In 2 *Cor. xi.* 23, in a pithy and nervous style, Paul exclaims, "in deaths oft;" and *Rom. viii.* 36, he applies to himself and his fellow Christians, *Ps. xliv.* 22, "For thy sake we are killed all the day long." St. Paul died unto sin once for all. Many die unto sin so imperfectly that they are alive and ready to get up out of the coffin every morning in season to die again that day; then they quote, "I die daily," a perfectly irrelevant proof-text, in justification of their playing fast and loose with sin.

St. Paul's death to sin had no resurrection unto sin. So should ours be. 1 *Tim. i.* 15 is our last perverted text in this chapter. Our readers may be surprised to learn that Paul the aged, in the fulness of his faith and love and professed holiness (1 *Thess. ii.* 10), was, at the time he was writing this epistle, actually outsinning all the sinners on the earth. This is the interpretation of some who search the Scriptures with the microscope to find proofs that sin must continue in the heart and crop out in the daily life of the best Christian so long as he is in the body. They emphasize the present tense "of whom *I am* chief." Let us read the context and see whether Paul is describing his past or his present character, "Who *was before* a blasphemer, and a persecutor, and injurious." Now, it is a rhetorical usage for a writer describing past events to change to the present in order to render his narrative more lifelike and impressive. This is called the historical present tense, which people of common-sense are in no danger of confounding with a real present, especially when the historian begins, as Paul does, by advertising the reader that he is narrating past events. The spirit of inspiration assumes that his readers will exercise the same good sense in reading the Bible as they do in reading other books.

St. Paul had been the chief, or a chief, of sinners. He was now the chief of saved sinners.

Gal. v. 17, "So that ye cannot do the things that ye would." Alas, how many unsanctified souls have made this astounding mistranslation the pillow upon which they have slept the sleep of death! There is no "cannot" in the original, nor in the *R. V.*, which is word for word the version of John Wesley a century and a quarter before: "The flesh lusteth against the Spirit, and the Spirit against the flesh, in order that ye may not do the things that ye would."

The doctrine taught by Paul is that in the regenerate, but not in the entirely sanctified, there is a struggle going on, the purpose of which is this: When ye would do the works of the flesh the Spirit strives to prevent you, and when ye would follow the leading of the Spirit, the flesh opposes. This warfare ceases when "the flesh is crucified" (verse 24) and "the body of sin is destroyed."—(Rom. vi. 6.) Of this mistranslation Wesley says, "It makes Paul's whole argument nothing worth; yea, asserts just the reverse of what he is proving." The author was once giving a Bible Reading on the subject of practical holiness, when an official of his church arose and read this mistranslation, alleging the impossibility of living up to his moral ideal. With such a conception of God as a hard master he soon after became so demoralized as to wreck a national bank and flee to Canada, where he died. Apologies for sin, and extenuations of sin as unavoidable, are fraught with the utmost moral peril.

XIII.

STUMBLING-BLOCKS REMOVED.

Setting an Electric Light in the Seventh Chapter of the Epistle to the Romans.

The seventh chapter of Paul's Epistle to the Romans is still quoted by some persons as a proof that the hereditary propensity to sin, called by theologians original sin, must continue in the heart of the believer so long as he lives.

1. But, if it prove that sin, as a principle, must exist, it also demonstrates far more clearly that sinning, by repeated, wilful violations of the known law of God, is the best moral state into which the abounding grace of our Lord Jesus Christ can bring the believer under the dispensation of the Holy Spirit, the Sanctifier. For habitual sins, of voluntary omission and commission, make up his every-day life. He does not do what he knows to be morally obligatory, and hateful sins he is constantly committing. Such a life must be under continual condemnation, inconsistent with justification. Hence, this chapter disproves justification more cogently than it does entire sanctification. This is our first objection to that interpretation of this chapter which makes it the portrait of a regenerate soul.

2. Our next objection to such an exegesis is that it makes the gospel as great a failure as the law in its reconstruction of human character. But this idea is flatly contradictory to the whole tenor of the New Testament. "For what the law could not do, in that it was weak through the flesh, God sending his own Son in the likeness of sinful flesh, and *as an offering* for sin, condemned sin in the flesh." — (Rom. viii. 3, *R. V.*) But what has this to do with regeneration and sanctification? The next verse assures us that the purpose of the mission of the Son is, "That the righteousness of the law might be fulfilled *in us* [not in Christ, as the imputationists vainly teach], who walk not after the flesh, but after the Spirit."

The contrast between the inefficiency of the law and the efficiency of the gospel is seen again in *Heb. vii.* 19, 25, "The law made nothing perfect;" "Wherefore he is able also to save them unto the uttermost [completely, DELITZSCH, WESTCOTT, and others] that come unto God by him." Still more explicitly this contrast appears in Heb. ix. 9, 14, "The sacrifices could not make him that did the service perfect, as pertaining to the conscience [of sins, Heb. x. 2] ... How much more shall the blood of Christ ... purge your conscience from dead [sinful] works to serve the living God." We must brand that exposition as false which degrades "the glorious ministration of the Spirit" to the low level of the "ministration of condemnation and death." — (2 Cor. iii. 7-18.)

3. We cannot accept that exegesis which violates the first rule of interpretation, — the law of non-contradiction. No passage is to be explained in such a way as

to make the writer contradict himself in the same document.

(1). In *Rom. vi.*, "We are dead unto sin;" "our old man is crucified, that the body of death might be destroyed." Again, "Being made free from sin, ye become servants of righteousness;" "ye have your fruit unto holiness." In chapter viii. we read, "For the law of the Spirit of life hath made me free from the law of sin and death." It must be, therefore, that St. Paul, in chapter vii., is not portraying a regenerate man, but a convicted Jew, who, under the glare of the law, sees himself a sinner, and resolves to achieve perfect rectitude in his own strength, without divine grace, and makes a series of failures so sad as to extort the wail that has been repeated through all the non-Christian ages, "O wretched man that I am!"

(2). Again, St. Paul must not in one text be so understood as to contradict the disclosures of his inner life in all other texts where he has drawn aside the veil. He nowhere else intimates that sin dwells in him. He requests prayers for himself in every epistle, for success in his ministry of the gospel, but never for the conquest of inward foes, never for the completeness of his spiritual life. He frequently testifies to deadness to sin (*R. V., Am. Committee, Gal. ii.* 20), "I have been crucified with Christ; and it is no longer I that live." *Gal. vi.* 14, "But far be it from me to glory, save in the cross of our Lord Jesus Christ, through which the world has been crucified unto me, and I unto the world." 1 *Thess. ii.* 10, "Ye are witnesses, and God *also*, how holily, and justly, and unblamably we behaved ourselves among you that believe."

How could a man living in the seventh chapter of Romans have the face to exhort the Corinthians thus (1 *Cor. xi.* 1), "Be ye imitators of me, even as I also am of Christ."

4. Our difficulties increase. Character is never predicated from a tendency which is under control, but rather from that inner principle which habitually dominates the conduct. If St. Paul is describing himself, or personating some other regenerate person, he cannot be classified as spiritual, since he confesses, "I am carnal, sold under sin." Are we to understand that carnality is the dominant principle in the regenerate? The phrase, "sold under sin," is the strongest expression which the Holy Spirit uses in the Scriptures for the full depravity of an unsaved man. It implies willing slavery in the drudgery of sin. He had no power to redeem himself.

We can conceive of true Christians with controlled depraved tendencies (1 Cor. iii. 1–3); but we have no ability to conceive how one under the perfect mastery of the flesh can be other than a "natural man, not having the Spirit. — (Jude 19, *R. V. margin*.)

In *Rom. vii.* 7–24 there is no term which implies the new birth, or spirituality. In the whole contest the Spirit does not appear on the field as one of the combatants. "The inward man" is not the new man, but the mind, including the æsthetical sensibilities which admire the beauty of holiness while repudiating its obligation. The two parties to the contest are the moral reason antagonizing the depraved appetites and passions, the upper story of the house at war with the basement on the plane of nature. This is entirely different from the strife of the Spirit against the flesh, in the case of the regenerate Galatians (chapter v. 17, *R. V.*), who had not advanced to the extinction of depravity by the Holy Spirit in entire sanctification, but were seeking perfection in the flesh, i.e., outward Jewish ordinances.

5. The best scholarship discredits this chapter as the photograph of a regenerated man. The Greek Fathers, during the first three hundred years of church history, unanimously interpreted this scripture as describing a thoughtful moralist endeavoring without the grace of God to realize his highest ideal of moral purity. Augustine at first followed this interpretation, till in his collision with Pelagius he found verses 14 and 22 quoted by his opponent to prove that the natural man can appreciate the beauty of holiness. To cut him off from these proof-texts he deviated from the traditional exegesis, and championed the new theory that this chapter is a delineation of the regenerate. Calvinian annotators have quite generally followed him, with notable modern exceptions, such as Moses Stuart and Calvin E. Stowe. The trend of modern scholars, whether Calvinian or Arminian, is now toward the view of the Greek Fathers. Among these are Meyer, Julius Müller, Neander, Tholuck, Ewald, Ernesti, Lepsius, Macknight, Doddridge, A. Clarke, Turner, Whedon, Beet, and Stevens of Yale.

To our interpretation it is objected that there are two utterances which strongly imply a state of grace. The first is the 12th verse, "Wherefore the law is holy, and the commandment holy, and just, and good." The second is the 22d verse, "For I delight in the law of

God after the inward man." It is asserted that an unregenerate man cannot form high moral ideals and contemplate them with delight. The assertion betrays an ignorance of human nature under the spell of depravity. It still has power to create splendid ideals, and revel in contemplating them. Some even account their admiration of virtue as a very good substitute for its presence. Isa. lviii. 1-4. Drunkards admire temperance, yet yield to the clamor of the alcoholic appetite; rakes admire purity and seek it in marriage, while they still visit "her whose house is the way to hell." The poet Thomas Moore thus describes Thomas Jefferson, the author of the Declaration of Independence,

"[He] dreams of freedom in his slave's embrace."

Fallen humanity is a paradox. You will find it in all the pagan literatures, especially the Greek and Latin poets. We quote Ovid as a specimen:—

"My *reason* this, my *passion* that persuades;
I see the *right*, and I approve it too;
Condemn the *wrong*, and yet the wrong *pursue*."

Says Canon Mozley, in allusion to this very chapter, "Man possesses a moral nature, and, if he has intellect enough, he can put his moral ideas into words, just as he can put metaphysical ideas; nor is his doing so *any test of his moral condition.* Take any careless person of corrupt habits out of the thick of his ordinary life, and ask him to state in words what is his moral creed. Has he any doubt about it? None. He immediately puts down a list of the most sublime moral truths and principles. But so far as relates to himself, as soon as these truths are formally and properly enunciated, their whole design and purpose is fulfilled." They are not a law to him.

Some who wish to adopt our interpretation are perplexed by the last verse of the chapter. If the two sentences of the verse were interchanged they would be relieved. But, in the present order, the doctrine seems to be taught that after victory, "through Jesus Christ our Lord," there is a lapse into the old struggle. Not so. The last sentence of the chapter is an epitome of the whole struggle between the "mind," or moral reason, and the flesh, or sinful proclivity. The emphatic words are, "*I myself*," alone, on the plane of nature, without the aid of Christ, can do no better than to render a dual service, with the mind serving the law of God, by my admiration of its excellence, but with the flesh, the law of sin, by such a surrender as carries my guilty personality with it. After this recapitulation the pæan of permanent victory resounds through the entire eighth chapter.

The exposition will be greatly illuminated by observing that vii. 5 contains the thesis of vii. 7–25, and vii. 6 the thesis of viii.

XIV.

ST. PAUL'S CLASSIFICATION OF THE CORINTHIAN CHURCH IN TWO CLASSES.

IN 1 *Cor. ii.* 14 St. Paul describes the natural man as utterly devoid of spiritual perception. Spiritual realities "are foolishness unto him;" and "he cannot know them, because they are spiritually judged or examined" (*R. V.*). Christ foretold this state of things when he declared that "the world," the aggregate of natural men, "cannot receive the Spirit of truth, because they see him not." They have in exercise only sense-perception and reason, neither of which apprehends God and spiritual things. Spiritual intuition is an attribute of spiritual life; and spiritual life is absent, because unbelief bars out the Holy Spirit, the Lord and Giver of life. Hence, St. Jude describes "natural or sensual [animal, *R. V., margin*] men as having not the Spirit." Just the opposite is the characteristic of spiritual men, "Now we have received not the Spirit of the world, but the Spirit which is of God, that we *might know* the things that are freely given to us of God." While the natural man is, by the perverse attitude of his will, an agnostic, the spiritual man is an epignostic, having a clear perception of divine realities, which he is enabled to speak of, not in the terms of grovelling human philosophy, but in the words which the Spirit teacheth (1 *Cor. ii.* 13, *R. V., margin*), "interpreting spiritual things to spiritual men."

Having clearly defined these two classes, the natural and the spiritual, the Apostle to the Gentiles encounters a difficulty in attempting to classify the Corinthian church. It will not do to call them natural, because they have a low degree of spiritual life, they are babes in Christ. They are on the resurrection side of the unbridged chasm between death and life. The term "babes" implies life, and the words "in Christ" imply regeneration and vital union with Christ. Moreover, they are addressed as "sanctified in Jesus Christ."

These words import that the principle of holiness had been lodged in their hearts, indicating their calling "to be saints," when that principle should achieve the exclusion of every antagonistic principle, i.e., when they should be sanctified wholly, body, soul, and spirit. St. Paul sees such a transformation already begun in the Corinthian disciples that he thanks God always for the grace of God which was given them, and for their enrichment in all utterance and all knowledge, so that they came behind in no gift. After this description, there is no ground for impeaching their discipleship to Christ. Why, then, does the apostle hesitate to rank them as spiritual? Because their spirituality is soiled and tainted with carnality. Inbred sin is still active though not regnant. In the language of Joseph Cook, "they possess a predominant, rather than a perfect similarity to God in moral character, loving what he loves and hating what he hates." While the trend of their being is upward, there are strong downward proclivi-

CLASSIFICATION OF THE CORINTHIAN CHURCH. 79

ties which distract and endanger. Jealousy, strife, and schism are not fruits of the Spirit, but works of the flesh not yet crucified, although dethroned; the strong man being not yet cast out, though bound in chains.

In this perplexity St. Paul, unable to call the Corinthians either spiritual or natural, without flattery and void of fear, bluntly declares, 1 *Cor. iii.* 3, "Ye are yet carnal," — mere *men of flesh*. He charges their unchristian acts to an unholy state. He traces their perverse doing to a lingering perversity in their being, which must be rectified before they can be truthfully denominated perfectly spiritual.

We must not suppose for a moment that these babes in Christ were wilfully transgressing the known law of God, for such sin would forfeit their adoption. Their fault was in not leaving the elementary principles and pressing on unto perfection, and in remaining chronic babes so long that they had taken on the unlovely characteristics of dwarfs. Babes as having least of earthly mould and freshest from the hand of God awaken our admiration; but protracted infancy awakens pity rather than delight. They are weak and sickly, unable to do a man's day's work in the Lord's vineyard. They are dyspeptic, turning away from those strong truths and high experiences which make gigantic believers who fight manfully the good fight of faith; while the dwarfs, equal in age to these stalwarts, linger in the nursery, and cry for the milk-bottle out of cradles which they have no ambition to outgrow. It is not strange that the spiritual forces become weak, and the old nature, which should have been moribund, becomes so fully developed as to threaten to unhinge the believer's right relation to God. Practically ciphers in the church, they are doctrinally weathercocks whirled about by every wind of doctrine by the sleight of men. They are "dull of hearing," and more dull of understanding the higher possibilities of grace attainable through the Holy Spirit appropriated by faith. What bungling teachers are these! Wherever they are found in the pulpit, they are "unskilful in the word of righteousness." Yet this very word, of whose deep significance they are experimentally ignorant, is the sword of the Spirit, which they know not how to wield effectively in the battle into which they have rushed unbidden and unprepared.

In a church of which I was pastor, the desire was publicly expressed for a revival in which many sinners should be converted. A wise woman, who sorrowed over the lack of spiritual development in the members of that church, arose and said, "What should we do with the converts? We have no place for them; the cradles are all full."

The Corinthian church is not the only church in which the nursery furniture is in greater demand than are the weapons of war — not the only church to many of whom it might be said, "Are ye not carnal?" But if many who are truly regenerate have depravity still dwelling — not reigning — in them, does not this fact demonstrate the truth of "the residue theory"? It is certain that there was a residue of sinful proclivity marring the character, disturbing the peace, and threatening the unity of one apostolic church.

The same marked distinction between two kinds of disciples of Christ occurs in

CLASSIFICATION OF THE CORINTHIAN CHURCH. 81

Phil. ii. 20, which is thus translated by Alford: "For I have none else like-minded with myself who will really care for your affairs; for all [my present companions] seek their own matters, not those of Jesus Christ." The only two wholly consecrated men in whom self had been crucified among the preachers in Rome, when Paul penned the epistle to Philippi, were himself and Timothy. Says Alford, "No weakening of the assertion must be thought of, as that of the 'all,' meaning *many* or *most* or *care more* about their own matters," as many annotators have tried to do. "The word 'all,' and the assertion that they seek their own, not the things of Jesus Christ, are absolute." — ALFORD. Meyer and Ellicott indorse this view strongly. Says Wesley, "For all" but Timothy "seek their own — ease, safety, pleasure, or profit. Amazing! In that golden age of the church could St. Paul thoroughly approve of one only among the laborers that were with him? And how many do we think can now approve themselves unto God?"

This sorting of Christians into two kinds, the self-crucified and those in whom self lives, the wholly and the partially sanctified, is a delicate business for which only an inspired apostle is competent. While we fallible mortals may wisely shrink from drawing the line, we should remember that this line is clearly discerned by the eye of Omniscience. O Lord, to which class do I belong? In which is the greatest safety, happiness, and usefulness? There can be but one answer.

XV.

PRAYERS FOR THE SANCTIFICATION OF BELIEVERS.

> "Blest are the pure in heart; wouldst thou be blest?
> He'll cleanse thy spotted soul; wouldst thou find rest?
> Around thy toils and cares he'll breathe a calm,
> And to thy wounded spirit lay a balm;
> From fear draw love! and teach thee where to seek
> Lost strength and grandeur, with the bowed and meek."

THE Epistle to the Philippians has been called the joyful epistle. It is full of commands to rejoice. This is because it is the outgushing of love, the fountain of joy in the heart of the writer. No epistle is so warm in its expressions of affection. In some passages St. Paul seems to exhaust the words of endearment in the Greek language, in his eagerness to pour out the impetuous river of his love. Read in proof of this *Chapter iv.* 1, "Wherefore, my brethren, beloved and longed for, my joy and crown, so stand fast in the Lord, my beloved." Love of a worthy object is the secret of bliss. The apostle had found that secret. The Holy Spirit had penetrated his heart to its very depths, and had abundantly shed abroad love to God and men, especially to believers in Jesus Christ. There was a very strong tie which bound him to the brethren in Philippi: he had suffered for them in the stocks, under the lash, and in the nether prison. Sacrifice and suffering for others invest them with a peculiar preciousness. In a course of lectures at Yale University on pastoral duties, the speaker insisted that love is the only adequate motive to a successful ministry, — love of the souls of the people. He was asked, "How can I get this love?" The answer was defective, because it did not recognize the Holy Ghost as the Inspirer of love. The speaker, H. W. Beecher, replied, "Go to work in earnest for the salvation of souls, and make sacrifices for them, and you will begin to love them." This is true in the case of a pastor already filled with the Spirit of God. In the absence of the spirit-baptism, self-sacrifice for others, especially the vile and thankless, is a difficult if not impossible achievement. It requires great love to prompt to self-abnegation and voluntary suffering ; and this love is of God. But where such love has been enkindled by the breath of God, it becomes amazingly intensified by our self-denial and patient toil for those who are dead in sin. When they are raised to newness of life by the resurrection power of the Spirit, and are wearing the image of Christ, a bond of love is knit between the pastor and the converts stronger than can be found elsewhere on earth. Hence St. Paul's love for the churches which he had planted amid tribulations, and also his overflowing joy. In the beautiful procession of the fruit of the Spirit, in Gal. v. 22, joy follows love. Wishing the Philippians to mount up to the highest and purest joy, he prays that their "love may abound yet more and more in knowledge." — Chapter 1. 9. There is no such thing in earth or heaven as love in a finite being becoming perfect in volume or degree of strength. The more that men and angels know of God the more they will love him. As knowledge of God is capable of eternal increase, so there will be scope for endless advancement in love and joy. Mathematicians prove that there is a curve of such a nature (the hyperbola), that it will forever approach a straight line in the same plane, but never touch it. Such a curve is the human soul in its capacity for ever-increasing knowlege and love of God. Among finite aptitudes this talent of eternal growth is a faculty having semi-divine dimensions. In it God's image gleams out most clearly. The knowledge, in this text, in which love mounts up to higher and higher degrees, is *epignosis*, experimental, certain, and clear. It is the heart of the believer touching the heart of God. The head of pride is always agnostic, the heart of love is always epignostic (not in the dictionary, but signifies knowing certainly).

Turning now to another prayer of St. Paul in 1 *Thess. iii.* 12, 13, we find that there is to be an ever "increasing and abounding love one toward another, and toward all men," in order to establishment in holiness. It is taught elsewhere in St. Paul's epistles that love is the element in which holiness exists (*Eph. i.* 4; 1 *Tim. i.* 5); but here we are assured that this love must have a man-ward, as well as a God-ward direction. Hence, a tart holiness, a bitter holiness, a sour holiness, an envious holiness, is a contradiction and an impossibility. Nor will the careful student of Paul's magnificent lyric on love, in 1 *Cor. xiii.*, find any such combination possible as perfect love and arrogance, or censoriousness, or self-conceit, or headstrongness. "Love," when purged of all dross, "suffereth long and is kind; love envieth not; love vaunteth not itself, is not puffed up, and doth not behave itself unseemly." Professors of heart purity, especially those who associate themselves together almost exclusively, are in danger of taking on some of these unamiable qualities, and of cherishing uncharitable feelings towards those Christians whose weaker wings of faith have not borne them up to the Pisgah tops of grace. As a safeguard against this peril we recommend a frequent and searching self-examination, with this chapter as a touch-stone. The result would be an increase in the number of "hearts unblamable in holiness before God," whose "eyes run to and fro throughout the whole earth, to shew himself strong in behalf of them whose hearts are perfect towards him." — 2 Chron. xvi. 9.

The interpretation is erroneous, that the establishment in holiness, " at the coming of our Lord Jesus," signifies the completion of our sanctification at that time. Rather, it will be in that day that the *result* of the Spirit's perfect purifying work in this life will be exhibited to the universe. The same remark applies to that strong proof-text (1 *Thess. v.* 23, *R. V.*), "And the God of peace himself sanctify you wholly; and may your spirit and soul and body be preserved entire without blame at the coming of our Lord Jesus Christ." The aorist tense of the verb " sanctify," denoting singleness of action, as distinguished from continuance or repetition, strengthens our position that there is no *post mortem* cleansing taught in these passages. This remark is for the special benefit of some good, and otherwise orthodox, theologians, who reject the modern philosophical inference that a change of relation to

God's law from condemnation to justification, in certain cases, may take place after death, but look with favor on the doctrine of the completion after death of the sanctification which began in the new birth. The latter is as destitute of scriptural foundation as the former. The only purgatory for sin is in the blood of Christ. To assert that this purgatory stretches out from death to the Day of Judgment is to pass over the gulf between Protestantism based on the Bible, and Romanism built on traditions. Prayer for the unsanctified dead would logically follow. Let me rather pray : —

> " O thou great Power! in whom I move,
>   For whom I live, to whom I die,
> Behold me through thy beams of love,
>   Whilst in this vale of tears I sigh;
> And cleanse my sordid soul within
> By thy Christ's blood, the Bath of sin!
>   No hallowed oils, no grains, I need;
>   No rags of saints, no purging fire;
>   One crimson drop of David's seed
>   Is all the cleansing I desire."

XVI.

ST. PAUL INVENTS STRONGER WORDS FOR COMPLETE DELIVERANCE FROM SIN.

WHEN the gospel came into the world as a message from God, it selected one of the many languages of men for the communication and preservation of its revelation of truth. The Greek tongue was honored by being chosen as the golden pitcher in which to convey down the ages the water of life to a thirsty and dying world. But some words had become so steeped in sensuality that they could not be used. They carried such a savor of impurity about them that the Holy Spirit abstained from bringing the truth of God into polluting contact with them. One of the three verbs signifying "to love" had become so saturated with lustful ideas that it was utterly unsuitable to express the holy love which is the central principle of Christianity. Hence it and its derivatives were rejected. In some instances new words were coined, as the noun *agápe*, love, which is not found in the so-called profane writers.

It is our purpose in our course of Greek Testament readings now begun to limit our researches to those changes and inventions in the language which followed the day of Pentecost. The study of the newly coined words will be specially instructive, as showing very plainly what truths of the gospel are so far above natural religion and Mosaism as to require newly created forms of expression. We will endeavor to make ourselves intelligible to the non-Greek reader. As it will be necessary to indicate the word under criticism, we will write it in English letters. Our present reading will set forth the words invented by St. Paul to express *the thoroughness of the Spirit's work in entire sanctification.* It would seem that the inspired apostle foresaw the future denial of this vital truth in nearly every age of the church, and he determined to fortify it with the strongest possible terms in the Greek, and to strengthen these terms by putting them together in novel compound words.

Col. ii. 11 contains a notable instance of strengthening his assertion of the completeness of the cleansing of the believer, by the invention of a noun found nowhere else in the whole range of Greek literature. The word is *apekdusis,* "*putting off* the body of the flesh" (*R. V.*), not "of the sins" of the flesh, as in the *A. V.*, which is a gloss teaching deliverance from sinning. The *R. V.* teaches the greater deliverance from the sin-principle or tendency called original sin. Let us scrutinize Paul's invented compound noun, made up of two prepositions, *apo* and *ek,* and the verb *duo,* all signifying the putting off and laying aside, as a garment, an allusion to actual circumcision. Meyer's comment shows the strength of this word: "Whereas the spiritual circumcision divinely performed consisted in a complete *parting and doing away* with this body [of sin], in so far as God, by means of this ethical circumcision, *has taken off and removed* the sinful body from man [the two acts are expressed by the double compound], like a garment drawn off and laid aside." The italics are Meyer's. If this does not mean the complete and eternal separation of depravity, like the perpetual effect of cutting off and casting away the foreskin, then it is impossible to express the idea of entire cleansing in any human language. This radical change of nature from sinful to holy is effected "by, or by means of, the circumcision of Christ," i.e., which is produced through Christ by the agency of the Holy Spirit procured by him. We do not accept the suggestion of Meyer that this Christian transformation is represented in its *ideal* aspect. God does not tantalize his children with unattainable ideals. He does not command perfection where it cannot be realized through his grace. He is not a hard master, reaping perfection where he has sown only imperfection. "His commandments are not grievous."

1 *Thess. v.* 23 is a text which implies that the regenerate are not entirely purified, and that they may be in answer to prayer. This implies that it is in this life. The expanded "amen" after this prayer, "Faithful is he that calleth you, who will also do it," is a declaration that it is God, and not death, who is the author of this work. There is an important word, *holoteleis*, which is found nowhere else in the New Testament nor in the Septuagint. It is an adjective in form with an adverbial meaning (Kuhner, 264.3). If Paul intended to pray that the Thessalonians might all be sanctified, there were three every-day adjectives which he might have used to express "all." He employed this unique term,

meaning "wholly to the end," or "quite completely," because he had realized in his own experience the uttermost sanctification, and he saw that it was the privilege of every believer. This rare and peculiar word is rendered in the Vulgate *per omnia*, "in your collective powers and parts." "Marking," says Ellicott, "more emphatically that thoroughness and pervasive holiness which the following words specify with further exactness." He thus translates it: "But may the God of peace himself sanctify you wholly, and may your spirit and soul and body be preserved whole without blame in the coming of our Lord Jesus Christ." A Greek version of the Old Testament was made by Aquila in which this word occurs in Deut. xiii. 16, to express the idea of "every whit." We have been explicit in defining this word as indicating the completeness of individual sanctification which is presently presented in detail, and not the cleansing of the totality of the Thessalonian church — may God sanctify you all. Of course the apostle's prayer for the entire purification of the individual includes every individual in the church.

But there is another word in this verse that occurs nowhere else in the New Testament except in James i. 4. It is *holoklaron*, "whole," an emphatic predicate referring to all three following substantives, — spirit, soul, and body. The SPIRIT is the highest and distinctive part of man, his real personality, responsible and naturally immortal, whereby we are receptive of the Holy Spirit through saving faith in Jesus Christ. In the unregenerate it is crushed down and subordinated to the animal *soul*, the seat of the passions and desires which we have in common with the brutes. The next

ST. PAUL INVENTS STRONGER WORDS. 91

component of man, for the entire sanctification of which Paul prays, is the *body*, the material envelope of the immaterial personality and its animal propensities. He says much in his epistles about the sanctification of the body, " Know ye not that your bodies are members of Christ? Know ye not that your body is a temple of the Holy Ghost? glorify God therefore in your body."— 1 *Cor. vi.* 15-20, *R. V.* The body is sanctified wholly when its members are used by the rectified will only " as instruments of righteousness unto God." Paul in this detailed sanctification leaves no more place for sin continuing till death than he does in 2 *Cor. vii.* 1, where " all filthiness of the flesh and of the spirit " is to be cleansed in the act of " perfecting holiness." This word for " whole " which Paul has used only in this place signifies intact, possessing all that belongs to it, and having nothing superfluous. Sin is an excrescence, a deformity which this peculiar word excludes.

In conclusion, on this point we would say that the *spirit* is preserved blameless in its wholeness when the voice of truth always rules it; the *soul* when it resists all the charms of the senses; and, lastly, the *body* when it is not abused as the instrument of shameful actions.

Heb. vii. 25, " Wherefore also he is able to save to the uttermost," etc. The Greek for " uttermost " is *panteles.* This is the only place in the New Testament where it is used, except negatively, " in no wise," in Luke xiii. 11.

It is a strong compound word, meaning "all to the end." The *R. V., margin,* is " completely." This is its true meaning, " perfectly, completely, to the very end," says Delitzsch, " but without necessarily any reference to time." Again he says, "Christ is able to save in every way, in all respects, *unto the uttermost;* so that every want and need, in all its breadth and depth, is utterly done away." This annotation is a perfect answer to his argument in his Biblical psychology in proof of "the unabolished antinomy" in Rom. vii. "The law in the members" warring until death against the law of the mind, and bringing the Christian at his best earthly estate into captivity to the law or uniform sway of sin. Let us believe the exegete rather than the theologian. It is always safer to trust an honest and scholarly expounder than a warped and traditional dogmatist. Modern interpreters unanimously reject the idea of some of the ancient annotators that "uttermost" has here reference to illimitable future time. Besides being unscholarly, this view involves the heresy of Canon Farrar's "eternal hope" for wicked souls after death.

Why was Paul constrained to invent these new and strong terms? Because he was divinely called to describe what never existed before Pentecost, and for that reason had no name, — human souls entirely sanctified through the mission of the Comforter. Why did he not do the same wonderful works before Pentecost, seeing that as God he was omnipresent and omnipotent? He had not the same tools to work with, the completed facts of the gospel ending with the ascension of Christ from the footstool to the throne. "Sanctify them through the truth."

XVII.

ST. PAUL'S NEW WORDS FOR SUPERABOUNDING GRACE.

WE will next examine the newly coined words to express *the victory over sin and the superabounding grace accessible to believers since the coming of the Paraclete on the day of Pentecost.*
Col. ii. 15, "Having spoiled principalities and powers, he made a shew of them openly, triumphing over them in it" (the cross). Here and in one other passage Paul uses the verb *thriambuo*, to triumph. It is found but twice in the Bible, and only as descriptive of pentecostal grace, or, as in this text, of Christ's complete victory over all evil angels and spirits, even the highest in dignity and power. The cross was the Waterloo defeat of all malignant personalities. In what way? Let me explain. Love is power. The highest expression of love is the highest power. The cross is the highest manifestation of love possible in the universe. When Christ, the Son of God, voluntarily bowed his head in death, as a self-sacrifice for men, even for his enemies, he shook the empire of sin to its very foundations. His last cry on the cross, with a loud voice, was the shout of eternal triumph and victory. In a celebrated cathedral in Europe there is be-

hind the altar a cross, with a ladder leaning against it, as if it had been just used in taking down the body of Christ. Beyond a hill in the background of the picture are seen the heads of four men who are bearing it reverently to the tomb. At the foot of the cross a stream of blood is running down the hill towards the spectator. In rapid flight from that crimson rill is seen a serpent instinctively hastening from his conqueror — the painter was a good theologian. But how does this victory of Christ help the Christian when hard pressed by the tempter? It gives great courage to continue the fight, when we are assured that we are battling with a vanquished foe, and that the victor is still in the field and within call, shouting to all his soldiers, "Be of good cheer, I have overcome the world." Faith makes his victory ours.

Rev. xii. 11, "And they overcame him [Satan] by the blood of the Lamb, and by the word of their testimony." The blood of atonement, so appropriated as to prompt to unceasing testimony, is the infallible weapon of victory. So long as Satan could point to the broken law, he could say, "Your case is hopeless, there is no pardon, no mercy in law; it is a straight-edge to lay on your character and show its crookedness. It cannot make you straight. It must condemn you. So all your attempts to be righteous are vain. You would do wisely to throw off all allegiance to that hard Master who reaps where he has not sown, whose law is impracticable, and whose commandments are grievous." But the death of Christ puts a new hope into the despairing soul. It brings to an end the reign of law, so far as it is the ground of pardon. The blood of Christ lays a practicable basis for the forgiveness of sins. Thus the devil and his hostile powers are deprived of their strength, which rested on the law as the sole ground of justification.

2 *Cor. ii.* 14, "Now thanks be unto God, which always causeth us to triumph in Christ." The *R. V.* reads, "always leadeth us in triumph," not as the conquered, but as the ministers of the victory, the soldiers of Christ, who are in the triumphal procession to share the honor. The difference between the same unique verb, to triumph, used here, and the ordinary *nikao*, is that it implies not only victory, but the most public display of it. In Roman triumphal processions incense and perfumes were burnt near the conqueror with different effects, pleasing some but sickening others; to which custom the apostle beautifully alludes in the next verse, "For we are a sweet savor unto God, in them that are saved, and in them that perish." This passage is an encouragement to every consecrated laborer in the Lord's vineyard. No faithful labor will lose its reward. The number of them that are saved may not require large figures in the statistical report; the number that perish may be much larger. Nevertheless, he who scans motives and notes faithful work in obscure places, unappreciated by man, is preparing a triumph for him at the grand Review. Of this he has day by day a foretaste furnished by the indwelling Comforter. Hence he is a victor in every place and every hour.

Says Chrysostom, "Thanks be to God who *triumphs us*, that is, makes us illustrious in the eyes of all. Our persecutors are the trophies which we erect in every land." The eighth and last beatitude of Jesus, the last because it is the sweetest and richest, is pronounced upon them that are persecuted for his sake. St. Paul had tasted persecution again and again. "Of the Jews five times received I forty stripes save one; thrice was I beaten with rods, once was I stoned." Yet so gloriously did God sustain him that he could express his superiority to all his sufferings for Christ, only by borrowing the pageantry of the Roman general making a solemn and magnificent entrance into Rome after an important victory. This God's abounding grace enabled him to do "always" and "in every place." Let the Fainthearts and Littlefaiths in the church study these words of the great apostle and take courage, and put unwavering trust in the Captain of their salvation.

Rom. viii. 37, "Nay, in all these things we are more than conquerors through him that loved us." Here St. Paul's habit of inventing stronger terms expressive of victory than any found in the Greek language appears again in strengthening the every-day verb *nikao*, to conquer, by prefixing the preposition *huper*, the Latin and English *super*. "We are supervictorious." This compound verb is found nowhere else in the whole range of Greek literature. This struggle to lay hold of adequate expressions, this straining of ordinary speech till it breaks out in unheard-of inventions, indicates the greatness of the writer's conception of God's wondrous grace surpassing the believer's utmost need.

Rom. v. 20, "But where sin abounded, grace did much more abound." Here St. Paul invents a term which he repeats in 2 Cor. vii., making the strong compound verb "superabound," the original of which is unique in both sacred and secular Greek. Why these daring inventions by a man of fine literary taste, educated in the University of Tarsus, the greatest centre of scholastic culture east of Athens? Classical authors usually abstain from the use of words coined by themselves, regarding them as barbarisms. Why did St. Paul deviate from a fundamental canon of rhetoric? The river of divine grace flowing through his soul was too full for its ordinary bed; it must overflow its banks, and cut for itself a broader channel, and become an Amazon for all the thirsty nations and generations. The constraint of the Holy Spirit caused these deviations from the standard of reputable use, and prompted this outburst of invented words. There is no other explanation. I want no other. This magnifies God's mercy and love. It shows how the richness of grace transcends the poverty of nature. In our second text (2 *Cor. vii.* 4), " I superabound in joy," we have a phrase that matches St. Peter's " joy unspeakable and full of glory."

Why should so many persons in Christian lands, and some even in the Christian church, be eagerly running to earthly springs to slake their thirst, while the heavens are pouring down Niagaras of living water?

"Love divine, all love excelling,
Joy of heaven to earth come down."

1 *Tim. i.* 14, "The grace of our Lord abounded exceedingly." Here St. Paul prefixes the *super* to another verb, which itself signifies to superabound, giving it the force of "exceedingly to superabound." This verb, *huperpleonazo*, appears nowhere else in the entire

volume of Greek literature. Before the outpouring of the Holy Spirit, "faith" and "love" in human souls were streams so small that they needed no wider terms for their description. Thanks to God for bringing me into being in the glorious dispensation of the Comforter! It is preferable to the days of Christ's flesh.

No New Testament writer except St. Paul uses the compound verb *huperballo*, to exceed, excel, surpass. He has written it five times as descriptive of the graces of the Holy Ghost, who has been aptly styled the communication of God, as the Son is the revelation of him. The texts are 2 Cor. iii. 10, "The glory that excelleth;" ix. 14, "Exceeding grace;" Eph. i. 19, "Exceeding greatness of His power to us-ward who believe; ii. 7, "The exceeding riches of His grace;" iii. 19, "The love of Christ which surpasseth knowledge." We have not time to unfold their wealth of meaning. Let each reader do this for himself.

No other writer in the New Testament has used the noun "*huperbole*," transferred into English as hyperbole. The texts in which this is applied to spiritual blessings are 1 Cor. xii. 31, "And a still more excellent way show I unto you;" 2 Cor. iv. 7, 17, "More and more exceedingly an eternal weight of glory." They are well worth studying by those who are aspiring for a large view of God's promises, as a preparation for their realized fulfilment through increased faith.

XVIII.

ST. PAUL'S NEW PHRASES, — WITHOUT SIN, WITHOUT STUMBLING, WITHOUT SPOT, WITHOUT OFFENCE.

THE wonderful change wrought in believers by the outpouring of the Holy Spirit is very noticeable, especially to the student of the Greek Testament. Strong words not found in the Old Testament, nor in the four Gospels, are either invented by the apostles or borrowed from classical Greek, to convey an adequate conception of the heavenly glory which has come into earthen vessels.

Jude 24. One such word, *aptaistos*, "from falling," St. Jude uses in that remarkable ascription with which this brief epistle concludes. The *R. V.* reads, " Now unto him who is able to guard you from stumbling." This is more difficult than the *A. V.*, inasmuch as the unsteady walker is more prone to stumble than to fall. The indwelling Spirit in his fulness can save even from stumbling.

Of course this does not signify intellectual mistakes. It is salvation from moral failures, however slight. Hence the Vulgate, the supreme standard in the Roman Catholic Church, has *sine peccato*, "without sin." This is the real significance of this adjective.

Christ has sent down from heaven a personal guide, who is able to keep every Christian from the commission of sin. Let every doubter try it for himself. Satan is very busy in keeping in circulation the falsehood that freedom from sin is impracticable and impossible in this world. He who believes this lie will continue to commit sin. He will stupefy his own conscience with the idea that sin is inevitable. Soon he will begin to fight against the scriptural doctrine, "Whosoever is born of God doth not commit sin." There is no doctrine that the devil more cordially hates than the possibility of holiness perfected this side of the grave. When he gets a Christian minister to take his view, and to advocate the necessity of sinning, he is specially well-pleased. His personal attention to that parish is no longer required. The word *aspilos*, "without spot," is used four times in the New Testament; once as descriptive of Christ as a lamb without blemish, 1 Pet. i. 19, and thrice in the portrayal of Christian character. Let us look at these latter in detail.

2 *Pet. iii.* 14. " Be diligent, that ye may be found of him in peace, without spot, and blameless." This is the end towards which we are exhorted to make an effort. Some may object that this spotlessness is not to exist in us during our earthly probation; it is only to be found in us in the day of judgment, to which the context points. If it is found in us, then it must have been in us before death, unless we assume that it is the work of death, or of some sanctifying agency after death. Neither of these last alternatives is supported by the holy Scriptures. But the other two texts de-

termine the time beyond all controversy. 1 *Tim. vi.* 14, "That thou keep this commandment without spot, until the appearing of our Lord Jesus Christ." This is the divinely inspired charge of Paul to Timothy, relating the manner of his life while in this world. God makes the same requirement of the laity as he does of the ministry. Both are to be equally pure. This is certainly indicated in our next text.

James i. 27 includes keeping ourselves "unspotted from the world" as one of the essential elements of pure religion. This seems as impossible to the man of weak faith as it would for a white-robed lady to dance among dye-tubs or tar-buckets without being smirched. But "all things are possible to him that believeth." This world needs a gospel which gives victory over sin. There are two stages of this victory. The first is deliverance from sinning. The new birth introduces the sin-sick soul into a state of triumph over actual sins, giving him the ability not to sin. "There is therefore now no condemnation to them that are in Christ Jesus;" that is, no consciousness of acts of wilful sin. Justification saves from sinning, but not from the tendency to sin, improperly called sin, because it lacks the voluntary element essential to guilt. Controlled tendencies to sin are consistent with non-condemnation, or justification.

But in these proclivities to sin, though repressed, there is peril and cause of inward strife, the flesh warring against the spirit and the spirit against the flesh. When this war ends by the extinction and annihilation of the flesh as the lurking-place of the sin-principle, there is deliverance from sin also, as well as from sinning. Justification, implying regeneration, saves from sinning; entire sanctification saves from sin.

Much like this word is another used by Paul three times, and found in no other New Testament writer. This word is *aproskopos*, "without offence" "toward God and men," as in *Acts xxiv.* 16. This was the kind of conscience the Apostle to the Gentiles "exercised himself to have alway." He has left on record no confession of his failure to hit the high target at which he aimed. There is no doleful lamentation over crooked paths; no self-reproach for falling below his own splendid ideals. His own unoffending life gave him the vantage-ground in exhorting others to the same style of character. In Phil. i. 10 he prays "that love may abound yet more and more in perfect knowledge and all discernment, . . . that ye may be sincere and void of offence." Note that this is "against the day of Christ" (Ellicott), as a probationary preparation for the judgment, and hence it is a proof-text for entire holiness, inward and outward, this side of the grave. In 1 Cor. x. 32, Paul exhorts to unoffending conduct far beyond the realm of ethics in the domain of things morally indifferent, such as eating flesh when it might occasion a weak brother to stumble. Here he appeals to his own perfectly unselfish example as a model for the Corinthian church. "As I also in all things please all, seeking not my own advantage, but that of the many, that they may be saved."

In his *First Epistle to Timothy*, Paul three times employs another adjective expressive of purity, found nowhere else in sacred Greek. It is *anepilaptos*, "irreproachable," or "irreprehensible," applied first to candidates for sacred orders (*iii.* 2), then to Timothy himself (*vi.* 14), and finally to the believing widows (*v.* 7) and, by implication, to all Christians. It is a strong ethical term, implying that one is not worthy of reprehension, even if he should be reprehended by his fellow-men.

We come now to *amomatos*, "without rebuke," found only twice in the New Testament (*Phil. ii.* 15), "that ye may be children of God without rebuke," and (2 *Pet. iii.* 14) a text already quoted, "that ye may be found in him without spot and blameless," or without rebuke.

There is another word for unblamable, *amomos*, used by Paul three times in portraying perfect Christians. *Eph. i.* 4, "According as he hath chosen us [believers] in him before the foundation of the world, that we should be holy, and without blame before him in love." Love is always the sphere in which holiness and blamelessness are found. *Eph. v.* 27, "That it [the church] should be holy and without blemish." *Col. i.* 22, "Unblamable and unreprovable in his sight;" not merely in man's sight, who is incapable of penetrating the invisible springs of action wherein real character lies. Jude 24, *R. V.*, "And to set you before the presence of his glory, without blemish in exceeding joy." We are not to be found faultless in some dark corner of the universe, where flaws and flecks would be unnoticed, but faultless amid the splendors of his ineffable glory. This is what divine grace as mediated by the Holy Spirit, the Sanctifier, is able to do for the weakest saint who perseveringly trusts in Jesus Christ, the adorable Son of God and Saviour of men.

Another once-used word, *ametakinatos*, "unmovable,"

occurs in 1 *Cor. xv.* 58, "that ye may be unmovable," like the granite cliff unshaken by the tornado and the tidal wave. Such vertebrate Christians men and women dwelling in houses of clay may become when "strengthened with might by his Spirit in the inner man."

XIX.

ST. PAUL'S "ELECTION" IS UNTO SANCTIFICATION.

IT is our purpose in the present Reading to discuss the post-pentecostal nouns expressive of sanctification and holiness. They are four in number. They were not used in the four Gospels because the Agent who produces holiness was not yet given as the Sanctifier. He is called the *Holy* Spirit, not to distinguish him from the Father and the Son, who are equally holy, but to designate his office, to create and conserve purity in believing hearts. It may be that he was not sent to do his official work before Christ's ascension, because his instrument, the sword of gospel truth, was not completely forged and tempered, like a Damascus blade. Gospel truth is a series of historical facts beginning with the manger-cradle and ending with the ascent from God's footstool to his throne. There may have been another reason for delaying the gift of the Paraclete. It is reasonable that the incarnate Son of God should be glorified in heaven before he should be glorified on earth. For the work of sanctification glorifies Christ, inasmuch as faith in him, implying perfect self-surrender to him, is the indispensable condition.

The great word for sanctification is *hagiasmos*. It

occurs ten times in the New Testament. St. Paul uses it nine times and St. Peter once. In the *A. V.* it is translated by "holiness" five times, and five by "sanctification." The *R. V.* always renders it by "sanctification." This is the more accurate version, since the ending *mos* in Greek means an act, as does the ending *tion* in English, while the ending *ness*, as holiness, signifies a quality or state.

Hence the revisers have furnished five new proof-texts to the definition of sanctification *as an act* in the catechism of the M. E. Church. Ans. 57. "Sanctification is that act of divine grace whereby we are made holy." The act is that of removing impurity existing in the nature of one already born of the Spirit. Deliverance from sin as a tendency born with us is the act of God through the Holy Spirit.

2 *Thess. ii.* 13, "God chose you from the beginning unto salvation in sanctification of the Spirit and belief of the truth." The election was made in view of the foreknown purifying work of the Holy Spirit wrought on the human condition of freely believing gospel truth. All foreknown, persevering believers are foreordained unto eternal life. This is the key to the first chapter of the Epistle to the Ephesians. Instead of "us" read "believers," to whom the epistle is addressed, "the faithful in Christ."

1 *Pet. i.* 2, "Elect . . . in sanctification of the Spirit," because it is the Spirit who accomplishes the cleansing. The human condition here is "obedience," a synonyme for faith, as disobedience and unbelief are interchangeable terms in the Greek. Rom. vi. 19, "Even so now present your members as servants to righteousness

unto sanctification," the goal of Christian purification in the present life. This is the aim of every regenerate man who places his mental and bodily powers at the disposal of righteousness, as a ruler over him. The purpose of justification, as here stated by St. Paul, is to open the way for entire sanctification. The same truth is stated in other words in verse 22, "But now being made free from sin [as a despot], and become servants to God, ye have your fruit unto sanctification, and the end eternal life."

The power of sin is broken by regenerating grace. The ripe fruit of this state of victory over actual sin is sanctification, which is viewed as done not at death, but before we reach the end, which is eternal life. The plain teaching of this text is that amid this wicked world the sanctified man is to stand laden with luscious fruit many years before he is called to his eternal reward. "Ye are the salt of the earth." "Ye are the light of the world."

Heb. xii. 14, "Follow after peace with all men, and the sanctification without which no man shall see the Lord." Only holy beings can rise to the sight of the Holy One. Whenever the Scriptures speak of the divine vision as the prerogative of the sanctified, it is a blissful, spiritual perception of God here and now. "Blessed are the pure in heart, for they shall see God." When the heart is purged of sin the eye is purged of film. President Edwards, even when a young man, had such enrapturing communion with God, and such a perception of his glory, that He seemed to be the only solid reality, while all earthly things seemed unsubstantial and shadowy. "No man knoweth the Father but the

Son, and he to whom the Son reveals him." The Son reveals the Father by sending the Holy Spirit to anoint the inward eye with eye-salve. The same truth is implied in the declaration, "He that loveth not knoweth not God." The implication is that love has eyes. But where does evangelical love come from? Turn to Rom. v. 5, and you will find the secret. "The love of God hath been shed abroad [a Niagara outpouring] in our hearts through the Holy Ghost which was given unto us."

Spiritual perception comes from love, love comes from the Spirit, who perfectly fills the sanctified heart to the exclusion of the sin-ward trend. Hence sanctification gives clear spiritual eyesight. It is the assurance of faith, or faith merged into certain knowledge, *Eph. iv.* 13. "Unto the unity of the faith and of the knowledge of the Son of God" — not two unities, as the faulty punctuation teaches, but one, as in Westcott and Hort's Greek Testament. To all doubting and hence weak Christians let me speak a word of cheer. Keep on trusting in Christ. The path of faith leads to the wide open door of knowledge, where the sun shines day and night all the year round. "For I KNOW him whom I have believed." An ill use is sometimes made of *Heb. xii.* 14, by quoting it as a threatening against the regenerate who do not realize the completion of the work of inward cleansing. There are no threatenings in the Word of God against the persevering sons of God. "If children, then heirs; heirs of God and joint heirs with Christ." Heirship hinges on sonship, not on development into perfect manhood. Hence it is neither scriptural nor wise to take Mt. Sinai for your pulpit when you preach entire sanctification. Preach this glorious doctrine, "always drawing, not driving." — WESLEY.

The word *hagiasmos* is sometimes used to denote either the act of God, or the believer's own act of preservation of the holiness imparted by the Holy Spirit, as in 1 *Thess. iv.* 3, 4, where abstinence is enjoined from fornication, to the conscience of the pagan world at that time an act of utter moral indifference, as it is to this day. Another text for the act of preservation is 1 *Tim. ii.* 15, "If they continue in faith and love and sanctification with sobriety."

For holiness as a quality there are three words in the Greek Testament, used only by St. Paul, and each used only twice. We come now to a word not found in classical Greek — *hagiotaes*, 2 *Cor. i.* 12. "For our glorifying is this . . . that in holiness and sincerity of God, not in fleshly wisdom . . . we behaved ourselves in the world." This is a very emphatic profession of holiness. The same word is found also in *Heb. xii.* 10, "That we may be partakers of his holiness," not in degree, but in kind. This is the recovery of the lost moral image of God, a glorious possibility to every believer.

Hagnotaes is a word not quite unknown in classical Greek. St. Paul uses it in 2 *Cor. vi.* 6, "In pureness." This is another instance where holiness is unequivocally professed. In 2 *Cor. xi.* 3, St. Paul again employs the same term to express his fear lest the Corinthians had been "corrupted from the simplicity and the *purity* that is toward Christ." The peculiarity of this word is that it means purity, and not consecration. That is true also of the next term, *Hagneia*, in 1 *Tim. iv.* 12, and *v.* 2, "In purity," "in all purity." These texts prove the possibility of inward cleanness in this life, for they both relate to intercourse in human society as now constituted.

XX.

ST. PAUL MAGNIFIES THE MEANING OF PERFECTION.

IN prosecuting our purpose to exhibit those words invented by the apostles, especially by Paul, to convey down the ages the fulness of that grace which came on the day of Pentecost — and came to stay, glory be to the Giver — we now examine the new terms expressive of sanctified and perfected character. The immediate aim of the gospel is the transformation of man's depraved moral nature; the ultimate end is to glorify God in this transfiguration of human spirits restored to the image of their Creator.

The word *teleiotaes*, perfectness, occurs but rarely, not only in profane, but also in Biblical Greek. It first appears in the New Testament after the outpouring of the Spirit. It is used only twice.

Col. iii. 14. "And above all these things *put on* love, which is the bond of perfectness."—*R. V.* Meyer's translation is very instructive — "*in addition to all this, however*, put on *love by which Christian perfection is knit.*" His idea of Paul's meaning is that "Love is to be put on like an upper garment, embracing all, because love brings it about, that the moral perfection is established in its organic unity as an integral whole." The substance of this exegesis is that all the individual virtues are first brought to perfection by love, and then these separate factors are united by love into a symmetrical whole. How love accomplishes this is beautifully shown in Paul's immortal eulogium of this perfect architect of Christian character in 1 Cor. xiii., where love is spoken of first, as the central sun, and all the other virtues are rays, radiating therefrom. But in Col. iii. 14, to our surprise, it is mentioned last. This was a rhetorical necessity, because of the figure in verse 12, of putting on the virtues as different articles of apparel, compassion, kindness, humility, meekness, longsuffering or patience, and a forgiving spirit. Love, from its very nature, in so far as it includes in principle the collective virtues, necessarily has assigned to it, in the making of the Christian's perfect toilet, the place of the upper garment. He is then fit to mingle in the society of archangels, and in this court-dress be presented to King Jesus himself. May neither the reader nor the writer of these words, through lack of this garment, " be ashamed before him at his coming." How natural the precept that follows the description of a saint faultlessly arrayed in the wardrobe of a complete righteousness. " Let the peace of Christ" (*R. V.*), that holy satisfaction of mind wrought by Christ through the Spirit, the blessed inner rest and delicious repose, "arbitrate in your hearts." It is very gratifying to find John Wesley, the heroic defender of Christian perfection in a darker age, so perfectly vindicated by Meyer, pronounced by Dr. Schaff, " the ablest exegete of his age." He even uses the very phrase, " Christian perfection," for which Wesley was almost snowed under by hostile pamphlets written by his clerical brethren of the Anglican Church. The world moves, thank God.

Heb. vi. 1, " Therefore let us cease to speak of the first principles of Christ, and press on unto perfection." — *R. V.* This is the only other passage where this Greek word for perfection is found. It is here represented not as something realized by the lapse of time, or by unconscious growth, and, least of all, attainable only at death. We are exhorted to press on against wind and tide, till we reach this "land of corn and wine and oil," and take up our abode. For the Greek preposition "unto" here embraces both motion to a place and rest in it, and cannot mean an aim at an unattainable ideal. Delitzsch insists that the verb " press on " is used very appropriately here with *epi* (unto), of the mark or object aimed at : it combines the notion of an impulse from without with that of eager and onward pressing haste. To De Wette, who says that perfection here signifies merely a fully developed line of teaching, Delitzsch replies, that "it refers to life as well as to knowledge ; to both word and action." Advanced doctrines are valuable only as they open the way for progress in holiness. Here perfection "refers especially to the fulness of spiritual knowledge manifesting itself in a Christian profession as the antithesis of babyhood," spoken of in *Heb. v.* 13. " Every one that partaketh of milk is without experience of the word of righteousness ; for he is a babe." This can be no other than the profession of Christian manhood, "a perfect man unto the measure of the stature of the fulness of Christ ;" i.e., in which one receives the fulness of Christ, the completeness of what he has to impart, a state of grace in which Paul not only was, but one in which he confidently expected to continue. " And I know that when I come unto you, I shall come in the fulness of the blessing of Christ."—Rom. xv. 29, *R. V.* Says Dr. Whedon, "When Heb. vi. 1 is adduced as an exhortation to advancing to a perfected Christian character, it is no misquotation. It is the noun form of the Greek adjective rendered full age in the chapter v. 14, and signifies *adulthood.*"

1 *Pet. i.* 13 is very inadequately translated in the *A. V.;* Dean Alford and the *R. V.*, margin, give the correct rendering: "Hope perfectly for the grace that is being brought unto you in the revelation of Jesus Christ." The word *teleiose*, "perfectly," is found in the New Testament only here. It is very rare in classic Greek. Hence the widely different versions of this word in this text; as, "to the end," "perfectly sober," and "hope perfectly." The last is the true rendering. Why did Peter employ this unusual phrase? Because there was none which could so fully express his idea of that complete deliverance from doubt which he experienced on the day of Pentecost, and which every believer may to-day experience who by faith receives a personal pentecost. He will henceforth hope without doubt or dejection, with full devotion of soul. So hope, that nothing more in the line of assurance can be desired. The grace which is the object of this perfect hope is being brought to us now, for the present tense is used. "There is," says Bengel, "but one revelation, which takes place through the whole time of the New Testament, by the two appearances of Christ." Thus, also, Luther, Steiger, and others. The bestowment of grace at the second advent is not according to the analogy of faith, and is foreign to the diction of Christ

and his apostles. They never hint any activity of grace when the Judge stands at the door. The Holy Spirit, the organ of God's grace, is never named in connection with the day of judgment. 2 *Cor. xiii.* 9 contains another once-written word, *katartisis,* "perfection;" more exactly, "perfecting," as in the *R. V.* "Your complete furnishing, perfection in Christian morality." — MEYER. "Complete symmetry of Christian character." — WHEDON. "Perfection generally, in all good things." — ALFORD. This is the burden of Paul's prayer for the church-members in Corinth. Paul had too good sense to spend his breath in praying for what was impracticable in this life, and for what would come to them as a matter of course in the hour of death.

Eph. iv. 12, "For the perfecting of the saints." Here is another once-used word, *katartismos,* "perfection." It has nearly the same meaning as the last word we have discussed, signifying, however, that perfection is an act rather than a process.

Says Bishop Ellicott, "The nature of this definite perfecting is explained in verse 13," "Till we all attain unto the unity of the faith and of the perfect knowledge of the Son of God." — DEAN ALFORD. Here are not two unities, but one; faith merging into certain knowledge of Christ revealed to the spiritual perception, as Paul testifies in Gal. i. 16, "When it pleased God to reveal his Son in me." The clear inward revelation of the Son of God is the first effect of entire sanctification, as distinct vision is a sequence of purging the eye of its film. Perfect vision argues perfect purity. *Rom. viii.* 29 and *Phil. iii.* 21 disclose the model on which our moral characters as well as our glorified bodies are to be fashioned, in a word not found anywhere else in Greek literature. This word is *summorphos*. There is no English equivalent. The word "copy" comes nearest to it. The Latin *fac-simile* comes still nearer.

We are each of us to be a kind of living, speaking, and working photograph of Jesus Christ. That we may be conformed to the image of the Son of God is the grand aim of all the acts of God in calling the sinner, in justifying and sanctifying the believer, and finally in glorifying him, soul and body, who perseveres in his loyalty to Christ. All whom the omniscient eye foresees as persevering believers has God predestinated to bear the image of his Son, that the Son of God by eternal generation may stand at last with the host of sons by the Spirit of adoption, "a row of glorified brothers, with Jesus at the head."

> "How can it be, thou heavenly King,
> That thou shouldst us to glory bring?
> Make slaves the partners of thy throne,
> Decked with a never-fading crown?"
>
> C. WESLEY.

Rom. viii. 17, In harmony with this inspiring and ennobling thought, St. Paul has used a word not found except in the Epistles. This is *sungklæronomos*, "joint-heir." A personal equality, based on equality of possession, is thus designated. As all American citizens are equal in rights before the law, so all God's sons, including him who bears the unique title of Only Begotten, are equally entitled to the Father's regards. They are "joint-heirs with Christ" in the *fact* of sonship, though not in the *degree* of love.

2 *Tim. iii.* 17, *Artios* is in the New Testament a once-used word. It signifies perfect in qualification for service, rather than in internal virtues or attributes of character. " That the man of God " — a Christian, not a professional title — " may be COMPLETE, furnished completely to every good work " (*R. V.*), by his ability to use the sword of the Spirit, the inspired Scriptures. Every believer should not only know the word of God for his own spiritual health and growth, but he should be skilled in its use for the salvation of others. There should always be two petitions in his prayers, — " Lord, bless me, and make me a blessing."

The ordinary words for " perfect " and " perfection," common to the Gospels and Epistles, I have omitted, because they are not " New Bottles."

XXI.

ST. PAUL'S DOCTRINE OF THE ANOINTING.

ANOINTING in the holy Scriptures is either material, with oil, or spiritual, with the Holy Spirit. At his baptism Jesus was baptized with the Spirit, the first person in human history to receive this highest honor possible for men to receive or for Heaven to bestow. For in the Old Testament, anointing was the official inauguration into three of the highest offices of the Hebrew nation, — king and prophet (1 Kings xix. 16), high priest (Lev. xvi. 32), and king (1 Sam. ix. 16). These three offices were typical of a great personality to come in the latter days, called the Messiah, the Christ, or the Anointed One (Ps. ii. 2; Dan. ix. 25, 26; Luke iv. 18). The nature of this anointing is foretold as spiritual: "The Spirit of the Lord is upon me; because the Lord hath anointed me to preach good tidings to the meek." Jesus of Nazareth appropriated this prophecy when he said, "This day is this Scripture fulfilled in your ears." This spiritual anointing being one of his chief credentials, the fact is recorded in John i. 32, 33; Acts iv. 27; x. 38. But the astonishing fact that this unique honor may be shared by all his true disciples, however humble and obscure, down through all the coming generations, was not clearly revealed in the Gospels. It was one of those truths which even his apostles were not able to understand till they had received the anointing itself on the day of Pentecost (2 *Cor. i.* 21). Says Paul to the Corinthians, " Now he which stablisheth us with you in Christ, and hath anointed us, is God." More exact is Meyer : " He who makes us steadfast after he has anointed us." This shows the relation of this anointing to the development and stability of the Christian character. To anoint the eyes with eye-salve is a figurative description of that instantaneous purging of the inward eye of the film of inbred sin, by the incoming of the Sanctifier, imparting the power of clear spiritual perfection (Rev. iii. 18). All that is said about the anointing as the privilege of all believers occurs very naturally after Pentecost. Hence the Greek *chrisma* is not found in the four Gospels ; and it occurs in the New Testament only three times, and all of them in the First Epistle of John : " But ye have an unction from the Holy One, and ye know all things." — ii. 20. In my limitation of "all things " to all spiritual truths, " necessary to life and godliness," I was once criticised by Gilbert Haven, editor of *Zion's Herald*. He said that my exclusion of philosophy and science from the "all things " was a needless limitation, since Christianity is the tree on whose branches all kinds of knowledge are found in perfection. There is a large kernel of truth in the criticism of my translated friend. The most Christian nations are the most scholarly, inventive, and progressive. Those who have the least of God's Spirit have the least intelligence. Many an individual, quickened by the Holy Ghost, has been aroused from mental stagnation to an inquiry after truth, which has led him through the whole range of biblical truth and its outbranchings into all the sciences and philosophies. The unction of the Holy Spirit is the highway to all knowledge. This is especially true of an insight into theology. Says that seraphic Scotchman, Samuel Rutherford, "If you would be a deep divine, I recommend to you sanctification;" i.e., the anointing.

In connection with the word *chrisma*, St. John explains the origin of antichrist. All who have the *chrism*, or anointing, know and honor the *Christ*, the anointed. "As long," says Dr. Whedon, "as we possess the holy *chrism* we will adhere to holy *Christ*." All who do not receive and retain the sanctifying *chrism* reject or abandon the *Christ*, and become anti*christs*, because of the absence of the enlightening *chrism*. (1 *Cor. xii.* 3, *R. V.*) "No man speaking in the Spirit of God saith, Jesus is anathema; and no man can say Jesus is Lord, but in the Holy Spirit." The doctrine of the supreme divinity of Christ, revealed to the soul only by the anointing, protects all the other doctrines of the evangelical system. Hence the Holy Ghost is the only conservator of orthodoxy. The thumbscrew, as a substitute, is a stupendous failure, as is proven by the ghastly history of the Inquisition. The soft doctrines of liberalism creep into churches which do not honor the Third Person of the adorable Trinity, except with their lips, while their hearts are without his indwelling. Departures from him, whether new or old, are always departures from the evangelical standard.

1 *John* ii. 27, "The anointing which ye receive of him abideth in you, and ye need not that any one teach you; but as his anointing teacheth you concerning all things . . . abide ye in him" (*R. V.*, marg.). Here *chrisma* of the Spirit is twice used with emphasis on his teaching office — of which we have already spoken — and his conditional abiding. He will abide in us so long as we heed the injunction, "Abide in him." When the Paraclete takes up his abode in the heart, he intends to stay forever, if the conditions are favorable. Neglect will obscure his brightness, weaving a veil of increasing thickness over his face; and unrepented wilful sin will cause him to leave in grief, to return no more forever. "The sixth chapter to the Hebrews may affright us all," says Rutherford, "when we hear that men may take of the gifts and common graces of the Holy Spirit, and a taste of the powers of the world to come, to hell with them." There is no state of grace this side of glory from which the soul may not finally fall. Yet permanency is the peculiarity of the anointing in the case of the persevering believer. The presence of the Comforter in the sanctuary of the heart, filling it with light, love, and joy, strongly inclines the person to persevere, so that he may freely determine to persist in faith and obedience. Of those who truly receive this anointing, in the fulness of its illumination, strength, and bliss, few ever realize its entire withdrawal. We teach no antinomian anointing when we say this.

Another peculiar office of the *chrisma* is that of sole teacher of certain facts, which it alone can assuredly certify to the exclusion of all other instructors. What are these facts? Adoption into the family of God, and the remission of sins. These facts the anointing declares so authoritatively as to supersede the necessity of any other source of direct certitude. The anointing also creates the soul anew, and makes it conscious of newness of life. Sooner or later, according as the pupil of the Holy Spirit is diligent in scholarship, the anointing imparts the more abundant life, and perfects the enkindled love by exterminating lingering carnality through spiritual circumcision. Then the anointing Spirit shines on his own perfect work in the consciousness of him who now believes with the full assurance of faith. On many other questions he may wisely consult teachers and books, and above all the Book of books. Here he will find marks of the new birth, and tests of his purity by which the testimony of the anointing may be confirmed. He will find directions how to walk in white through a world of pollution without defiling his garments whiter than snow, washed in the blood of the Lamb. He will find the Bible an infallible directory to eternal life. He will find in it a highway along which all who are inspired with "the higher life" walk; on which no unclean foot ever passed, nor lions, nor ravenous beast, only the ransomed of the Lord returning to Zion with songs and everlasting joy upon their heads.

XXII.

ST. PAUL ARRANGES A BOUQUET OF CHRISTIAN GRACES.

BEFORE the day of Pentecost the apostles had experienced the new birth. Proof. First Negative. The absurdity of giving to unregenerate men the great commission to disciple all nations (Matt. xxviii. 19, 20), with the promise of Christ's gracious presence. If Christ, the Head of the church, sent forth unconverted men to convert the world, his church would be justified in following his example of knowingly ordaining unsaved ministers of the gospel. But our positive proof that the apostles were in a state of grace before the effusion of the Spirit is found in Christ's own declarations. "I am the vine, ye are the branches," "Now ye are clean through the word," "They are not of the world, even as I am not of the world." Yet the pentecostal gift wrought a wonderful transformation in these men who had already been born again. The changes wrought in them required the application of terms not found in the four Gospels. Let us examine them. In Eph. iv. 32, is the adjective *eusplanknos*, "tender-hearted." In 1 Pet. iii. 8, it is rendered "pitiful." This virtue proud Rome despised, and treated its possessors with contempt. When in the Flavian Amphitheatre, or Colosseum, where gladiators were led into the arena to butcher one another on festive days, if anyone in that vast assembly of eighty thousand was seen to shed a tear, the police immediately arrested such an offender against good order and excluded him from the building. He manifested a weakness not in harmony with Roman iron-heartedness, which was called *eusplanknos*, "strong-bowelled," spirited, bold, undaunted. St. Paul and St. Peter use the same word; but they read into it a sense entirely different — compassionate, tender-hearted. The heart of steel, which boasted of its ability to resist all appeals to the natural sensibilities, is still the same strong heart; but it is strong to express the divine tenderness which has been poured into it from above, as a fruit of the Holy Spirit. Hence the word used by profane writers to signify iron-heartedness is used after Pentecost to signify the sympathetic and pitiful heart. Therefore we may say that the fulness of the spirit has actually converted at least one Greek word from a heart of stone to a heart of flesh. This is an earnest of the transfiguration and glorification of all the languages of this Babel earth by the gospel of Christ in its universal triumph.

There are three words for gentleness which are new bottles to hold the pentecostal wine. The first is *chraestotaes*, "benignity," kindness, and gentleness. The most noted instance of the use of this word is found in *Col. iii.* 12, where the apostle makes a fragrant bouquet, by grouping together all the virtues which characterize a divine philanthropy. "Put on therefore, as the elect of God, holy and beloved, bowels of mercies, kindness, humbleness of mind, meekness, longsuffering, forbearing, and forgiving, and above all these things put on love, which is the bond of perfectness." All these flowers have the smell of heaven upon them. The only soil on earth into which they can be successfully transplanted are human souls cleansed and filled by the Holy Spirit. Genuine kindness is a divine attribute brought down from heaven by the Son of God. Then it was "that the kindness and love — Greek, *philanthropy* — of God, our Saviour, toward man appeared." — *Tit. iii*, 4. St. Paul is the only writer in the New Testament who uses *aepios*, "gentle." This word etymologically indicates a gentleness that expresses itself in the form of affability, a kindness which has its value, despite the proverb that "kind words butter no parsnips." In 1 *Thess. ii.* 7, St. Paul professes the gentleness of the softly-speaking nurse cherishing the children committed to her care. In 2 *Tim. ii.* 24, he insists on the necessity of this quality in every true "servant of the Lord." He "must be gentle unto all men, apt to teach, patient in meekness, instructing those that oppose themselves."

The last of the three post-pentecostal words for gentleness is *epicikeia*, "fairness," mildness, called by Matthew Arnold, "sweet reasonableness." It pertains more especially to exterior demeanor, to intercourse with others, while the grace of *praotaes*, "meekness," with which it is joined as descriptive of Christ in 2 *Cor. x.* 1, is rather an interior disposition and an absolute virtue. This relative excellence, so aptly described by Arnold, Christians are commanded in *Phil. iv.* 5 to make known unto all men. The unfortunate word "moderation," found in the *A. V.*, has been used as a couch of sloth by many when exhorted to strenuous Christian effort. We are glad that the *R. V.* has used the word "forbearance" instead of "moderation," thus removing this couch from beneath the spiritual sluggard.

In *James iii.* 17, the wisdom that is from above is first pure, then radiant with all the lenient and gentle graces. These demonstrate to worldlings the heavenly origin of the evangel which we are commanded to preach to every creature by devout living as well as by persistent testimony. It is the absence of these fruits of the heavenly vine which obstructs the spread of the gospel at home and in pagan lands. The pagans have keen eyesight. They are studying the question whether Christianity is a mere ideal system, not adapted to men under the dominion of sin, or whether it is a practical scheme of deliverance from the guilt of sin, the love of sin, and the indwelling of sin; in other words, whether the missionary is as good as his book. The great need of the world is not more professors of Christianity, but more Christ-like men and women. Professors may be multiplied on the plane of nature where the gospel has become fashionable. But Christ-like people are the creation of a supernatural agency, even the Holy Spirit in his personal inworking and abiding. That Christianity may attain its maximum power to transform men and elevate society, there must be a radical work wrought with nominal believers who not only do not shine themselves, but, what is worse, they obstruct rays which radiate from truly consecrated souls. It is not only true that one sinner destroyeth much good, but one dead church member casts an eclipse on many souls who would otherwise see Christ, the Light of the World.

In conclusion, we say that the surprising contrast between the teachings of the New Testament and that of the philosophers and moralists is in the importance it assigns to the milder virtues, and the discount it places on the heroic virtues, reversing the order of their importance. The work of the Holy Spirit in the fulness of his incoming and abiding in the believer is conspicuous in the development of those virtues which proud philosophy despised, although their universal diffusion would increase the happiness of mankind greatly.

XXIII.

ST. PAUL SHOWS THE CERTAINTY OF SPIRITUAL KNOWLEDGE.

WE close this extended series of readings by showing the effect of the outpouring of the Spirit in quickening the spiritual perceptions and giving a certitude of God and of spiritual realities. We will limit our Reading to the study of only two compound words employed by the apostles after the day of Pentecost to express the fulness, clearness, exactness, and certainty of their spiritual knowledge.

Heb. x. 22. The first word is *plaerophoria,* "most certain confidence." "Let us draw near with a true heart, in full assurance of faith." The key to the meaning of this noun is found in the use of its cognate verb in 2 *Tim. iv.* 5. "Make full proof of thy ministry;" and in 2 *Tim. iv.* 17. "That the preaching by me might be fully known." The verb here used was used by Justin, the martyr, when examined by the prefect Rusticus. Said the prefect, "Do you suppose that you will ascend up to heaven to receive some recompense there?"—"I do not suppose," was the martyr's ready correction, "but I know and am perfectly assured." This means that the fulness of the Spirit enables us to come to God without any hesitancy, disbelief, or diffidence as to our right and fitness through the blood of Christ to draw nigh to the Holy of Holies, the place of God's presence. This right is far higher than that of the Israelite when sprinkled with the blood of the first covenant at the base of Mt. Sinai. For the true believer in Christ has a superior qualification, being provided with holiness inwrought by the Holy Spirit, to enter into the sanctuary, or Holy place, where God dwells. For all believers are priests, and have the priestly prerogative of access to God, not granted to the Hebrew laity.

Heb. vi. 11, "But we earnestly desire that every one of you do show the same diligence with regard to the full assurance of hope unto the end." This teaches us that converted Hebrews had a full conviction and a joyous assurance, which they are exhorted to keep unshaken to the end of their Christian course. On this text Wesley bases his doctrine that to some at least is granted the highest degree of divine evidence of persevering grace, and of eternal glory. See his notes. J. Fletcher concurs. See his, " Checks," vol. ii., p. 659, note.

This idea harmonizes more perfectly with Calvinism than with Arminianism. For this reason Methodists have generally abstained from preaching a state of grace not attainable by all, but bestowed on a few favored ones — the assurance of eternal salvation.

Col. ii. 2. That the gospel abundantly satisfies the demands of reason and the intellect is shown where "the full assurance of understanding" is spoken of, beautifully expressed by Meyer as " the lofty blessing of full certainty of Christian insight," the whole riches of which may be attained by all believers in Christ who claim their heritage by faith. The cumulative fulness of spiritual certitude described in this verse is surprising indeed, as we shall very soon see. This full assurance of the intellect is grounded on the testimony of the Spirit.

This word is found also in 1 *Thess. i.* 5. "Much assurance." This is interpreted as expressive of the assured persuasion on the part of the preachers who had proclaimed the gospel in power and in the Holy Ghost. They did not preach with an interrogation point at the end of every utterance, as if in doubt themselves.

Much is said in the New Testament, especially after the day of Pentecost, about knowing God, and our adoption into his family, and the indwelling of his Spirit, and the certainty of spiritual realities. The ordinary word for knowledge in classic Greek is *gnosis*. But Paul added an intensive prefix to it, changing it to *epignosis*, giving it a stronger meaning. Peter in three instances follows Paul's example. Hence this Bible reading is constructed upon the word *epignosis* found in the Greek Testament, inadequately translated in most of the versions, though I have a version by Dean Alford which has it accurately translated, which version will be used in a part of this Bible Reading. The subject is the Christian's privilege to know God without a peradventure or a doubt, to be certain of the forgiveness of sins, and of the indwelling of the divine Comforter and Sanctifier. The object of the lesson is to show that God has laid down no foundations for doubt, or for uncertainty, in this important matter. For it is a matter of transcendent interest to every human being. To know God is eternal life; and some are without the knowledge of God. I speak this, says the apostle, to your shame.

I am to discuss the question of how far we may know God in this life. There is no dispute among Christians that we have a revealed knowledge of God in his word; but this does not satisfy, because it is indirect and roundabout. It is designed to be a stepping-stone to a better kind of knowledge. It is a knowledge through testimony, the testimony of others coming down to us through the centuries that are past; the latest testimony given is eighteen hundred years old. We want a more certain knowledge than that. We want a direct knowledge. Men wish to have a knowledge of God at first hand if it is a possible thing. Hence the philosophers have sought after this direct knowledge of God, and they have not succeeded very well. They are called theosophists. They have sought through physical operations, through magic, and some of them have thought they could find God at the bottom of their crucibles, in the laboratory of the chemist. We have even the German fire philosophers, who labored very hard to find God by chemical processes. A great many, especially in India, thought they found God by intense thought, going away by themselves and sitting down and thinking, and thinking, and thinking upon one subject. And some of them say they have had a mental illumination which has enabled them to grasp God as an object of direct knowledge. These are called the philosophical theosophists.

I sympathize with this desire to have a direct knowledge of God, clear and satisfactory, the knowledge of God in spiritual realities; but I abhor what is called theosophy, because it ignores the revealed knowledge of God, and does not seek God through his word. It seeks him through other agencies such as I have just described. The great difficulty with these people is that they apply the wrong organ to spiritual knowledge. They apply the intellect, the head instead of the heart. It is very much like applying the ear to the rainbow in order to perceive its beauties, and the eye to an oratorio in order to delight in its music. We know God through love. St. John tells us that. He that loveth not knoweth not God. I may have the intellect of an archangel, but if I do not love I will not know God. That is the difficulty with theosophy.

Its second great difficulty is that it knows nothing of the Holy Spirit. God reveals himself to us through his Son Jesus Christ, but he communicates himself to us through the Holy Spirit. This is the beautiful relation of the three persons in the Trinity,—God the Father, revealing himself to the world, to our intelligence, to our faith, rather our intelligent and reasonable faith, in his Son Jesus Christ, but giving a direct and experimental knowledge of himself by communicating himself to our spiritual intuitions through the person of the Holy Ghost.

After the Holy Ghost was given, a word comes into the Greek Testament which is not found in the four Gospels, a strengthened form of the word knowledge, *epignosis*, meaning exact, clear, full, perfect, satisfactory knowledge; of course not exhaustive knowledge of God and of spiritual things. All these adjectives are used by the various great scholars of the age now living, and some who have passed away, — by Meyer, Bishops Lightfoot, Ellicott, and Westcott, and Dean Alford, and many others.

Now let me read a few passages in which this word occurs, and you will see how much it adds to the strength of the New Testament. Perhaps the question may arise in your mind why the revisers did not translate this strengthened word for knowledge, by the use of the adjectives which I have given. The revisers of the New Testament were far more conservative than the revisers of the Old Testament in some particulars, and they hesitated to put in two words instead of one. They hesitated to put in the adjectives which I have indicated — *full, clear, perfect, exact, certain;* though some of those very men in their commentaries do thus translate it.

The first passage is *Rom. i.* 28, "And even as they did not like to retain God in their knowledge [full knowledge, clear knowledge, certain knowledge], God gave them over to a reprobate mind, to do those things which are not convenient" or becoming. If you will read that first chapter of Romans, you will be struck with the fact that in several places it is said God gave people over to certain things, and those things were the things which they liked, and God gave them over because they did not like a full and clear knowledge of Him. He gave them over to some very unworthy and base things. So that they exchanged monotheism, or the knowledge of the one God, for images of four-footed beasts, and birds, and creeping things, and began to worship them.

In *Rom. iii.* 20 the word occurs again. "Therefore by the deeds of the law there shall no flesh be justified in his sight, for by the law is the FULL knowledge of sin."

Men may have a knowledge of sin without the written law. The pagans all over the world have a knowledge of sin, a somewhat indefinite knowledge; but when God's law is preached to them, they begin to have a knowledge of sin that puts them under condemnation, weighty condemnation, and they begin to cry out after the mercy of God. So the adjective "full" brings out that fact — that the law or revelation is requisite to the full knowledge of sin, as well as the full knowledge of God. Bishop Taylor in his preaching says that first he broadswords his congregation with the law — cuts them down, cuts their hearts through and through with the law. In his great tour through Southern Africa, made in 1867, among the Kaffirs, he generally preached two days in each place; and the first day he preached on the Ten Commandments, and the second day he preached on the day of Pentecost, and the outpouring of the Spirit. The Kaffirs were converted a hundred in a day, seven thousand in all.

Rom. x. 2, "For I bear them record that they have a zeal of God, but not according to *exact* and *certain* knowledge."

The Jews had some knowledge of God; but they did not have a full knowledge of him, because they did not recognize his Son through whom he reveals himself to men. Hence he says, "I bear them record that they have a zeal of God, but not according to definite knowledge." A zeal to know God, and to serve him, very imperfectly and very fanatically, because they rejected the grand organ of divine revelation, which is the divine Logos, the eternal Son.

Now turn to *Col. i.* 9, 10, "For this cause we also, since the day we heard it, do not cease to pray for you, and to desire that you might be filled with the PERFECT knowledge of his will in all wisdom and spiritual understanding."

Mark the strength of the expression. Filled with knowledge, filled with a *thorough* knowledge of God's will. That shows us the path of duty pretty clearly. It pours the light upon us. A thorough knowledge of God's will, in all wisdom and spiritual understanding; or spiritual sagacity, spiritual sharp-sightedness.

Phil. i. 9, "And this I pray, that your love may abound yet more and more in knowledge."

That is, in *full* knowledge. The strengthened word is used here. And in all judgment, all perceptivity.

Just mark the strength of these terms here for knowledge, both of them. Abound yet more and more *in knowledge and in all perceptivity.* It is a very strong expression. I call your attention to the fact that this 9th verse justifies me in saying that love is the organ of knowledge, the knowledge of God. "And this I pray, that your love may abound yet more and more." Love is the sphere in which knowledge, full, clear, satisfactory, experimental knowledge, dwells.

Heb. x. 26. This throws light upon a very perplexing question, "For if we sin wilfully after that we have received the knowledge of the truth, there remaineth no more sacrifice for sins."

A man wrote me the other day, an eminent preacher,

wanting that passage explained to him. There is used here the strengthened form of the word knowledge. If we sin wilfully after that we have received a clear, full, undoubted, thorough, satisfactory, and experimental knowledge of the truth, there remaineth no more sacrifice for sins. What does he mean? He is writing to the Hebrews. If a converted Hebrew backslid, where did he backslide to? He slipped back into Judaism. If a Jew had been converted and brought into the full, experimental knowledge of the truth, and then had deliberately gone away from Christ and rested again in Judaism, of course he rejects not only Christ, but the whole system of truth of which he is the centre. He can find no salvation now in Judaism. There is no salvation there for him. I do not say that every Jew is going to be lost. Many pious Jews may be saved on the same ground that the pious pagans may be saved, if they have the spirit of faith and the purpose of righteousness. They may never have seen a New Testament; they may have been brought up under such circumstances that the light of Christian truth has not had any chance to shine in their minds, and they can be saved on the same basis that the pious pagan or the pious Mohammedan may be. What do I mean by the spirit of faith? The disposition to grasp the object of faith were it presented. What do I mean by the purpose of righteousness? The disposition to walk by the rule of the divine requirements, the Ten Commandments, if that rule were made known.

Now we will read this passage again, calling attention to the fact that the word "sin" in the present tense denoting continuousness here signifies not a single act of sin, but a course of sin. If a Christian Jew enter upon a career of sin, a continuous course of sin, wilfully, after he has received the full experimental knowledge of the truth of God's salvation, and then deliberately turn away from it, and go back to Judaism, he would find in Judaism no sacrifice adequate to meet his case. If he should repent and come back, there is still virtue in the all-sufficient sacrifice of Jesus Christ to save him. That is my understanding of this difficult passage.

2 *Peter* ii. 20. This is in the same line. "For if after they have escaped the pollutions of the world through the FULL knowledge of the Lord and Saviour Jesus Christ, they are again entangled therein, and overcome, the latter end is worse with them than the beginning. For it had been better for them not to have *fully* known [here is the strengthened verb] the way of righteousness, than, after they have perfectly known it, to turn from the holy commandment delivered unto them."

2 *Tim.* ii. 25, "In meekness instructing those that oppose themselves; if God peradventure will give them repentance to the *full* or *certain* knowledge of the truth."

The word "acknowledging" in the King James Version is the word which I am speaking of, the word for full knowledge.

2 *Peter* i. 1-3, "Simon Peter, a servant and an apostle of Jesus Christ, to them that have obtained like precious faith with us, through the righteousness of God and our Saviour Jesus Christ: Grace and peace be multiplied unto you through the CERTAIN knowledge

of God, and of Jesus Christ our Lord; according as his divine power hath given unto us all things that pertain unto life and godliness, through the knowledge of him that hath called us to glory and virtue."

Huxley, the great scientist, in the year 1869 invented a new term, *agnosticism*, which was caught up by all the people that did not know God and his salvation, and were filled with doubt upon the subject, and were running into various forms of scepticism and materialism, and they all of them began to apply that word to themselves, and began to boast that they were *agnostics*. We can find many people here, in the Athens of America, who are saying, with manifest pride, "I am an agnostic, I am an agnostic." What does an agnostic mean? It means an *ignoramus*. That is the exact meaning of the word. How do they use it? They use it to mean that they do not know whether God exists, and they do not know that he does not exist. They do not wish to be called atheists. So they take this position: Is there a God? I do not know. Is atheism true? I do not know. Is there a hereafter after death? I do not know; there is not sufficient proof. God is so great and infinite, the human mind is so narrow and finite, that it cannot have a knowledge of God. Then they say that God is unknown, and therefore he is unknowable. We have no faculties by which we may know him, because the finite cannot grasp, cannot comprehend, infinite. That is the great trouble that intellectual men are in now. They cannot find out that there is a God and be certain about it. Let them come forward for prayers. Let them repent of their sins. Let them cry, "God be merciful to me a sinner!" Let them keep that up a few hours, and they will begin to find out that there is a God. And if they keep it up a few hours more they will find out that he is a pardoning God. If they come in the name of his Son, Jesus Christ, turning away from their sins, their pride, abandoning every other hope and every other plea, casting themselves upon the broad merit of the atoning death of Jesus Christ, they will find the pardon of their sins. And if they keep on and plead the promises made with respect to the day of Pentecost, they will find a personal pentecost, the fulness of the Holy Ghost, God imported by the Holy Ghost into the very centre of their beings.

That is the great trouble with the agnostics. They are applying the wrong organ to the question of spiritual knowledge. Let them come and seek God with the heart, believing in his Son, and they will soon find their feet standing upon the everlasting rock of certainty. Gladstone says, "Although I cannot embrace the mountain with my arms, I can touch it with my hand. Knowledge may be positive, though it is not exhaustive."

In *Titus i.* 1, the same word occurs. The strengthened Greek word occurs in all these passages. " Paul, a servant of God, and an apostle of Jesus Christ, according to the faith of God's elect, and the CERTAIN knowledge of the truth which is after godliness." The short epistle of Philemon has the same word in it in the sixth verse. "That the communication of thy faith may become effectual by the FULL knowledge of every good thing which is in you in Christ Jesus."

You do not know, what good things are in you until you receive this knowledge by the Holy Spirit, revealing himself, revealing God to you; translated in our version, by the word "acknowledging." We do not know ourselves, our real worth, till we know God by a heart experience.

I suggested that there was one writer that dared to translate these passages aright. Dean Alford, in his commentary, calls attention to the fact in all these cases. In his version he puts in the adjective in many of the passages, some of which I am now about to quote.

Eph. i. 17, "That the God of our Lord Jesus Christ, the Father of glory, would give unto you the Spirit of wisdom and revelation in FULL knowledge of him."

I call your attention to these because some of you might imagine that I am developing this Bible Reading out of my own imagination. Dean Alford was one of the most eminent men of England, a divine in the Church of England, who spent his life on the Greek Testament. In his notes he is very emphatic upon rendering this term by some such adjective as this.

God has laid down no foundations for doubt; he does not want people to walk in the mist, not knowing whither they go. If you will have faith in the Lord Jesus you will be brought out into a large sphere of knowledge. Dean Alford, I believe, enjoyed what he himself insisted upon in his commentary. I was touched the other day in reading in the Encyclopædia Britannica a little account of him, where it gives what is written upon his tombstone, "The lodge of a pilgrim on his way to the New Jerusalem." He knew God and he had a sense of the reality of spiritual things. He knew that there is a new Jerusalem to which he would come.

Eph. iv. 13, "Till we all attain unto the unity of the faith, and of the PERFECT knowledge of the Son of God, unto the full grown man, unto the measure of the stature of the fulness of Christ." — ALFORD.

This remarkable text was made for such a discussion as this. Christ has gone up on high. He has sent down or called into activity various orders of ministers, apostles, prophets, evangelists, pastors, and teachers, "for the perfecting of the saints, unto the work of the ministry, for the edifying of the body of Christ till we all come" — this is the final and grand aim of the whole — "till we all come in the unity of the faith and of the perfect knowledge of the Son of God." Not two unities, but one. Every version and every manuscript of the Greek, except the last critical ones issued from Cambridge, have a comma here in the wrong place, a comma after faith. What is the unity? It is faith becoming knowledge, faith merging into knowledge, faith ending in knowledge, the oneness of faith and knowledge. Till we all come in the unity of faith and of the knowledge of the Son of God. All true faith ends in knowledge, and the knowledge is perfect knowledge, according to Dean Alford's translation. Not exhaustive knowledge, but experimental, and hence, perfect knowledge, in the sense that it excludes doubt. Agnostics say no man can know God because God is so large; no man can know him because the finite cannot fathom or grasp, or reach clear round the infinite. Bless your dear soul, must a knowledge be perfectly exhaustive in order to be positive? Do you know the Atlantic Ocean? You have seen a part of it, have you not? but you have not gone from bottom to top, from the North Pole to the South Pole; you have not been upon every single yard or square foot of it. But you are positive that you know it. A knowledge of a fact does not depend upon our having an exhaustive analysis of it. We may have a certain satisfactory and positive knowledge without having an exhaustive knowledge. Till we all come in the unity of the faith and of the perfect knowledge of the Son of God. And that we cannot fathom. No man knoweth the Son but the Father. This is one of the grand proof-texts of his divinity. No man has a sounding-line long enough to fathom the Son of God but the Father. Nevertheless, we may have *certain* knowledge of him and be *perfectly* sure that we know him and are united with him. We may be positive and certain of it without a doubt, because the Son of God reveals the Father to us who believe.

Col. iii. 10, "And have put on the new man, which is being renewed unto PERFECT knowledge after the image of him that created him." — ALFORD.

That shows a work of grace after the new birth. Have put on the new man, which is renewed, being renewed, in perfect knowledge, after the image of him that created him.

Col. ii. 2, "That their hearts may be confirmed, they being knit together in love, and unto all the riches of the full assurance of understanding, unto the THOROUGH knowledge of the mystery of God." — ALFORD.

Most of the manuscripts put in as an explanation of

what the mystery of God is — Christ even Christ. Thus is it in the revised New Testament. The King James version reads, "Of God, and of the Father, and of Christ." But I call your attention here to the cumulation of phrases, as if Saint Paul had strained the Greek language so we could almost hear it snap, to pile up phrases strong enough to express his own conception of the clearness of the knowledge which we may have of Jesus Christ. "Unto all riches!" When anything is superlatively excellent, St. Paul always brings out this word "riches;" riches of grace, riches of assurance, riches of knowledge, and so on. Unto all riches! Not some riches. "All riches of the full assurance of understanding!" God provides for men's intellects as well as for their hearts. To the perfect or thorough knowledge of the mystery of God, which is Christ.

1 *Tim. ii.* 4, "Who willeth all men to be saved, and to come unto the CERTAIN knowledge of the truth." — ALFORD.

Yes, that is God's wish, not his decree. He wishes all men to be saved, and to come to the certain knowledge of the truth. Hear this, ye who walk in darkness. You are not walking according to God's will. Mr. Spurgeon one day in his sermon spoke of having had a great conflict with doubts. The deacons took him aside and asked him why he did not confess that he had been stealing horses, or stealing sheep, or something of that kind. They said it was just as bad to doubt God as it was to violate his law. And Mr. Spurgeon said that he stood reproved. He never would again doubt God, or confess his doubts of God. The deacons were right. It is not God's will that we should walk in doubt, but in the certain knowledge of truth.

2 *Tim. iii.* 7, " Ever learning and never able to come to the FULL knowledge of the truth." — ALFORD.

Did you ever see any such persons? Our churches are full of them. The purpose of this Bible Reading is, if there are any readers of this class, that they may be shamed out of their living in this wretched state. Take God at his word! Put his promises to the test, and see if you do not mount up above the mist to a place where the sun shines day and night all the year round!

2 *Peter i.* 8, " For these things being in you, and multiplying, render you not idle nor yet unfruitful towards the PERFECT knowledge of our Lord Jesus Christ." — ALFORD.

The things spoken of here is the list of Christian virtues, beginning with faith. " Giving all diligence, add to your faith, virtue [or courage]; and to virtue, knowledge; and to knowledge, temperance [or self-control]; and to temperance, patience; and to patience, godliness; and to godliness, brotherly kindness; and to brotherly kindness, love. For if these things be in you and abound, they will make you that ye shall neither be barren nor unfruitful in the perfect knowledge of our Lord Jesus Christ."

Now, do not say that all this perfect knowledge is going to be after you are dead! A great many people are putting every good thing beyond the river of death, and living on starvation rations here. Just take the promises of God, and enjoy them this side of the river. This is the divine purpose. There is a very great comfort and very great strength in it.

At the suggestion of Joseph Cook and Dr. McCosh

the word *merognostic, knowing in part* (1 Cor. xiii. 12), has been invented and put into the so-called "Standard Dictionary." Whether this new word will become current in the English language we are not certain. It may be convenient to express our narrow view of God's providences and our limited intellectual conceptions of his nature and works. It is certain that Paul did not need it to express his experimental knowledge of God in Christ, his personal Saviour and Lord. As regards the assurance of Christian truth, Paul was neither a *gnostic*, implying a conceit of spiritual knowledge ; nor an *agnostic*, professing ignorance of revealed truth ; nor a *merognostic*, having only doubtful glimpses of divine verities ; but he was an *epignostic*, rejoicing in perfect assurance of spiritual realities. This last word, invented by the author of this book, has as yet no standing in reputable English, but it is easily derived from *epignosis*, and is quite intelligible to the Greek scholar, indicating one who knows God in Christ beyond a doubt. Although the term may not be in the dictionary, the reality is in the heart of every one who claims his full Christian heritage. Thus endeth this reading of the Scriptures. May it be to God's children, wandering in the dark forests of spiritual uncertitude, a blazed path out into the sunny clearing where they can see the open gates of the celestial city.

XXIV.

SOME OF THE DIFFERENT MEANINGS OF THE WORD "FLESH."

It is quite a remarkable fact that none of the words of Christ have been perverted into proof-texts in support of sin in the heart of the believer. The only exception is the twist given by the Plymouth Brethren school of teachers to John iii. 6 : "That which is born of the flesh is flesh." They interpret the Greek perfect tense "has been born" as implying that the flesh remains unchanged till physical death. Hence they infer that the sin-principle must inhere in the believer so long as he dwells in a house of clay. Their fallacy lies in transferring to the Gospels the Pauline use of the term *sarx*, "flesh," as a synonym for sin. It is never so used in the four Gospels. Cramer, in his Biblico-Theological Lexicon, arranges the meanings of this word under six classes. In the first five there is no hint of sin. The sixth definition embraces the peculiar Pauline signification : "*The sinful condition of human nature in and according to its bodily manifestation.*" Then follows an exhaustive list of quotations, filling more than one quarto page, all taken from the epistles, chiefly from those of St. Paul. There is not one taken from the four Gospels, which are abundantly quoted under the five shades of meaning which do not imply sin. He classifies *John iii.* 6 under his third definition: "*That which mediates and brings about man's connection with nature.*" In this text, "That which is born of the flesh is flesh," the term flesh " means the whole of human nature apart from the life-giving Spirit. This can but produce flesh." — ALEX. MC-LAREN. Says Pres. Timothy Dwight, "The flesh is to be understood here in the physical, not in the moral, sense."

Meyer insists that the Pauline view should not be "attributed to John, because it is strange to him." With Weiss and Julius Müller, we understand Jesus to say that the new birth has for its sphere the immaterial part of human nature, "as the corporeal birth only produces the corporeal, sensual part." Henceforth the regenerate is free from the dominion of the animal nature; and if he claims the full heritage of the believer, he is entirely filled with the Holy Spirit, the Sanctifier, and walks in the newness of the *Holy* Spirit as the efficient principle of the Christian Life.

Turning now to the apostolic epistles, we find in 1 John i. 8, a text which every doctrinal opposer of entire sanctification as a present possible experience hurls with an air of triumph against its advocates, as deceiving themselves and not having the truth in them. Just what St. John means will be seen when we find what great errors he is writing against. He lived long enough to see the germs of so-called gnosticism springing up to corrupt the church. Their basal error was dualism, two eternal, uncreated principles in conflict, good and evil, the latter making its abode in matter, and identifying itself therewith in such a way as to be inexpungable by God himself. One branch of the gnostics taught that spirit is perfectly free from sin, and cannot be tainted or soiled by it, since sin is limited to the sphere of matter, and there is no bridge nor pontoon from one to the other. Hence the human spirit is sinless, though its material envelope may be foul with lust, debauchery, gluttony, and drunkenness. The favorite simile of the gnostics was, the sinless soul in a polluted body is like a golden jewel in a pigsty, encompassed by filth, yet without mixture with it. He who embraced this philosophy had no need of the blood of Christ as the ground of the forgiveness of sin, because his spirit, his real personality, had no sin to be forgiven, no pollution to be cleansed. This is exactly what St. John means when he says, 1 *John* i. 8, "If we" — i.e., any gnostic — " say we have no sin," needing the atonement, "we deceive ourselves, and the truth is not in us." But if any one abandons his false philosophy, confesses his sin, and makes a clean breast by his full acknowledgment and genuine repentance, "He is faithful and just to forgive us our sins, and to cleanse us from all unrighteousness." This exegesis is in perfect harmony with the announced purpose of the epistle, ii. 1, "That ye sin not." It avoids making John flatly contradict himself when he says (iii. 9), "Whosoever is born of God doth not commit sin." Above all, it avoids the absurdity of recommending a medicine as a perfect cure, and in the same breath branding every testimony to such a cure through its use as a piece of self-deception, or an unmitigated lie. John advertises the blood of Christ

DIFFERENT MEANINGS OF THE WORD "FLESH." 149

as the perfect antidote for all unrighteousness. Is he now so illogical and demented as to denounce as untrustworthy every one who declares himself healed through the application of this antidote? Is this the way to interpret a writer of ordinary common-sense? Does such an exegesis honor the Spirit of inspiration by which John wrote? Let him answer who perverts this text into a divine negation of holiness of heart and life in this world. In this very epistle St. John writes: "For this purpose the Son of God was manifested, that he might destroy the works of the devil." What are these works of the devil but human hearts defiled by sin through the wiles of Satan? Who are more evidently protecting the works of the devil than they who deny the power of the Son of God to accomplish the purpose of his mission, and decry the witnesses to his perfect saving grace?

We have seen writings in which *James iv.* 5 is quoted in proof of the impossibility of living without sin. Let us examine this text. The *R. V.* hints that there is a different reading in the Greek. Instead of "dwell," it has the causative "made to dwell." There are two marginal readings, from which we are quite sure of the meaning. The fourth verse, in Old Testament style, stigmatizes the apostasy of the righteous as spiritual adultery, the divine covenant being viewed as the marriage of God's people to himself: "Ye adulteresses, know ye not that the friendship of the world is enmity with God?" To preserve Christians from this worldward tendency, which is spiritual adultery, God has caused his Spirit to abide within them, to watch over their fidelity, most jealously desiring our undivided love for the heavenly Bridegroom. This exegesis of the fifth verse brings it into beautiful harmony with the fourth, by carrying out the figure of spiritual wedlock by the appointment of the indwelling Spirit as its guardian, to keep believers faithful to their marriage vow. There is no reference to the human spirit in this verse; much less is there permission for envy to dwell therein. It is the Holy Spirit jealously desiring our perfect love to God.

1 *Pet. v.* 10. It is alleged that St. Peter in this text intimates that this perfect heart loyalty to God cannot exist here and now, but only "after ye have suffered a while." Our answer shall be a quotation from Dean Alford's notes: "'His eternal glory in Christ Jesus' belongs to 'hath called;' and 'when ye have suffered a while' belongs to the same words, 'hath called,' not to what follows, as is decisively shown by the consideration that all four verbs — perfect, stablish, strengthen, and settle — must belong to acts of God on them *in this life*, while these sufferings would be still going on." Our paraphrase conveys the exact meaning, "May the God of all grace, who hath called you unto his eternal glory in Christ [not now, but], after ye have suffered a little while, himself [now, immediately] perfect, stablish, strengthen, and settle you [without waiting to do or to suffer more]."

XXV.

OLD TESTAMENT STUMBLING-BLOCKS REMOVED.

THERE are several misunderstood passages in the Holy Scriptures which seem to justify an unholy life; texts which apparently teach that sin is necessary to the present state, and Christian perfection, or deliverance from inbred sin through the Holy Ghost shedding abroad the love of God in its fulness in the heart, is a chimera. It is the object of this chapter to show that no word of the Holy Scriptures, properly interpreted, upholds, or in the least extenuates, sin as an act, or as a state or tendency.

1 *Kings viii.* 46. In his prayer at the dedication of the Temple, Solomon represents various future national exigencies for which he implores the intervention of Jehovah bringing deliverance. Among these is national sin followed by national captivity. "If they sin against thee (for there is no man that sinneth not), and thou be angry with them," etc. Here the stumbling-block is in the parenthesis, which seems to declare, with the Westminster Catechism, that every man, after all that grace can do for him, is continually sinning. If this is man's normal condition, there is no pertinency in the supposition, " If they sin." It is very much like the governor of Massachusetts at the laying of a corner-stone of an

insane asylum, being reported as saying in the dedicatory address, "If any citizen of this commonwealth becomes crazy, and there is no citizen who is not crazy, let him come here and be cured of his mental maladies." All the readers would say that there is a contradiction in the speech, through the blunder of the reporter or the printer; and they would immediately correct the parenthetic clause, and make it read thus: "For there is no citizen who *may* not be crazy." Now, an examination of this text in the original Hebrew develops the fact that the word for "sinneth" is in the future tense, the only form in the Hebrew for expressing the potential mood. (See Nordheimer's Grammar, § 993, Green, § 263, Rodiger's Gesenius, p. 238, d.) The corrected rendering then would be, "For there is no man who *may* not sin;" i.e., there is none impeccable, none that is not liable to transgression. Thus the alleged criminal imperfection is not a declared fact, in any sense whatever, but only a declared possibility. The text properly translated gives no support to the doctrine of the necessity of sin in a believer. Accordingly the Latin Vulgate, the standard of the Roman Catholic Church, has *non peccet*, "may not sin," as also the interlineal translations in the Antwerp, London, and Paris Polyglots; and in the latter two we have the same rendering of the Syriac and Arabic versions.

The same criticism and correction apply to *Eccl. vii.* 20, which should read thus: "For there is not a just man upon earth, that doeth good, and may not sin," the verb, to sin, being future, to denote a contingency, a possible, not a positive, future event. A little scholarship applied to these texts would greatly improve the theology of some people.

Job ix. 20, "If I justify myself, mine own mouth shall condemn me: if I say, I am perfect, it shall also prove me perverse." This verse lies just as strongly against justification as against entire sanctification. In the evangelical sense, in which God is the justifier and the sanctifier of the believer in his Son, this verse contradicts neither. Job disclaimed justification by works and absolute perfection. That he had evangelical perfection, unfaltering faith, unquestioned loyalty, and perfect love, the root of all obedience, God's testimony ought to be conclusive, " Hast thou considered my servant Job . . . a perfect and an upright man, one that feareth God, and escheweth [is shy of] evil?"

The true state of the facts is this: Job's professed comforters were three universalists of the old school, who viewed the present life as the sphere in which perfect justice is displayed, and rewards and punishments are exactly meted out. Hence, the greatest sinner must be the greatest sufferer in this life, and *vice versa*, the greatest bodily sufferer must have been the greatest criminal on earth. Job, the greatest sufferer, must therefore be the greatest sinner. This logic Job resented, and he refused to plead his perfect integrity upon any such platform of theological errors. He believed that afflictions befall good people for disciplinary ends and not for punishment solely. Hence, should he prove his own spotless purity, his own sufferings would not shake his demonstration, or militate against God's absolute justice, because he has other reasons than penalty for inflicting physical suffering. For Job to adopt the theology of his three friends and then declare his own perfection would have been an impeachment of the divine administration which would certainly "prove him perverse." Nevertheless, we are not left in uncertainty respecting his consciousness of inward and outward holiness : "My lips shall not speak wickedness, nor my tongue utter deceit ; till I die I will not remove mine integrity [moral wholeness] from me, my righteousness I hold fast, and will not let it go : my heart shall not reproach me so long as I live." — Job xxvii. 2–6. This is certainly what Dr. Whedon would call a very tall profession of spiritual perfection, not made to impeach God's righteous administration, but to confound and put to eternal silence the wretched errors of his three professed friends.

Psalm xxxvii. 23, 24, is quoted as implying that every good man will fall into sin at times, and that God in his great mercy will not utterly cast him away. The truth is, there is no hint of sin in these verses. None of the versions intimate that a falling into sin is meant, but rather into adversities, distresses, and troubles, out of which God will at last give him a happy issue.

In *Psalm xiv.* 1–3 God looks down upon the human family aside from divine regenerating grace, and sees every one by nature and by practice corrupt and sinful. St. Paul, in Rom. iii. 10, quotes this passage to prove the universal depravity of our race, as proving the necessity for that scheme of universal redemption in the blood of Jesus Christ, the Son of God, which he is proceeding to unfold in this theological epistle. No one has a right to pervert this text into proof that there are none righteous in the kingdom of grace.

Psalm cxix. 96, "I have seen an end of all perfection : *but* thy commandment is exceeding broad." No text in the Old Testament is more frequently quoted against Christian perfection, usually with an air of triumph, as though that doctrine is pulverized by the crushing momentum of this verse. Let us examine it. The original word for perfection in this passage is a once-used word in the Hebrew Bible. Hence its meaning is with scholars a matter of dispute. But many of them agree that it is the complete ending and vanishing away of anything. Thus Martin Luther renders it, "I have seen an end of all things, but thy law lasts." Hence, the word perfection not being in their version, the Germans have no difficulty with this text. All earthly things end, but the Bible lasts. This rendering makes the text concordant with Isa. xl. 6–8. and 1 Pet. i. 24, 25. "All flesh is as grass. The grass withereth, and the flower thereof falleth away: but the word of the Lord endureth forever." That the idea of this text in the alphabetic psalm is the evanescence of the earthly and the eternity of the spiritual, especially of divine revelation, is proven by the Septuagint version, "I have seen the end of every finishing up, but thy commandment is very wide," while the Vulgate reads, *Omnis consummationis finem vidi*, literally, "I have seen the end of every consummation." We confidently make the assertion that no candid scholar, however strong his prejudices against evangelical perfection, or loving God with all the heart, after a thorough study of this text, will ever again hurl it against this precious scriptural doctrine and blessed conscious experience of myriads of his saints.

XXVI.

ENLARGEMENT OF HEART.

It was the Psalmist who, according to the Septuagint version, testifies (*Ps. cxix.* 32), "I ran the way of thy commandments, when thou didst enlarge my heart." In his early spiritual life there was in this Old Testament saint the same straitness, slowness, and lack of momentum, which characterize young Christians in modern times. His service had been enforced by the law and its penalties. Duty was a word which had not been written over and almost concealed by the superimposed capitals which spell Love. But it seems there was a crisis in his religious life where constraint ends and joyous liberty begins; where irksomeness disappears, and spontaneity in service is a permanent characteristic. The crisis which separates these two experiences is the enlargement of the heart. This is a figure for what St. John calls "perfect love," and which St. Paul elsewhere describes as "the love of God shed abroad in the heart by the Holy Ghost;" though he once, at least, employs the Old Testament phrase (2 *Cor. vi.* 11), "O ye Corinthians, my mouth is opened unto you, my heart is enlarged." Reverse the order of these clauses, and we have the cause and the effect. A full heart makes an unloosed tongue. The inquiry is al limportant, When is this crisis reached? Some say, "Never this side the dying bed." But no Scripture proof of this dismal doctrine is ever given. It is not true that the believing soul must be a partly filled goblet till it is overflowed by the waters of the river of death. Others say: All souls at the new birth are deluged with love to the brim; a love that drives their chariot-wheels as swiftly as the mysterious electric current drives our street-cars up and down our tri-mountain city. Such a steady motive-power is not the experience of multitudes, yea, the vast majorities who are truly regenerate. Their inertia is great, and the impelling power is feeble. Indeed, something worse than inertia is to be overcome; a strong opposition often arises within, which it takes all their strength to overcome. They have not a heart at leisure from itself to concentrate upon the work of God. True it is that a few Christians, like John Fletcher, very soon after their birth into the kingdom, because of a correct apprehension of their privilege in the dispensation of the Spirit, are deluged with divine love and become giants in faith. The mass of believers are mere babes in spiritual development. They see days of great weakness, and are often on the verge of surrender to the foe. Some, alas, throw away their arms, and run away from the fight, and never renew the battle. Others fight all their lives with foes in their own hearts and never overcome and cast them out. They have been told by their preachers that this war in the members is the normal Christian life. Hence, believing their preachers instead of the Word of God, they limit his power by their unbelief, and never gladly run, but always sadly drag themselves along the heavenly way. This large class of Christians need enlightenment and encouragement, and not denunciation. They need to dwell in thought upon "the exceeding great and precious promises," that they may have an experience of the "exceeding greatness of God's power to us-ward who believe." They need to lock arms with St. Paul and walk through his glorious epistles, and get his large view of the extent of Christ's saving power, since he has sent down the Holy Spirit, the Sanctifier. They should study the new Greek words which Paul coined to express the fulness of divine grace and the wealth of privilege which are the heritage of those who fully believe; such as that translated by "more than conquerors" (Rom. viii. 37), "much more abound" (Rom. v. 20 : 2 *Cor. vii.* 4), "and the grace of our Lord abounded exceedingly with faith and love." — (1 Tim. i. 14.) Especially should they ponder that declaration of God's ability to save, found in 2 *Cor. ix.* 8, in which are two "abounds" and five "alls," — " God is able to make all grace abound towards you, that ye always having all sufficiency in all things may abound unto every good work." They should daily repeat St. Paul's prayer for the Ephesians, emphasizing each petition, especially the ascription at the close (*Eph. iii.* 20), " Now unto him that is able to do exceeding abundantly [*superabundantly, above the greatest abundance.* — A. CLARKE] above all that we ask or think, according to the power that worketh in us." There is not sufficient familiarity with the promises on the part of professed Christians. While unbelievers neglect the threatenings, believers are prone to neglect the promises of the

ENLARGEMENT OF HEART. 159

Holy Scriptures. Again, the growing failure to magnify the Holy Spirit results in constraint, and in the legal spirit, instead of the freedom of the evangelical spirit, inspiring courage to run through troops of foes. How many so-called evangelical Christians there are whose creed is practically as defective as was that of the first believers in Ephesus, — "We have not so much as heard whether there be any Holy Ghost" as receivable into the heart.

This important item dropped out of a Christian's faith palsies his tongue, paralyzes his hands, and enfeebles his feet. If he is a preacher, his message will be delivered in the weakness of uncertainty and doubt. Splendid rhetoric, and oratorical tones and attitudes, are beggarly substitutes for the unction of the Holy Ghost. The anointed pulpit will always be mighty. The Spirit inspires fearlessness, imparts freedom of utterance, enkindles zeal and unconquerable love of souls. All of these are elements of genuine eloquence. They furnish the man, the subject, and the occasion.

The formal prayer-meeting would be transformed by the enlargement of the heart. Dumbness, the penalty of unbelief (Luke i. 20), will find a ready and glad utterance, and the dry harangue will be replaced by the hallelujah.

Let the heart of Protestantism be enlarged by the fulness of the Comforter, and rivers of salvation would flow out unto the ends of the earth, vitalizing those organizations which he can use, and sweeping away those which have been devised as substitutes for his regenerating and sanctifying power.

XXVII.

SPIRITUAL CIRCUMCISION.

The Old Testament and the New contain, not two different religions, but one in different stages of development. Well did Augustine say: "In the Old Testament the New lies hidden; in the New Testament the Old lies open." The essential principle of Judaism and of Christianity is the same,—supreme love to God. The great Teacher and Lawgiver sums up the law, and the prophets, and all human duty, in this great word LOVE. It is the natural and necessary inference from the unity of God, as opposed to polytheism; hence it follows the "*Shema,*" the first words every Hebrew child is taught to speak (*Deut.* vi. 4, 5), "Hear, O Israel: the Lord our God is one Lord: and thou shalt love the Lord thy God with all thine heart, and with all thy soul, and with all thy might."

We are here met by the question, "Can genuine love be evoked by command? Is it not the free, spontaneous outflow of the heart towards the object for which it has affinity? How, then, can a soul void of all affinity for God love him supremely?" This question is more important than the theological puzzle, the origin of sin in a holy universe, inasmuch as the cure of an evil is of far higher interest to the sufferer than its genesis.

If we turn to Rom. viii. 7, we shall be appalled at the vastness of the multitude to whom the great command of both the law and the gospel is an utter impossibility, "because the carnal mind is enmity against God." But before we rashly accuse God of injustice, in reaping obedience where he has not sown ability, let us further read our Bibles, and get the whole of the divine purpose in this case. It is possible that a scheme of wondrous mercy may be found instead of severity. It is remarkable that most of those who find fault with God have the least knowledge of his revelation. Turn again to the Old Testament at *Deut. xxx.* 6, and the difficulty vanishes and God's moral character is vindicated. He proposes, by a direct, supernatural interposition of his almightiness, with man's free consent, to perform a piece of spiritual surgery, to cut away the carnality which prevents love and invites enmity, and to clear the way for the natural up-springing of love, filling to the brim every faculty of intelligence and sensibility, — "And the Lord thy God will circumcise thine heart, to love the Lord thy God with all thine heart, and with all thy soul, that thou mayest live," or have real and eternal well-being. Carnality in the least degree is obstructive of love of the purest and most perfect kind.

The question now arises, " Who are entitled to this heart-circumcision?" As natural birth within the old covenant was a necessary condition of circumcision in the flesh, so the new birth under the new covenant is the necessary condition of that spiritual circumcision without which perfect love cannot exist. This is beautifully proven by St. Paul in 2 *Cor. vii.* 1 ; read in connection with the last verse of the preceding chapter. "Having therefore these promises,"—things promised, especially adoption as "sons and daughters,"—the work of entire sanctification is to be perfected in so thorough a manner as to exclude every "filthiness of the flesh," —all tendencies to those sins which find expression through the body,—"and of the spirit," every taint of the spirit prompting to sins independent of the material organism, as pride, unbelief, rebellion, hatred, etc. The doctrine taught by St. Paul is that spiritual circumcision follows spiritual sonship in order to the perfecting of holiness. Impenitent sinners are nowhere in the Holy Scriptures exhorted to holiness, to perfection, to fulness of the Spirit, but rather to repentance and the new birth. Only they who "have been made partakers of the Holy Ghost" can be filled with the Spirit, only they who have become believers can mount up to the altitude of perfect faith, and only they that have life are capable of having the more abundant life. We now come to the questions: "Who is the author of heart-circumcision in New Testament times? and in exactly what does it consist?"

The answer to both of these questions is found in *Col. ii.* 11, *R. V.*, "In whom ye were also circumcised with a circumcision not made with hands, in the putting off of the BODY OF THE FLESH in the circumcision of Christ;" i.e., that which he provides for believers through the efficacy of his atonement. Here we have a full account of spiritual circumcision, or entire sanctification. For judicial clearance from the guilt of "the sins of the flesh," through justification by faith, is not here described, as King James's Version of a defective

MS. teaches, but rather the perfect riddance of the flesh itself, the sin-principle in depraved humanity. "The 'body of the flesh,'" says Bishop Ellicott, "is practically synonymous with 'the body of sin,' in Rom. vi. 6, and is designedly used in this place to keep up the antithetical allusion to legal circumcision, which consisted in the cutting away and laying aside of a *part* (Ex. iv. 25), the circumcision by Christ in putting off the *whole* body of the flesh. Similar reasoning is found in John vii. 23, where Christ contrasts the greatness of his work on the Sabbath, in bestowing perfect and entire healing on the cripple, making an entire man whole, with the insignificance of circumcision, which purified only part of a man, making him only ceremonially clean. But we have not done with Col. ii. 11. We call the attention of every Greek scholar to the strength of the original noun, "putting off." It is a word invented by Paul and found nowhere else in the Bible, nor in the whole range of Greek literature. To show the thoroughness of the cleansing by the complete stripping off and laying aside of the propensity to evil, the apostle prefixes one preposition (*apo*) denoting separateness, to another (*ek*) denoting outness, and thus constructs the strongest conceivable term for the entire removal of depravity. In Col. iii. 9 he uses the same strong combination of words, in the form of a participal (used nowhere else in the New Testament except in Col. ii. 15, "having stripped away from himself the [hostile] principalities and powers"), to show how completely the "old man," as well as "his deeds," has been "put off," if the believer has realized the full extent of gospel salvation.

We have now ascertained that Christ is the originator of heart-circumcision, and that it figuratively signifies entire purgation from the defilement of sin.

Let us now inquire for the agent who effects this wonderful deliverance in which the scheme of redemption reaches its climax. For this purpose we turn to *Rom. ii.* 29, and we find a photograph of a real Jew, "who is one inwardly; and circumcision is that of the heart, in the spirit," i.e., says Meyer, "in the HOLY SPIRIT in the definite sense, and as distinguished from the spiritual conditions and tendencies which he produces."

Thus we find the whole Trinity engaged in the circumcision of the human heart. The Father instituted the symbolical rite, and intended its spiritual efficacy; the Son originated its causal ground, his atoning blood; and the Holy Spirit is both the sphere in which holiness exists, and the agent who introduces it into the soul. Well may the believers thus soliloquize with Faber:—

> "Oh, wonderful, oh, passing thought!
> The love that God hath had for thee,
> Spending on thee no less a sum
> Than the undivided Trinity!"

We are often asked for scriptural proofs of the instantaneousness of entire sanctification. We add to those which are customarily quoted as indicating momentary action, because of the tense in the Greek, all the texts in the Bible in which the circumcision of the heart is spoken of. It is a remarkable fact that this is the only kind of circumcision which the spirit of inspiration thought worthy of mention, except in Jer. ix. 25, from the entrance of Joshua into Canaan, to the circumcision of John the Baptist, a period of 1,450 years.

The conclusion to which this Bible Reading conducts us is that entire sanctification, as an act, is the divinely appointed gateway into perfect love as a state. As the act is always followed by the state, and the state always implies the preceding act, entire sanctification, and loving God with all the heart, are practically equivalent phrases. By perfect love we mean pure love. It is perfect in kind, but is capable of infinite increase.

There were three remarkable transition points in the religious development of Abraham. The first was *separation* from his kindred and country at the divine command. It is a mistake to say that this separation was because the kindred and country were polytheistic —an environment unfavorable to the growth of monotheism. This would argue the removal of all modern Christian converts out of heathendom to some other country in order to the attainment of the highest spiritual excellence. Our missionaries do not approve of such a segregation. God separated Abraham from his native country, because he would make him the founder of a national and localized religion in a country best adapted to this purpose.

The call of Abraham is typical of that call of the Holy Spirit which sooner or later comes to every sinner, to turn away from all known sin as a preparation for saving faith in Christ.

The second point of transition in Abraham's life was his *justification* by faith. He believed in Jehovah; and he counted it to him for righteousness. St. Paul cites this as a conspicuous instance of justification by faith under the old covenant. Abraham had exercised faith in obeying the call to separation; but it was what theologians style prevenient rather than saving faith.

Twenty-four years after Abraham's first call, and several years after his justification, he passed the third and final transition in his religious career, which in modern parlance would be called his *spiritual perfection*. (*Gen. xvii.* 1.) When he was ninety years old and nine, Jehovah disclosed to him his almightiness under the name of El-Shaddai, Almighty God, as the ground of a new commandment, "Be thou perfect." With this injunction was the institution of circumcision as necessary to the perfection required, demonstrating typically that spiritual circumcision, or entire sanctification, is the gateway into Christian perfection, or pure love, styled by John "perfect love which casteth out all tormenting fear." For in "the self same day" in which Abraham was commanded to walk before God and be perfect, he submitted to the painful rite of circumcision, the removal, in Hebrew conception, of that bodily impurity with which he was born. Here we find a striking type of original or birth sin, denied by all the self-styled modern liberalists, put away by "the circumcision of Christ" through the agency of the sanctifying Spirit, not by a gradual outgoing of native depravity, but by the heroic treatment of instantaneous excision. Hence, the doctrine of spiritual circumcision is a two-edged sword, cutting away Pelagianism with one edge and gradualism with the other. The first is the denial of inbred or birth sin, and the second is the denial of its instantaneous extinction when faith lays hold of him who is able to save unto the uttermost.

Some persons may insist that there was a fourth crisis in the life of the father of the faithful, — the supreme test of his faith in obeying the command to offer up Isaac. It was a crisis, but not a transition from one state of grace to another. God found Abraham perfect in loyalty and love, and demonstrated this fact to all the coming generations of Bible-readers. The three marked epochs in his life were his separation, his justification, and his entire sanctification, the beginning of his perfect walk before Jehovah, and not before misjudging mortals.

XXVIII.

THE "OVERCOMETHS" IN THE REVELATION.

In the message of Jesus Christ to the seven churches there recurs a favorite verb on which the destiny of each individual member turns. As the conditions of salvation are the same in all ages, we should understand what is implied in this verb to overcome, and how vast and various are the rewards which will follow the victory.

Chap. ii. 7, "To him that overcometh will I give to eat of the tree of life, which is in the midst of the paradise of God." There is implied here that the Christian life is a perpetual warfare. For the verb in every message is in the present tense, which denotes, not singleness of action, but continuousness. There are foes which may be conquered so completely by the stroke of the omnipotent Holy Spirit that they are said to be crucified and destroyed. In *Rom. vi.* 6 one of these foes is spoken of by name, "our old man." So long as he lives in the regenerate he is plotting to regain his lost dominion. Hence there is no safety except in his capital punishment. A dethroned, wicked king is always a menace to the successor, and a nucleus for a rebellion. On the principle, "better one die than many," wise statesmanship brings him to the block, as the stern guardians of Britain's liberties brought Charles I. Till that event there must be warfare with an enemy within. Afterwards the war is not what the Romans called an "intestine," but a "foreign" war. Many people think they must carry a civil war in their breasts till they drop into the grave. Not so the inspired apostles after the day of Pentecost. What are the foreign foes with whom we may never make a truce? One of them is the world, a term comprehending the sum total of the influences hostile to the spiritual life which flow from our social environment, its maxims, fashions, and principles. To these there must be a constant resistance. Pleasures which becloud the spiritual vision must be denied; business must be conducted on the principles of New Testament morality, although these yield less immediate profit than the principles of current commercial morality; and voluntary social alliances with unbelief must be refused at whatever cost. In every case, the spiritual must be put above the material. Everything that puts eternal life in jeopardy must be thrust aside or trampled under foot. Only clear-eyed faith can do this. "This is the victory that overcometh the world, even our faith." By faith the things not seen and eternal are brought near, and are made more influential over conduct and character than things seen and temporal.

Another foe is the personal devil who will be spoken of hereafter. The reward here promised carries us back to the gates of our lost Eden, makes the sentinel cherubim sheath the flaming sword and open the bolted gate, and lead the conqueror to the tree from which Adam never ate. In *Chapter xxii.* 14 we have a more minute description of those who will ultimately have access to this tree, "Blessed are they that wash their robes."—*R. V.* Of course the purifying medium is the blood of the Lamb, as in chapter vii. 14, where the washing and the whitening of the robes are spoken of, the former, according to Hengstenberg and J. Fletcher, denoting regeneration, and the latter entire sanctification.

It is remarkable that what the human race lost in the first three chapters of Genesis, believers gain in the first three in the Revelation. Had the Scriptures a different close they would make us all pessimists. As it is they open wide the door of hope.

Chap. ii. 11, "He that overcometh shall not be hurt of the second death." This is the negative side of the reward figuratively expressed as eating of the tree of life. In a physical sense he may "be hurt" by the fires of martyrdom, but such is his grip of faith that he is lifted above the second death, defined in chapter xx. 14 as the "lake of fire." When Polycarp was threatened by the proconsul with death by fire, he replied, "Thou threatenest me with the fire that burns for an hour and in a little time is extinguished; for thou knowest not of the eternal fire that is reserved for the ungodly." It is utterly impossible in the present life to have any appreciation of the unspeakable horror of the second death. Physical death, in point of suffering, is of so little moment that Jesus Christ drops it entirely out of view in his description of the future of the believer. "Whosoever liveth and believeth in me shall never die." It is for our spiritual health to keep in mind what we are saved from as well as what we are saved to. In both these texts the exemption from the second death is expressed in a double negative, which gives great precision and certainty to the promise as it stands in the Greek.

Chap. ii. 17. For the special encouragement of the church in Pergamos, by reason of her dwelling where Satan's seat is, and where the fires of martyrdom had been kindled, a twofold reward is promised to the overcomer, — the hidden manna, and the white stone. The first symbolizes Christ himself, the true bread from Heaven. It is hidden, because our spiritual life, with its springs and nourishments, is "hidden with Christ in God." Every believer has meat to eat which the world knows not of. The best explanation of the white stone is that it was a small white marble ticket of admission to banquets. Both together, the manna and the stone, signify a heavenly feast with a right of way to it already assured. The new name is the new nature, as the name of Jacob was changed when the mysterious angel made him a "partaker of the divine nature." When Christ in his high priestly prayer (John xvii. 6) says, "I have manifested thy name," he means the revelation of the glory of his Father's moral character, — love, holiness, justice, wisdom, and truth. Only he who has experienced this blissful change can have any knowledge of it, except the second-hand knowledge, which comes from the life and testimony of the regenerate.

Chap. ii. 26, "To him that overcometh will I give power over the nations. And he shall rule them with a rod of iron," etc. This is a quotation from the Second Psalm in which this promise is applied to the Son.

The two texts are harmonized by the fact that appropriating faith mystically identifies the believer with Christ, in such a way that he may be said to reign in Christ, who also represents him. Though the saints have no subjects personally, yet are they *kings* in his royalty, sharing his glory; though they offer no sacrifices, yet are they priests in his priesthood, having his prerogative of access unto God; though they arraign no criminal, yet are they one with him in judgment, approving every judicial sentence. Even in this world the Christian governments dominate the pagan nations. But there is another promise, "And I will give him the morning star." In explaining these poetical words we will repress our imagination and use only our Biblical knowledge. In Chap. xxii. 16, Jesus styles himself "the bright and morning star." But how do I get a title-deed to this brightest star in the firmament? *Peter* (2 *Epistle*, *i.* 19) answers this important question. "We have a more sure word of prophecy; whereunto ye do well to take heed . . . until the morning star (ALFORD) arise in your hearts." Study the Scriptures with faith, and the Christ portrayed therein as a historical person will enter your consciousness as a glorious reality. You will ask for no other credentials in proof of his divinity. It would be like lighting a tallow-dip to see the sunrise. St. Paul needed no human testimonial "when it pleased God to reveal his Son in me," nor was there any asking advice of "flesh and blood" whether he should herald the true Messiah to all nations. He had the morning star which lighted up every step of his journey, from Damascus to Nero's block.

Chap. iii. 5, "He that overcometh shall thus be arrayed in white garments." — *R. V.* The word "thus" refers to the fourth verse, where it is said that, "A few names in Sardis which did not defile their garments shall walk with me in white; for they are worthy." These are they who have not sullied the purity of their Christian character by the stains of sin. They are to have the high honor of walking arm in arm with our glorified Redeemer. He could walk thus intimately with none others without soiling his own robe.

Chap. iii. 12, "Him that overcometh will I make a pillar in the temple of my God." We read in chapter xxi. 22 that there is no temple in the heavenly Jerusalem, but that "the Lord God Almighty and the Lamb are the temple of it." To be pillars in such a temple is to have a fixed and important place in the divine regard. In that glorious city, which is all temple, the victors of faith are its living stones and pillars. Many a worldly professor with a long purse, who has been regarded as a pillar in the church on earth, will be sadly disappointed in the future world. The eloquent J. N. Maffit was accustomed to scathe such, thus: "Ye worldly professors who think yourselves pillars of the church will soon find out that ye are only caterpillars in God's house." How different are those overcomers whom God will indorse first with his own name, and secondly, with the name of the New Jerusalem, and thirdly, with "my new name."

Chap. iii. 21, "To him that overcometh will I grant to sit with me in my throne," etc. I have always regarded this as the tallest promise in the whole Bible. Whenever I attempt in thought to scale its height, my head begins to swim and I give up the attempt. Does it mean that the law is to be so completely absorbed in love that we are no more to recognize its existence? Does it mean that God has so great confidence in the spiritual heroes who come up from earth's Waterloos and Gettysburgs with waving palms, that he can safely relax all authority over them, and seat them by the side of his crowned Son, reflecting the brightness of his glory. Says Bishop Butler, "There may possibly be in the creation beings to whom the author of nature manifests himself under this most amiable of all characters — this of infinite, absolute benevolence . . . but he manifests himself to us under the character of a righteous governor." It may be that after their earthly probation the overcomers are to be the beings spoken of by this profound writer. At any rate, the outlook from the summit of this promise, to him who has nerves steady enough to climb up to it, must be inexpressibly glorious.

Chap. xxi. 7, "He that overcometh shall inherit these things ; and I will be his God, and he shall be my son." — *R. V.* We need a large volume to exhaust all the blessedness implied in sonship and heirship to God. Let each of my readers write that volume for himself. It would be a great means of grace. This Bible Reading would be incomplete without noting the weapons by which we may overcome. These are found in *Chapter xii.* 11, "And they overcame him [Satan] by the blood of the Lamb, and by the word of their testimony." This contest is in the form of a criminal suit. Satan appears as "the accuser of our brethren." There is no use in bringing in witnesses to establish the spotless innocence of our brethren, for they have all sinned and cannot make that plea of a perfect past. What plea will prevail? Acknowledge ourselves sinners, and then cry, "for me, for me, the Saviour died." The blood of the Lamb is a plea that Satan cannot answer, especially when there is added the personal testimony to its cleansing efficacy. This rules the devil's accusation out of God's court. It is impossible for the righteous judge to condemn one bringing this plea, the blood of Christ attested by experience and perseveringly confirmed by a holy life before an unbelieving world. This is a fireproof safe which will stand the fires of the Judgment Day. There is no other.

XXIX.

WHY DID MOSES VEIL HIS FACE?

THE revision throws much light on this question, showing that the traditional answer is erroneous. That answer is, that the purpose of the veil was to subdue the excessive brightness, or to conceal it entirely, so that the Israelites could look at Moses and come nigh without fear.

Let us first study *Ex. xxxiv.* 29–35, in the *A. V.* and the *R. V.* The chief difference is found in verse 33. The *A. V.* reads thus: "And *till* Moses had done speaking with them, he put a veil on his face." The word "till" is in italics to indicate that it has no corresponding Hebrew term. The inference is natural that the veil is put on to allay the fear that kept the people at a distance. See verse 30. But the *R. V.* gives an entirely different meaning. "And when Moses had done speaking with them, he put a veil on his face." This "when" completely contradicts the notion that the purpose of the veil was to banish fear and to draw the people to hear the message of Jehovah. For he spake with unveiled face, and did not put on the veil till he "had done speaking." Why did he veil himself then? Certainly not to allay the fears of his brethren, and draw them into audience with him.

These ends had already been attained. In vain do we ask the Old Testament why the lawgiver veiled himself. Hence we turn to the New Testament. For the Bible has this peculiarity, that it is a self-explaining book when in the hands of the diligent student, who patiently confronts Scripture with Scripture.

Turn now to 2 *Cor. iii.* 7-18. St. Paul is contrasting the two dispensations, that of the letter that killeth, and that of the spirit that giveth life. The former he styles glorious, although it was the ministration of death written and engraven in stones. The allusion to the law engraven on the two tables of stone suggests the glory that finds expression in the shining face of Moses bringing them down from Mount Sinai. But it was a transient, not an abiding and eternal radiance, as was evinced by the fact that Moses put on a veil to conceal from the people the evanescence of that glory, symbolizing the transitoriness of the dispensation which he was introducing. It seemed to be suddenly revealed to him that he was founding, not a system of realities, but of shadows of coming realities. Methinks, as this great prophet was descending the steep slope of Sinai, he had a sudden vision of a greater Prophet, who would stand upon the earth after fifteen centuries, and found a dispensation whose glory should never wane, but wax brighter and brighter forever. The contrast of the solar light streaming eternally from the face of the coming Messiah, with the quickly dying splendors which momentarily glowed on his own countenance, of whose rapid fading away he was himself conscious, prompted the veiling of his face, lest the Israelites, "looking steadfastly on the end of that which was passing away," would read its symbolical meaning, the transitoriness of their religion, and undervalue its blessings, and turn away from its requirements in disgust. Hence the purpose of the veil. But now mark the use that Paul makes of this act in heightening the contrast between the law and the gospel. The pentecostal dispensation invests every believer with a glory which is not doomed to fade, but which will from its very nature eternally increase in brightness. We will never need a veil to conceal the vanishing glory. This is the privilege of the most obscure and illiterate disciple of Christ. Do you wish for proof? Harken, "But WE ALL, with unveiled face, reflecting as a mirror the glory of the Lord, are transformed into the same image from glory to glory, even as from the Lord the Spirit." — *R. V.*

How beautifully this describes the permanency of that experience which Christ promises through the abiding of the Comforter in the heart of the believer, spoken of by Paul elsewhere as the temple of God, the habitation of God through the Spirit. It is not evanescent, because it is the glory of the indwelling Christ, the same yesterday, to-day, and forever.

Thank God, all ye believers in the Holy Ghost, that we live not in a dispensation of shadows, but of realities, not of types, but of the glorious antitype, our adorable Christ, through whom we receive and daily enjoy the Spirit of truth, or the Spirit of reality, in contrast with all the adumbrations and unrealities of all the rudimentary dispensations of Gentilism, Patriarchism, and Judaism.

The dispensation of the Holy Spirit is never to be

superseded by anything more glorious on the earth. Its glory will not pale before any brighter dispensation. No future believers will ever need veils to hide the dying splendors of the abiding Paraclete. The indwelling Spirit is heaven below, just as it will be heaven above. For the river of the water of life, clear as crystal, proceeding out of the throne of God and of the Lamb, described in Rev. xxii. 1, is only a poetic conception of the joy of the Holy Spirit filling to the brim the spirits of saints below and saints above.

> "Angelic spirits, countless souls,
> Of Thee have drunk their fill;
> And to eternity will drink
> Thy joy and glory still."

The future permanency of the fulness of the Spirit is implied in St. Paul's assured declaration, "I know that, when I shall come unto you, I shall come in the fulness of the blessing of Christ." — Rom. xv. 29, *R. V.* Here is no expectation of the subsidence of the conscious fulness of the Spirit. His positiveness respecting the future undimmed brightness of the Son of God revealed within him (Gal. i. 16), seemingly excludes the possibility of his ever needing a veil to hide from men and angels the fading glory.

This fulness is the heritage of every child of God who claims it in the name of Christ, and this confidence of its future abiding belongs as a birthright to every persevering believer.

> "O little heart of mine! shall pain
> Or sorrow make thee moan,
> When all this God is all for thee,
> A Father all thine own?"

XXX.

AN EXPOSITORY SERMON.

"Herein is our love made perfect, that we may have boldness in the day of judgment: because as he is, so are we in this world. There is no fear in love; but perfect love casteth out fear: because fear hath torment. He that feareth is not made perfect in love."— 1 JOHN iv. 17, 18.

THE foundation of the Christian doctrines is laid in the word of God. We, Protestants, believe that no doctrine is to be received or enforced upon any person that is not found here in the open Bible. Nevertheless, the confirmations of a doctrine are found in our own experience. I believe all the doctrines of the Bible are confirmed in Christian experience, even the doctrine of the Trinity. You know that prayer reaches its highest development only in connection with that doctrine. If you do not, I do; and no one can have a real earnest grip on God who has no mediator between God and himself, no divine Christ, no personal Comforter. So that all the doctrines of the word of God find a response in human needs and in human experience. They are confirmed. The object of this Biblical exposition is twofold. First, to develop the doctrinal basis of the higher forms of Christian experience; and secondly, to encourage confirmatory testimony. And it is wise to keep these two running right along, side by side, grounding the doctrine in the clear exposition of the word of God, and then calling forth the witnesses to confirm its truth.

The text has two words in it — fear and love ; and these, by the way, make up all there is of religion. All pagan religions of the world are made up of fear, dread of their gods. The only religion in the world the substance of which is love came down from heaven in the person of the Lord Jesus Christ. Christianity is the only religion that ever existed upon the face of the earth, or ever will exist, the essence of which is love. We shall have something to say farther on with respect to the matter of fear and love in Christian experience.

A little exegesis now of the text, a little explanation of what it means. In the first place, the first verse we read has a dispute about it. " Herein is our love made perfect." If you look in the margin of your Bibles you will find it reads there, " Love with us." " Herein is love with us made perfect." There is a class of writers and teachers who insist that the love spoken of in that sentence is not our love toward God, but God's love toward us. The absurdity of that interpretation is found in the very declaration that God's love is ever made perfect. It always is perfect, and was from the beginning. The second difficulty is, that it is out of harmony with the context, for the word " love " before this text occurs in the following connection : " And he that dwelleth in love dwelleth in God." That is to say, he who loves God, and abides in that love, dwells in God. And the very next passage after this indicates that the love is the love which proceeds from the human heart. " There is no fear in love ; " not referring to God's love to us, but our love toward God. We contend, therefore, that the word "love" right along in these three verses refers to the human love, the love of a human soul going out toward God. The class of writers that we speak of, who prefer the other way, considering that this refers to God's love, do so because it stands in the way of their theory that no person can have perfect love who dwells here on the earth. I think John did not belong to that class of people. "Herein is our love made perfect;" the love which we have toward God, that we may have confidence or boldness in view of the day of judgment, not simply *in* the day of judgment. For John is speaking now of what the Christian feels in contemplation of the day of judgment; and this is the confidence which we have in view of the day of judgment, and this confidence is a token, an assurance, a declaration, that love has reached perfection in the heart. That is to say, it has excluded all antagonisms to itself. All dread, all fear, tormenting and servile fear, have been excluded; and the thought of the apostle is that this is the test of perfect love, love which has become pure and unmingled, excluding everything which is antagonistic to it, so that the person can contemplate the descending Judge without a fear.

How is it with you this hour, supposing this roof were removed, and you should see with these natural eyes of yours the great white throne descending, and the Judge of the quick and the dead seated thereon? What emotion arises in your heart in view of that, if you should think of it for a moment as a real fact? Is there a shrinking away, is there fear, is there dread?

AN EXPOSITORY SERMON. 183

I think I would meet him half-way. I think it is Bishop Simpson who uses this illustration. If you go into a machine-shop where the floor is covered with dirt and iron filings, you take a strong magnet and pass it near the floor, and every particle of iron will leave the dirt, and spring up and cleave to the magnet. And he says that when the Lord Jesus Christ shall come into the sphere of this world in his glorified person, the moment he descends into our atmosphere the magnetism of his glorified person will draw the body of every believer out of the dust to meet him in the air. There is no fear in perfect or pure love. This is the thought of John here. John was a very peculiar writer. He was not a reasoner like the Apostle Paul. Paul delighted to run off in long chains of logic. John was an intuitive man; he stood face to face with truth, and he declared it. He was very much like his Lord and Master. He had been so intimate with him that his spiritual intuitions were awake and clear. What was self-evident to him, in other people had to be reached by a long, laborious process of logic. John therefore announces, and when he attempts to reason he sometimes drops off one premise, and comes to his conclusion without it; and so we have to study to find out the missing link. There is a missing link here in our text, and it is this: The Judge will not condemn fac-similes of himself. And this is his syllogism, if we may construct it. The Judge will not condemn fac-similes of himself. We are fac-similes of the Lord Jesus. Therefore he will not condemn us, and we have no fear in view of the day of judgment. We are fac-similes of him. Why should we be afraid of judgment? He will not condemn those who are just like himself. That is the logic of John if you put in the missing link here.

"The sense of our text must be gained," says Dean Alford, the great English scholar, "by strictly keeping to the tenses of the text," especially the passage which I have just read: "Because as he is, so are we in this world." Some people alter the text and make it read thus: "Because as he *was*, so are we in this world." It is a great truth that we are as Jesus was in this world. He was abused, misunderstood, he was persecuted, villified, maligned, and at last they hung him up between two thieves; and he says himself, "As they have persecuted me, they will persecute you." It is a great truth that we are in this world very much as Jesus Christ was when he was here, misunderstood and persecuted as he was.

But that is not the utterance of John here. John uses the present tense and not the past. Suppose we alter another verb here in the text, we shall have a great truth, but not a truth that John announces. Because as he is, we shall be hereafter. As he is glorified we shall be hereafter; we shall stand a row of glorified brothers with Jesus at the head. Splendid truth! But John does not announce it in this text. And Dean Alford insists that we shall cling to the exact tenses in order to get the meaning. And the tense is this: Because as he *is*, to-day, in heaven, so we are in this world. In what respect is the likeness? I will give you Dean Alford's note on this subject. He was not considered a "perfectionist." He was regarded as very well-balanced, a very proper and conservative

Church of England man. So I give you his note upon it that you may see that I am not straining the passage at all. This is his note. He asks the question: Wherein is the likeness? As Jesus is to-day enthroned on the throne of the Father, so are we in this world. He says the likeness is not in the fact of trials and persecutions through which we are passing. It is not in the fact that we are the adopted sons of God, or beloved of God, as he, the only begotten Son, is loved of God. In the third place, it is not by our being not of the world, as Christ is not of the world. In the fourth place, it is not in the fact that we live in love as he lives in love ; but in the fact that we are righteous as he is righteous. This is the note of Dean Alford upon that subject,— that we are righteous in this world as he is righteous. And he confirms that position by quoting several passages in this very epistle to show that that is a favorite thought with John. He refers to the 2d chapter and 29th verse, " If ye know that he is righteous, ye know that every one that doeth righteousness is born of him." And in the 3d chapter and 3d verse you will find: " And every one that hath this hope set on him purifieth himself, even as he is pure." Dean Alford goes on to say that John refers to the fundamental truth on which our love rests, and says, " Because we are absolutely like Christ, because we are in Christ himself, because he lives in us — without this there can be no likeness to him." Hence, the likeness to Christ consists in the fact that we have the moral image of Christ, the righteousness of Christ, the holiness of Christ. Not an imputed holiness, but an imparted, an inwrought holiness, making us fac-similes of the Lord Jesus Christ.

We now come to the topic which we said we would speak of, — the fear and love that the Christian experiences. I have said that all pagan religions are made up of fear. There are four possibilities of the combination of fear and love.

In the first place, there is one class of people who have neither fear nor love. I do not refer to pagans, but to a class of people worse than pagans, — gospel-hardened sinners. They do not love God, and they have no fear. I am sorry to say that there is a large class of these in the country. The second class is made up of those who fear without love, and the very first step toward reaching the first class is to bring them into the second; bring them under conviction for sin and make them fear; uncap the smoking pit of perdition and let them look into it and see the dreadful end of the wicked. I believe in preaching the terrors of the law. I believe one great error of modern times is to omit the preaching of the law. John Wesley said there was a class of men that held gospel services, but for his part he held law and gospel services. And in order to bring men who have neither fear nor love into a better state, you must preach to them the law of God. As Bishop Taylor said: You must broadsword them with the law. Cut them to the heart; make them cry out for fear of the penalty of violated law. When sinners are thus convicted they have fear of God without love, and we are to treat them so as to point them away from Sinai, after they have had a glimpse of its fiery lightnings, to Calvary, and to the Lord Jesus Christ. The third class is made up of those who have both love and fear. I think, if a census was taken of the whole

Christian church by a competent person (and that competent person would have to have omniscience to read all hearts), he would find a very large number, I am afraid a majority, of the Christian church, whose Christianity is not spurious, but is in the mixed condition of fear, or dread, and love ; and that is their condition before God. The impulse to service is largely fear, not a mighty, resistless love moving them on as upon the wings of angels. The fourth class is the class spoken of by John in our text, love without fear, which he calls perfect love. I do not think that John, when he spoke of that class, was thinking of angels or imaginary beings. He was speaking out of the depths of his own experience. He knew the possibility of having love without fear filling all the soul. Love the impulse to service ; love moving glad souls further in every line of activity to which they are appointed by the Holy Spirit, or by the indications of divine Providence. I thank God for the possibility of living in this world in this blessed condition, divested of all fear that hath torment, all dread of God, all dread of the penalty or punishment of the law.

I call your attention to the exact language of John here. He says, perfect love casts out fear ; not represses it, not holds it down, but casts it out, separates it from the soul. What is dread ? What is fear ? Why, it is the first-born of sin. Study the second chapter of Genesis, when our first parents committed sin. What was the first-born emotion in their hearts when they heard the voice of God in the garden ? Dread, fear, a disposition to hide themselves. When, therefore, the first-born is cast out, you see that the mother, sin, is cast out also. If fear is cast out, we say the mother that breeds the fear is also cast out. For if sin remains in the heart, there must be more or less dread or fear.

Now, notice that John does not say of these persons who are not made perfect in love that they are not Christians. John is too sagacious for that. He does not throw stones at them. He does not say you are a guilty sinner because your love is a mixed love. What he does say is this, — that it is not made perfect, it is not complete, it is not pure; there are elements in it which give it a mingled character. The plain implication is that there are degrees in Christian love, and that it is possible for us to live and to love year after year with an imperfect love; and it is possible also for men dwelling on the earth, living in the body, surrounded by the various temptations of this probationary state, to be perfect in love, to have pure love.

But what is perfect love? If you should go back to the Old Testament you would find what perfect love is; for the Old Testament and the New are at the bottom all the same, and the same doctrines are taught. I turn to Deut. vi. 4, 5, for the answer to the question: "What is perfect love?" It begins with the celebrated, "Hear, O Israel: the Lord our God is one Lord." Every Jew babe born into the world is taught to say that verse. Then follows this: "And thou shalt love the Lord thy God with all thine heart, and with all thy soul, and with all thy might." That is the doctrine of the Old Testament, which is a definition of the perfect love which John speaks of in the New Testament near its close, showing the unity of the two dispensations, showing that true religion has always been in the world.

But somebody here starts up and says, "That is an impossible command. Thou shalt love the Lord thy God with all thine heart, mind, and strength." And he has a text to sustain him in the declaration. The text is this: "Because the carnal mind is enmity against God: for it is not subject to the law of God, neither indeed can be." Does God give impossible commands? John in this very epistle says his commandments are not grievous, not oppressive, not beyond our power to obey. Every command implies a promise of aid, of help to fulfil the command. And the command which I have quoted is the biggest command in the Bible, the all-including command of love toward God and love toward our fellow-men, for that follows necessarily from it. There accompanies, therefore, every command, a promise of grace to aid in keeping that command, an implied promise. What is the implied promise here? Turn to the same Old Testament. Deut. xxx. 6 shows how men will be assisted to obey this commandment. "And the Lord thy God will circumcise thine heart to love the Lord thy God with all thine heart, and with all thy soul, that thou mayest live." Here it is, then, in a nutshell. God does not give people impossible commands. When he commands you to love him with all your heart, he sends down the divine and blessed Holy Spirit to perform a surgical operation upon your heart, so that you may love him; to cut away the carnality from your being, to remove the depravity from your heart, and to give you ability to fulfil this great command. Circumcision is the type of the entire sanctification of the heart. The doctrine of spiritual circumcision comes into the New Testament in a rather remarkable form. I want to quote from Col. ii. 11, "In whom ye were also circumcised with a circumcision not made with hands, in the putting off of the body of the flesh, in the circumcision of Christ." Not the body of the sins of the flesh, but the body or totality of the flesh, the sphere of sin, as in Rom. vi. 6, where "the body of sin is destroyed." See the revision. The circumcision of Christ, that is, the circumcision which Christ affords through his mediation and through the gift of the Holy Spirit, is entire sanctification.

The doctrine of our text, then, is simply this : that the gateway into perfect love is spiritual circumcision or entire sanctification. Entire sanctification, like circumcision, is an instantaneous act, the gateway into a state, a continued state, in this world and forever hereafter, of loving God with all the heart and mind and strength. This love is perfect, we say, because it is pure. Not perfect in degree. I think I love God more to-day than I did yesterday. I love him more to-day because I have a larger capacity for love, an increasing apprehension. One element of our happiness here and in the world to come is in our growth and expansion and development, so that we shall know more of God, and the more we know of him the more we shall love him.

One of the popular objections against the doctrine of Christian perfection is that we teach the doctrine that God lays a bound before the Christian beyond which he cannot go. We do not teach any such doctrine. We teach the doctrine of arriving at a state of pure love, love that casts out all fear, love that takes hold of our enemies and loves them, the very love spoken of in the Sermon on the Mount, the very love spoken of by Christ when he said, "Be ye therefore perfect, even as your Father in heaven is perfect." The term perfection is misunderstood. It is a term which I used to skip when I was preaching in my earlier ministry, because of the opprobrium that has attended it. But one day I read this passage: "He that is ashamed of me or my words, of him will I be ashamed before my Father and his holy angels." I said then, I will find out what it means, and I will stand by it. This is one of his words. I have given you my explanation of it. I do not think it is an ideal perfection. It is an attainable one; one that may be wrought in the soul by the power of the Holy Ghost: a perfection we may receive here and now by a surrender of ourselves unto God, and claiming Jesus Christ as our wisdom, and righteousness, and sanctification, and eternal redemption, receiving the Divine Spirit for his full work upon our souls, for that work of spiritual circumcision of which we have been speaking.

XXXI.

SPIRITUAL DARKNESS.

PASTORS who closely question their church-members find many of them walking in darkness, the natural environment of all unbelievers and backsliders. It is unnatural for the true believer in Christ. With a double negative in the original, he declares, *John* 8, 12, "He that followeth me shall not [at all] walk in darkness, but shall have the light of life." Yet we find in all our churches some who are evidently fearing God and working righteousness, who diligently use all the means of grace, but complain that there is an incertitude about their path, and a foreboding that it may not lead to heaven's open gate. Sometimes this is the effect of a physical cause. I was once asked to help a despairing Christian woman into the light. I learned from her that after a joyful experience of several years the light within had entirely ceased and left her in Egyptian darkness. "But why are you here at Clifton Springs?" said I. "The plastering fell from the ceiling of my schoolroom and struck my head with a concussion that has shattered my nerves," was her reply; "and since that hour I have lost my grip upon God, and all sense of his favor." I assured her that he loved her now just as much as he did before, and that he was telling her so; but that the telephone was so damaged at her end of the line that she did not hear his comforting words. Ten years afterwards I met her with health restored and walking in the light of the Lord. The receiver had been repaired, and the heavenly messages were now heard. But in the vast majority of cases where there is no bodily disorder, the spiritual desolation and darkness must be traced to a moral cause : some sin, some neglect to obey the Spirit's voice, some culpable ignorance of God's promises, some lack of faith with consequent loss of love, some unholy temper, or some shrinking back from the surrender of every idol as the condition of perfect purity of heart, and of the full-orbed shining of the Sun of righteousness.

But others insist that there is another cause of the evil under discussion. They assert that it is the will of God ; that he often withdraws a sense of his favor arbitrarily for disciplinary ends ; that we derive spiritual benefit by these hidings of God ; that spiritual growth is the result of the diligent search to find him again ; and that alternations of light and darkness in the spiritual realm are as healthful as they are in the natural world. This was the position of Charles Wesley. In one of his poems he teaches that spiritual darkness is sometimes an act of divine sovereignty : —

> " Shall man direct the Sovereign God,
> Say he cannot use his rod
> But for some fresh offence?
> From saints he never hides his face,
> Or suddenly their comfort slays,
> To prove their innocence? "

His brother John insists that this desolate and joyless state is because of an eclipse of faith. Hence his sermon on the "Wilderness State," in which he proves that Christians pass into that state because of their unbelief, just as Israel sinned as the cause of their wilderness wanderings. In neither case is there arbitrary allotment. The fixed order of spiritual law has been violated, and its sequences are a sense of desertion, and a feeling of incertitude and discomfort. Charles continues:—

> "Nay, but he casts the righteous down,
> Seems on his beloved to frown,
> Yet smiles their fears to see.
> He hears their oft-repeated cry,
> Why, O my God, my Father, why
> Hast thou forsaken me?"

To refute his brother's error, John Wesley examines his Scripture proofs. The first is

Isa. l. 10, "Who is among you that feareth the Lord, that obeyeth the voice of his servant, that walketh in darkness, and hath no light? Let him trust in the name of the Lord, and stay upon his God." John argues very cogently that the character here addressed is not in a state of grace, but is under the law, convicted of sin, and trying to be justified by works. An awakened sinner has a painful dread of Jehovah, and walks in darkness. Penitent faith is the only way out. This text contains no proof that a persistent and obedient believer must sometimes be sovereignly thrust into darkness. The next text is *Hos. ii.* 14, "I will allure her, and bring her into the wilderness, and speak comfortably to her." "Hence," says J. W. "it has been inferred that God will bring every believer *into the wilderness*, into a state of deadness and darkness. But it is certain the text speaks no such thing; for it does not appear that it speaks of particular believers at all, but of the Jewish nation." The next text is *John xvi.* 22, "But ye now have sorrow," etc. John Wesley well shows that Christ is addressing his apostles only, on the theme of his own sorrowful death and joyful resurrection. The whole context proves this. "A little while [whilst I am in the tomb] and ye shall not see me." Hence their brief sorrow. "No inference can be drawn from hence with regard to God's dealings with believers in general." The fourth text is 1 *Pet. iv.* 12, "Beloved, think it not strange concerning the fiery trial which is to try you." "But this is just as foreign to the point as the preceding," says J. W., who renders the Greek thus: "Wonder not at the burning [martyrdom and its fiery sufferings] which is among you, which is for your trial." Says he, "Neither is this text anything at all to the purpose for which it is cited. And we may challenge all men to bring one text, either from the Old or New Testament, which is any more to the purpose than this." But Charles has hinted at another text in the following verse:—

> "Then let the patient, perfect man
>   His integrity maintain,
>   But not before his God;
>   The Lord may crush a sinless saint,
>   As once he left his Son to faint
>   And die beneath his load."

To this John makes no reply, for the obvious reason that the dereliction of Christ on the cross, in his unique atoning sufferings, cannot be logically quoted as a proof that God will treat all saints in this way. No man can have any proper fellowship with Christ in the atonement. He trod the winepress alone. We have no sounding-line long enough to reach the depth of that sorrow, which wrung from the Son of God the cry —

Matt. xxvii. 46, "My God, my God, why hast thou forsaken me?" Martin Luther, after several hours of silent meditation on these words, exclaimed, "God forsaken of God! I cannot understand it." It is certainly a great mistake to generalize the Son's abandonment on the cross by the Father, and insist that this adumbrates the normal experience of all believers. It flatly contradicts the promise in *Heb. xiii.* 5, "I will never leave thee, nor forsake thee," fortified by five negatives in the Greek, thus : —

"I'll never, no never, no never forsake."

We close with a word of apology for the great poet of Methodism. His high-strung, delicate, nervous constitution was subject to depressing, morbid reactions, in which he imagined himself forsaken by God, while he was as near to him as ever. Charles Wesley took his theology more largely from his feelings than did his brother, who rebuked this error, saying, "God does not play at bo-peep with his creatures." He insists that there are no arbitrary hidings of his countenance for our growth in loyalty and holiness; that joy and sunshine have a far more effectual purifying power than gloom and darkness; that light and love go hand in hand. Darkness breeds corruption; light purifies. In forming a union with us, God takes the first step; in sundering that union, we take the first step. He never sovereignly and causelessly deserts us even for an hour.

XXXII.

CONSCRIPT CHRISTIANS.

IN a recent struggle for a nation's life, when the volunteering spirit flagged, a conscription law was enacted. This law was designed to re-enforce the weak patriotism of multitudes who shrank from the hardships and hazards of the camp. The drafted soldiers did good service to their country, and their graves are honored as highly as the graves where sleep the volunteers. But there was a great difference in the character of the service. The one was spontaneous, free, and joyous, while the other was constrained, reluctant, and servile. The one felt no hardships, because love knows no burdens in the service of its object; the other, urged on by the fear of the law, felt that the knapsack on his shoulders weighed a ton.

The conscript is tormented with the temptation to play the poltroon in battle, and to desert his country's service. Every day in the camp he counts as a day subtracted from the happiness of life.

The volunteer rushes into the battle with patriotic songs, and is brought back on a stretcher mortally wounded; and when he turns his glassy eye, for the last time, towards the regimental flag, he thanks God for a country worth bleeding and dying for. Let us suppose that the conscript, noting this contrast with shame, prays to God for better feelings towards his country, and that there suddenly falls upon him a baptism of patriotism. His country now stands forth before his eyes "the chiefest among ten thousand, and the one altogether lovely." (Cant. b. 10.) His country's flag is no longer the symbol of a hateful despotism which has ruthlessly despoiled him of his liberty, but the emblem of the sweetest freedom. The temptation to desert never comes to him now. If the term for which he was drafted should end to-day, he would find a recruiting officer in an hour and enlist for the whole war, bounty or no bounty. So passionately does he love his native land that he covets the privilege of fighting till the last enemy lays down his arms, and the flag shall float over every acre of the redeemed Republic. What is this change which has taken place in this soldier? Love, instead of fear, has taken up its abode behind his will as the motive of his actions. Love is the magical transformer.

Perfect love casts out all fear.— 1 *John iv.* 18.

The reader may easily conjecture the application of this illustration.

There are in all churches multitudes of Christians arrested and pressed into the service of Christ by the constraining fear of the law. Though the goodness of God is certainly designed to lead men to repentance, it so manifestly fails that all successful preachers must follow the example of their Master, and proclaim the terrors of the law, and point to the drawn sword of justice flashing in the skies and ready to fall upon the heads of the impenitent. We do not deny that a kind

of feeble, invertebrate, or backboneless spiritual life
may exist where only the goodness of God is preached;
but for the production of a strong, victorious, spiritual
life, the law must be our schoolmaster to lead us to
Christ. (*Gal. iii.* 24.) In Greece and Rome a slave
was detailed, in aristocratic families, to be the *paida-
gogos*, or child-leader, whose duty it was to grasp with
his rough hand the hand of the boy, and lead his unwilling feet to the schoolroom. St. Paul asserts that
this is the office of the law, to be the child-leader to
bring us to Christ, the great Teacher.

This beautiful imagery illustrates the point where
the impelling power of fear is changed to love as the
motive of Christian service. When the law relaxes its
grasp we become dead to the law as a motor, and love
to Jesus, the Lawgiver, takes its place. Now, the difficulty with many believers is that they do not get out
of the hand of the child-leader and enter the school of
Christ. They seem to remain in the vestibule. In
plain terms, there is somewhat of legality and servility
in their service. They are in the condition of John
Wesley during the first eleven years of his ministry;
they are servants of God accepted and safe, but have
not yet received the spirit of adoption by which they
are assured of their sonship to God and joint heirship
with Christ. Hence, there is no sunshine in their souls,
no joyfulness in their service. They serve as under a
taskmaster. They deny themselves as the law of discipleship requires, but they secretly wish this hard requirement was abolished. They bear the cross much
as one Simon, who bore the cross of the fainting Christ
along the *via dolorosa*, the way of grief, from Pilate's
hall to the hill of Calvary. They sing : —

> " Look, how we grovel here below,
> Fond of these earthly toys;
> Our souls how heavily they go
> To reach eternal joys."

Some of our hymnologists have made the song still worse by altering the last couplet thus : —

> " Our souls can neither fly nor go
> To reach eternal joys."

A very discouraging condition, indeed, for souls called to scale the mount of God, to be destitute of both wings and feet, when the promise is, that " they that wait upon the Lord shall mount up with wings as eagles, and run and not be weary." — *Isa. xl.* 31.

The remedy is near at hand and attainable by all. It is the fulness of the Spirit coming into the soul through simple trust in Jesus Christ, who has promised to send the Comforter into the heart of every one who unswervingly trusts his word. That this is a conscious and permanent blessing, we infer from the promise that he shall *abide* forever, and from the assurance given to the disciples that they shall *know* him " for he shall be in you." John xiv. 17. It is the office of this divine Comforter to shed abroad the love of God in the heart. He will also bring to maturity the fruit of the Spirit, — love, joy, peace, etc. This is the grand cure of the ailments of the church, that army of the Lord, of which, at the present time, the majority belong to the invalid corps, and are serving their great Captain, not in the field, but in the hospital.

The only effectual impetus which shall set in motion a stationary church fast fettered by worldliness, indifference, and unbelief, is a pentacostal outpouring. The only way that this is to be obtained on a scale which shall be felt all through the world, is for each church, or group of churches, to gather in one place with one accord, and persist in prayer and faith, till the mighty effusion is poured down from the opened windows of heaven.

XXXIII.

SEMI-SPIRITUAL CHRISTIANS.

These are not nominal Christians so plentiful in every community, who by some misfortune became church-members before they were born again, or who began in the spirit, but ended in the flesh, after running well for a season. Gal. iii. 3. For it is a misfortune for the vine to have a fruitless branch, and to the dry branch itself to be in a position where it must be inevitably cut off and cast into the fire. We speak of a very large class of disciples who live in the twilight instead of the cloudless sunshine, who are in the condition of the world before the fourth day, when the sun was created. Gen. i. 14-19. As there was phosphorescence before the king of day poured his full light upon creation, so there is a degree of spiritual illumination before the Holy Ghost in full-orbed splendor rises upon the believing soul. We can never mingle with these Christians without commiserating their condition. They see just enough to be afraid. In a mist everything has a ghostly, spectral, terrific look. They are perplexed with doubts and harassed with fears. They are in the pre-pentecostal state of weakness and blindness. There was slight spiritual illumination enjoyed by the disciples before the glorified Lord Jesus sent down the Comforter. They saw men as trees walking, as did the half-cured blind man after Jesus had wrought an imperfect work upon him; for the perfect Jesus heals souls by stages, as he did this man's eyes, just in accordance with their faith. Mark viii. 24. The chief objections to the "higher life," or the conscious abiding presence of the Sanctifier, come not from the totally darkened worldling, whether within the church or without, but from these good people whose perceptions of Christian truth respecting the extent of gospel salvation under the new covenant are sadly distorted by their spiritual ophthalmia. How clearly the apostles and the Jerusalem church-members saw, after their souls became the habitation of God through the Spirit! Eph. ii. 22. What a rending away of the veil of Jewish prejudices! What a clear spiritual insight to read with ease what had before been enigmatical and dark! How the Scriptures opened beneath their gaze, the Spirit rendering the dark passages transparent, and uncovering mines of richest treasure in the open fields which they had trodden a thousand times before! But was not all that miraculous and exceptional, designed to give Christianity a good start, but never to be repeated after the apostolic age? "The day of Pentecost was a pattern day; all the days of this dispensation should have been like it, should have exceeded it! But, alas! the church has fallen down to the state in which it was before this blessing had been bestowed, and it is necessary to ask Christ to begin over again. We, of course, in respect to knowledge — intellectual knowledge of spiritual things — are far in advance of the point where the disciples were before Pentecost. But it should be borne in mind that when truths have once been revealed and made a part of orthodoxy, the holding of them does not necessarily imply an operation of the Spirit of God. We deceive ourselves doubtless in this way, imagining that because we have the whole Scriptures, and are conversant with all its great truths, the Spirit of God is necessarily working in us. We need a baptism of the Spirit as much as the apostles did at the time of Christ's resurrection." [1]

It would be a blessed day which should witness the descent of the Holy Ghost anew upon the whole Christian church. But to ask for this would be to ask for uncovenanted grace. For the majority of Christians are not in a receptive condition. Vessels must be emptied of earth before they can be filled with gold. There must be an intense thirst before Jesus will give these living waters. Even then there must be an unwavering faith, grasping the following truths:—

1. That the Spirit of Promise, the Comforter, is a person who has a work to do in your soul, after justification, anointing your eyes (Rev. iii. 18), and then revealing Christ to your astonished spiritual vision.— John xvi. 14.

2. That conversion was the beginning of this work, which awaits a more glorious consummation when the Sanctifier comes to purify you and to abide in you, giving you a spiritual apprehension of Christ and the Father. — Acts xv. 9.

3. That Christianity in respect to the extent of its spiritual privileges has not tapered off, but, since the

[1] Love Revealed; Bowen.

Holy Ghost proceeds from the Omnipotent Father, through the ever living Saviour (John xiv. 16), "yesterday, to-day, and forever the same" (Heb. xiii. 8), there must be the same wealth of blessing attainable now as in the upper chamber eighteen hundred years ago; and that if there is any change in Christian privilege, it must increase and not decrease, in accordance with the law of progress which runs through all the dispensations.

4. That simple, all-surrendering, persistent *faith* in the promises of Christ is the only condition; a faith that works by love, and a love that shines out through obedience.

5. Reliance on the testimony of those who witness to the coming and abiding of the Holy Spirit in their hearts, bringing them into a delightful union with Christ, though not laid down in the Scriptures as an indispensable condition of this great grace, is, nevertheless, very important, inasmuch as its absence indicates "hardness of heart and unbelief" as the condition of your soul. "And he upbraided them with their unbelief and hardness of heart, *because they believed not them which had seen him after he was risen.*" — Mark xvi. 14. The fact that the lives of some who profess to be living on the high table-land of a full trust in Jesus Christ do not comport with their lips should no more stumble you, than the admitted fact that there are both deceivers and deceived who receive the name of Christ in baptism should cause you to doubt the divinity of the gospel of Christ. There are not a few unimpeachable witnesses to a full trust in the blood of Christ, to an incoming fulness of love and joy, to the highest serenity of soul,

to a deliverance from the power of inward evil impulse, to a cleansing from inbred sin, and to the fulness of God, the crowning blessing, for which St. Paul prayed in Eph. iii. 19. Do not cherish unchristian prejudice against these brethren and sisters in the Lord's witness-box. Seek their fellowship, heed their counsel, enlist their prayers; for you will find that very many of them, in the language of Father Taylor, "are on speaking terms with God." Their names are known in the heavenly courts. Even if your close scrutiny should so sift them that they should be reduced from fifty, peradventure to forty-five, and then to forty, to thirty, and peradventure to ten, you will find that Christ has not left himself without witness in our age, that "he is able to save them to the uttermost who come unto God by him." This credence given to the testimony of believers filled with the Spirit is the starting-point in almost every case of successful seeking. This is the divinely appointed way of communicating a knowledge of this blissful Christ-life hidden within the soul. This accounts for the persistence in testimony which is thoughtlessly called hobbyism, and is ascribed to mental narrowness and shallowness, instead of a quenchless fire shut up in the bones. Hear them sing:—

> "I love thee so, I know not how
> My transports to control;
> Thy love is like a burning fire
> Within my burning soul."

Do not be deterred from this fulness of spiritual life by the fact that the world has long since pronounced every one of its possessors a madman. The world has some good ground for its verdict. A madman is one who sees, or thinks he sees, what others see not; and seeing such things walks accordingly. Under the intense illumination of the Father, Son, and Holy Spirit abiding with the believer (John xiv. 16-23) he sees what the blind world sees not, and shapes his conduct in accordance with the heavenly light. Hence, those who see not what he sees must think him beside himself, and express their pity that reason has been dethroned. If you are unwilling to be an unintelligible and sadly misunderstood person in the eye of the world, an enigma to your best friends who know not the experience of the indwelling spirit, we advise you to wait till you have conquered the world in so far as to live without its good opinion. By the grace of God the thing can be done. "Be of good cheer," says our great representative and exemplar, "I have overcome the world." — John xvi. 33.

An objection still arises in your mind, my semi-spiritual friend, which puzzles and disturbs you. How can a person be partly spiritual without being wholly spiritual? Say you, "I have been born of the Spirit, does not that classify me with the spiritual?" Just as Jesus was begotten by the Holy Ghost, and yet had the Spirit given him without measure at a later stage of spiritual development, after which his life, already of the Holy Ghost, took another form in the manifestation of that same Spirit, so is the divine life in your soul to be deepened and intensified beyond all your conception, if you will trust the promises of Jesus.

The fact that you are by nature depraved, and that the taint of original sin inheres even after justification, makes the need of a second work still more imperative. If the Christians in Corinth were in one breath styled "babes in Christ" and "carnal" (1 Cor. iii. 1), which is far worse than semi-spiritual, may you not be in that mixed state of Christian experience in which many Christians groan for deliverance?

XXXIV.

THE TEN SPIES — AN EVIL REPORT.

NUMBERS XIII. 32.

THERE is much more in the Old Testament histories than lies on the surface. Without adopting the fanciful hidden sense read into the Scripture narratives by Swedenborg and some extravagant modern typologists, we may without peril of dangerous error follow in the footsteps of inspired apostles when they assert that certain facts in the annals of Israel prefigure spiritual experiences in gospel times. St. Paul is certainly a sure guide in this matter. In the command, "Let there be light," he sees a type of the greater *Fiat Lux* in the heart of the believer, "to give the light of the knowledge of the glory of God in the face of Jesus Christ" (2 Cor. iv. 6). In the emergence of our globe out of chaos into order, beauty, and life, he sees a prophecy of a more sublime creative art, not in the realm of matter, but in the sphere of the human spirit (2 Cor. v. 17). He beautifully allegorizes the history of Sarah and Hagar to set forth the superiority of love-service to law-service (Gal. iv. 21-31). The writer of the Epistle to the Hebrews, assumed by us to be St. Paul, sets forth quite extendedly the deliverance of Israel from Egypt, and their wanderings in the desert, and their failure to enter into the promised land through unbelief, as a representation of the sad failure of many Christians to enter into some great spiritual blessing through their feeble grasp of the divine promise (Heb. iv. 1-11). Let us first settle the important question, What is this great blessing spoken of as the res that remaineth to the people of God? Some unwisely assume that Canaan is the type of heaven, and the rest which many Christian professors fail to attain is eternal life in heaven. The logical carrying out of the type as thus explained is something dreadful to contemplate. Of the million of adult Israelites who left Egypt but two entered Canaan; all the rest fell by the way under the frown of God. The antitype then would be that, of the myriads delivered from bondage to sin by pardon and the new birth, only here and there one finally attains eternal life. I must not thus explain the type of Israel's failure to enter the promised land.

In the third and fourth chapters of Hebrews, St. Paul, proceeding upon the maxim that "history is philosophy teaching by examples," from the failure of Israel, urges Christians to press with all earnestness into "rest." Eleven times does he use the term "rest" in the course of a short passage beginning with a quotation from Ps. xcv. 7-11, where the word "rest" is substituted for "the land" in Num. xiv. 23. The land was to be a type of the rest, not heavenly rest, but spiritual rest on earth. For five centuries, after enjoying Canaan, David urges the people, "to-day if ye will hear his voice, harden not your hearts," evidently pointing them to heart-rest in God. He could not have exhorted them to enter into rest in heaven, to-day, without urging them to suicide. Joshua gave physical, he could not give spiritual, rest. Only the greater Joshua can give this supreme soul-rest in this life. As God did not rest till he ceased from his creative works, so the Christian cannot rest till he ceases from his compensative works, vainly wrought as an adequate offset for acceptance with God. Faith in the great atonement is the only basis for the undisturbed repose of the soul beyond the reach of fears and doubts and sins. "For we which have believed do enter into rest." Let us thank God for this present tense, "do enter." Says Dr. Finney, "The truly believing soul rests from its own works. It sees salvation secured in Jesus Christ, and has no longer any motive to legal works. It works not from self nor for self; but its works are from Christ and for Christ. He works in the believing soul to will and to do, and, having no longer any occasion to work for self, the soul delights in rendering to Christ a full-hearted loveservice. True faith works love, and love does all for Christ. Thus the believing soul ceases from its own works." Hence it follows, if a soul will fully believe in Jesus to-day, it will enter into rest to-day. Again in the exhortation, "Let us labor therefore to enter into that rest," the original for "labor" is not a word signifying long and wearying toil, but it is radically the same as that found in the Septuagint version of Joshua iv. 10, "and the people HASTED and passed over." It would be absurd to exhort to hasten into heaven, but quite reasonable to urge the believer to hasten into the highest state of grace this side of glory: —

> Since thou wouldst have us free from sin,
> And pure as those above,
> Make haste to bring thy nature in,
> And perfect it in love.

We find no scriptural ground for making Canaan a type of heaven and Jordan the type of death. The love of Christ fully shed abroad in the heart by the Holy Spirit is the true Canaan, and death unto sin through entire sanctification, as the instantaneous deliverance from sin with power then imparted always to cleave unto God, is the believer's Jordan. This is the blessed rest to which Jesus invites laboring souls. Wisely indeed does the great poet of Methodism sing, —

> " Lord, I believe a rest remains
> To all thy people known;
> A rest where pure enjoyment reigns,
> And thou art loved alone.
> A rest where all our souls' desire
> Is fixed on things above ;
> Where fear, and sin, and grief expire,
> Cast out by perfect love.
> O that I now this rest might know,
> Believe and enter in!
> Now Saviour, now the power bestow
> And let me cease from sin."
>
> C. WESLEY.

God's ideal of Israel's possible future was a trustful and obedient nation marching in two or three months straight from Mount Sinai into Canaan by the way of Kadesh-Barnea, after they had received the Decalogue and had been sufficiently instructed in the Levitical law. They would be victorious in every battle, and in a very short time would exterminate every foe out of the land. What would Canaan typify in this ideal? A Christian experience well grounded in a knowledge of the law, the basis of the atonement which is the only measure of sin, advancing by rapid strides into a rest undisturbed by inward enemies, a rest from harassing doubt and tormenting fear, a rest filled with ever-increasing assurance, gladness, and strength. How different the picture of actual Israel through their perverse distrust of God and rebellion! See them rejected by him whose covenant they had broken, wandering wearily in the wilderness thirty-nine sad years in weakness, uncheered by hope, and doomed to die beneath the ban of that very God who longed to show himself strong in their behalf, if they had maintained their trust in him, and thus presented a character worthy of such interposition. They are still the people of the Abrahamic covenant. They are not as a nation cast off forever; but the blessings of the covenant are withdrawn, and they are shut out from the joyful sense of the divine favor. Alas! that this should mirror the sorrowful condition of many real Christians, who will doubtless be saved so as by fire. They have been delivered from the guilt of sin, their Egyptian taskmaster; through faith in the blood of Jesus, the Paschal Lamb, they have crossed the Red Sea of repentance, and have entered upon newness of life with the glorious possibility of perfect triumph over all their foes and a speedy settlement in perfect love; but, distrusting the ability of their great Leader, they falter and fail and grovel for years, and even scores of years, pitiable weaklings instead of conquering heroes.

The first indication of the paralysis of unbelief in Israel is their desire to send spies to ascertain whether God had told them the truth on two interesting points; first, Is Canaan worth conquering? and secondly, Is God able to conquer it through our agency? From the narrative in Num. xiii., we might infer that the scheme of sending the spies originated with Moses as guided by Jehovah; but his command, as found in Deut. i. 21, 22, was "fear not, neither be discouraged." What was the reply of the people to these brave words of faith? "And ye came near unto me every one of you, and said, we will send men before us, and they shall search us out the land, and bring us word again by what way we must go up." As if God did not know the way, and they must help him find it! Here is the primal error, this miserable business of the spies. If they had unwaveringly trusted God, they would never have sent the twelve spies. For Jehovah had assured them that the land flowed with milk and honey, and that he would drive out all their enemies, if they would go bravely forward and fight beneath his banner. How strangely like this is the conduct of many Christians. Christ reveals to them the Canaan of perfect holiness of heart, and sends his Holy Spirit to bring them in and establish them there forever. But instead of perfect confidence in this wonderful revelation and an unwavering reliance on the Divine Sanctifier, multitudes, yielding to a secret distrust of Christ's word and the cleansing efficacy of his blood, demand to see somebody who has been there; and they immediately send out a gang of spies whose names are Philosophy and Speculation and Investigation and Caution and Hesitation and Suspense and Suspicion and Uncertainty and Distrust and Doubt, whose surname is Thomas. This sorry set of spies is sent out to explore the land of Christian Perfection, and report whether Christ tells the truth about it and about the possibility of entering into it at once, when he commands his disciples to be perfect in love (Matt. v. 43-48). It does not take a prophet to tell beforehand what their report will be, "There are no perfectly holy men but dead ones." See that ye fail not after the same example of unbelief. Depravity naturally hates holiness, even that which still lingers after the new birth. There are animals born with an instinctive knowledge of their enemies. The young partridge, just out of its shell, will skulk and hide under the leaves at the first sight of a hawk; the mouse runs into its hole the first time he sees a cat; and the little kitten, before his eyes are open, will spit and curve his little back when a hand that has just touched a dog is placed near his nose. Slavery had an instinctive dread of liberty, and raised a bloody rebellion at the very thought of the possible supremacy of freedom. The flesh which lusteth against the Spirit, even in the hearts of believers, in their initial regenerate experience, shrinks back from the very words "sanctify you wholly," "cleansing from all sin," and raises up all sorts of doctrinal, scriptural, and philosophical objections and practical difficulties. The real difficulty is the heart's unwillingness to be crucified with Christ. This disrelish for evangelical perfection in young Christians is greatly intensified by the indifferent or hostile attitude of the older and more influential. A majority of Israel's leaders — for the spies were all princes of their tribes — reported adversely to marching immediately into Canaan. That report manufactured unbelief by the wholesale among the common people in the camp. "Our great and wise men say that we cannot conquer and cast out the Canaanites. It must be so, if our leaders say so." The detailed report of the ten cowardly spies is unfortunately lost. It would be interesting and instructive to read just what each said. But, perhaps, by a diligent study of the account and a judicious use of our imaginations, we can introduce these individual reports as they fell from their lips. Their names, who can call? If any one whom I am addressing can from memory speak one of them, let him arise and pronounce that name. We all know the two names attached to the minority report. The believing spies have written their imperishable names on the hearts of all the generations. God has embalmed them in the memories of all good men. In every Jewish and Christian age children are proud of the names Caleb and Joshua; and when the Son of God stooped down from the skies to become the Son of Mary, the heroic name of Jesus, the Greek of Joshua, was found to be the fittest name for the Lord of glory to wear among men. But no children are named after the ten spies:—

"Cancelled from heaven and sacred memory,
Nameless in dark oblivion let them dwell."

Yet God has put their names on record. In Num. xiii. they stand in the pillory of sacred history for the reproach and scorn of mankind. "Of every tribe of their fathers shall ye send a man, every one a ruler among them."

The tribe of Reuben was represented in the exploring expedition by Prince Shammua. It is easy to reproduce his report from the general characteristics of his tribe as discerned by the keen sagacity or supernatural insight of dying Jacob: "Unstable as water, thou shalt not excel." Indecision marks all the Reubenites. Their spy being called on first, not knowing on which side the majority will be, finds himself in a difficult position. He is averse to committing himself. He has a good opinion of the land as every way desirable; but he fears that he shall get the name of a radical and a fanatic, if he should boldly say, "We ought to march straight into it without a day's delay." That will not sound well. "I must look to my reputation. A good name is better than great riches." So, after praising the country, he says that on the practical question of immediate conquest he has not yet made up his mind. "I prefer to announce my views after my brother spies have reported. You may reckon me on the side of the majority when I find out what it is." A good type of a Christian lacking independence, positiveness, and inflexible firmness in standing on his convictions. If he is a layman, he is always taking his religious beliefs at second hand from his influential brethren; if he is a preacher, he inquires for what he may enjoy, profess, and preach, not in God's word, illumined by the Holy Ghost within him, but in the last debate of the Preachers' Meeting or Ministerial Club to which he belongs. Oh, for vertebrate men and women whose beliefs have become experiences, who have gotten hold of truth so precious that they are willing to suffer the loss of all things rather than to sell it out for human applause! (John v. 44.) Prince Shaphat of the tribe of Simeon next arises before the hushed assembly and expresses his view of the critical situation: "I cannot deny the excellence of the land. It is fertile, pleasant, and healthy. Just see this mammoth cluster of grapes and the enormous figs and pomegranates surpassing in both size and quality anything Egypt can produce. But — but — the people are more numerous than we. The odds are heavily against us. In my reading of history, I have discovered the important fact that the strongest battalions always win. It is best to take a sober, rational, and commonsense view of this matter, and consider it in proper military style. Numbers must decide in the long run. That is a very fanatical view which has gained some adherents in our camp, that five of us shall chase a hundred, and a hundred put ten thousand to flight. I stamp that sentiment as exceedingly visionary and perilous, if it should become so general as to shape our policy, and thrust us, all unprepared, into deadly conflict with these seven mighty nations. I counsel delay, till we have become stronger and our foes have grown weak. I have no good opinion of this foolish reliance on the supernatural. If we beat our foes, we must trust alone in our own muscle."

Here is the type of the naturalistic Christian! How strange a combination of words, in view of the facts of a miraculous gospel history, and of the spread of Christianity against such tremendous odds arrayed against it by Judaism and Paganism, by learning, wealth, and power, by imperial persecutions, and brutal mobs. Yet we live in a day when myriads wear the name of Christ, the Wonderful, from whose faith the supernatural has entirely evaporated. The naturalistic Christian may be known by his little faith in sudden conversions, and instantaneous sanctifications, and baptisms of the Spirit, and in discouraging efforts to promote sweeping revivals of religion. If the exact census of Christendom should be taken, we fear that a wide column would be filled with this class of professed Christians.

Prince Igal of the tribe of Issachar is now eager to report: "I bear witness to the truth of the old description of the land which had so delicious a sound around our cradles and in the brickyards of Egypt. It is a land which floweth with milk and honey.

"Being of antiquarian turn of mind, I recall that I saw in Egypt the records of Rameses II. chiselled in stone. That great king brought back from Canaan, he tells us, gold, glass, gums, cattle, male and female slaves, ivory, ebony, boats laden with all good things, horses, chariots inlaid with gold and silver, goblets, dishes, iron, steel, dates, oil, wine, asses, cedar, suits of armor, fragrant wood, war galleys, incense, gold dishes with handles, collars and ornaments of lapis lazuli, silver dishes, vases of silver, precious stones, honey, goats, lead, spears of brass, colors, beer, bread, geese, fruit, milk, pigeons — the plunder, in fact, of a rich and civilized country. The meadows of Palestine, its fortresses, its groves, and its orchards, are mentioned, showing that prosperity of every kind abounded. It is no savage nor unoccupied region, therefore, that is to be conquered by us, but a land strongly defended, full of people, and provided with all appliances for resistance. Nor is it without marked culture, for its libraries gave a name to some of its cities. But, nevertheless, in my reconnoissance of that interesting country, I was alarmed at the extraordinary stature of the people. They actually stand seven and eight feet high in their stockings. Our party of spies — you see that we are good-sized men — were as grasshoppers in their sight, and we felt like grasshoppers in our own sight. There is no use of attempting to cope with a race of demigods. It would be worse than a crime, it would be a blunder, for us pygmies to rush madly against a host of giants. Pause! Pause, fellow Hebrews! before you rush headlong into a position where a battle will be certain defeat, or a retreat a national disgrace or a national extinction. Meanwhile we are very comfortably off where we are: we have abundant cool, sweet water out of the rock, and bread rained daily upon the camp; and though the manna is rather flat to my taste, yet it is much better than nothing. I think we can very profitably spend a score or more of years here reflecting on the greatness of our deliverance from the yoke of Pharaoh. This eagerness to press forward to the land of promise indicates a lack of appreciation of the great emancipation of our nation. We ought not to forget this glorious event, as we evidently are forgetting, in our haste to push forward. There is something wrong in that song I have been pained to hear everlastingly resounding along the column as we have followed the pillar of cloud.

'Forget the steps already trod,
And onward urge your way.'

"We should hold the past in grateful memory, and magnify our abundant present blessings, and not dwarf them down by contrasting them with some great imaginary blessings in Canaan. In fact, we are already in Canaan as much as we ever shall be. This I can prove from Jehovah's own word in Ex. xxiii. 31, 'I will set thy bounds from the Red Sea even unto the sea of the Philistines.' We stepped into Canaan when we came up out of the Red Sea and set our feet upon the eastern shore. The great miracle is already past. God does only one great work for any nation. He does not deliver piecemeal. Yes, we are already in the promised land; though things are rather rough here, and not quite up to our expectation and God's promise. We have had too rose-colored anticipations.

' 'Twas distance lent enchantment to our view.'

"We shall be acting wisely to tone down our expectations to harmonize with our surroundings. Things will gradually improve as we get used to the climate and better acquainted with the inhabitants. We must rely on natural processes, — growth, education, refinement, and the softening effects of the fine arts. Let us move slowly and steadily forward with no more such spasms like our deliverance from Egypt. Spasms indicate weakness and not robust health."

Many a Christian secretly confesses that his experience is not what he expected when he embraced Christ. He does not find complete satisfaction in him. But when told to go forward into the goodly land of full salvation how strangely he acts; he looks round him for proofs that there is no better experience, and he takes a kind of sad delight in dragging down the rich promises of God to his own meagre realization. With such half-starved and stationary Christians the church is overstocked.

Palti, a prince of Benjamin, now takes the platform, and in a loud voice says, "My brethren, the land cannot be too highly praised. It is surpassingly excellent. Its valleys are fat with olives, and all you have to do with its terraced hills is 'to tickle them with a hoe and they will laugh into a harvest.' But I looked upon the land with the eye of a soldier and strategist. I observed that all the strong positions, the key points, are already occupied by our enemies. Their cities are stupendous fortresses crowning every high hill. Nature and art have made them absolutely impregnable. Why, you will scarcely believe me when I soberly say that their walls tower up into the very heavens. It is sheer presumption to think of dashing our heads against such munitions as these. I do not believe that the command to throw ourselves against these impregnable walls has been rightly interpreted. It is evidently figurative. It means that we are to contend against them with the arts of diplomacy, and to outwit them in statecraft, by and by, when we shall have reached a higher intellectual and political status. There must, of course, be treaties of peace, then we will get the best of these bargains, and reduce them to serfdom, and make them pay tribute to us. There must be some mistake about that command of an universal extermination. Why, the very thought is horrible! The banishment or destruction of every one of these seven civilized nations! The thing is without precedent in the annals of mankind. We cannot hope for anything better than a gradual melting of the two peoples into one nationality, Canaan taking on circumcision and our Abrahamic covenant, while we meet them half-way by giving up our clannish exclusiveness and bigotry, our groundless prejudice against the Gentiles, and our overnice rules of diet. I advise that we begin this process of assimilation as soon as possible. Let us immediately send a flag of truce and enter into peaceable treaty relations. By this means we shall lift our rude nation into cultivation, refinement, and wealth; for these Canaanites, as Prince Igal has just said, are polished, cultured, and rich, being of the same race with the great city of Tyre. Our sturdy Hebrew strength united with their elegance and taste will make a nation both heroic and splendid."

Many Christians think that the best way to conquer the world is to become just like it. Thus did not the Son of man, who was holy, harmless, undefiled, and separate from sinners, whose all-conquering moral power lies in his unlikeness to the world in spotless character.

Gaddiel, a prince of Zebulun, now speaks : " Sons of Abraham, the beauty and fertility of the land exceeds all the upreachings of man's imagination. It is beyond our most glowing dreams. It is a land worth fighting valiantly for, when we get fully ready. For it is folly for us to push headlong in our present unprepared condition. We lack military drill. We have had no experience in war except in a little skirmish at Rephidim near Mount Sinai. We need arms. For generations we have been in bondage. Slaves are never permitted to own arms. We must make arms by building forges and smelting iron and copper, which abound here in this wilderness. We must first get our materials, and then train our armorers to make shields, swords, spears, and battle-axes; for it will not do to depend on so rude an arm as the sling in besieging walled cities. To put ourselves in fighting order will take years. Discretion is the better part of valor. When we have a good military outfit you shall hear my voice for war, but not till then."

You will find many Christians of this procrastinating sort, distrusting God's promise of present complete salvation, and waiting in idleness for strength, which comes only through activity begotten of faith in God.

The vast audience of Israelites crowd near to the stand as Gaddi, a prince of Manasseh, stands up to report: "Hear, O Israel! if I were a painter I might transfer to your minds some idea of the indescribable loveliness and richness of Canaan. I hope to dwell amid its matchless charms, at least in my old age. For I see that its conquest is a work of many, many years. Although we are Hebrews, the chosen nation, we are human nevertheless, and we must proceed by the historic methods which have ended in success. We are a single nation marching against a strong confederacy of seven nations. We have no allies. It will be wise for us to form alliances with neighboring nations, and thus to multiply our strength. This will take time. This is the most reasonable course. The possession of reason argues that we should use it, and not go blindfold into battle and be butchered like sheep. What some people call faith I brand as sheer presumption. In addition to small arms, a want mentioned by my brother prince, we must have battering-rams, catapults, ballistas, and all the ponderous enginery of warfare. This will take more time."

Here is a type of the conservative Christian pleading for more and more time in which to get ready to be victorious over his spiritual foes within, not by a decisive battle, a crushing victory, secured by almighty power, but by a kind of easy human gradualism, which never comes to a deadly clinch with the foe within the heart.

Listen now to Ammiel, prince of Dan: "Children of Israel, enough has been said about the excellence of other people's land. What benefit is to come to our nation by aggravating them with descriptions of a country which they will never inhabit. Conquest by us is absolutely impossible. Our great-grandchildren may develop strength enough to drive out the Canaannites, should Israel hold together so long as a nation. I, for my part, am bold to say that we made a big mistake when we left Egypt, the great granary of the world, the centre of learning, the mother of the arts, and the fountain of religion. Although our liberties were somewhat curtailed there, we were tolerably well off under the protection of a strong government. I wish that we were well back again. As it is now, we are just nowhere. We are neither luxuriating in the vineyards of Canaan, nor drinking the sweet, cool waters of the Nile. We are just living from hand to mouth, roving about in this wilderness, with no chance to lay up anything for more than twenty-four hours ahead, and that, a little insipid manna. I confess that when I turn my eyes northward toward the Promised Land, I see only thunder-clouds of appalling blackness. The idea of our immediate conquest of that confederacy of strong and warlike nations on their own soil, where they will fight like tigers for their altars and their fires, and the sepulchres of their sires, is the greatest absurdity of the age. It is time this humbug was exploded, and the true state of the facts was made known to this easily duped multitude. I say, let us take the back track to Egypt. For this state of being nowhere I do not enjoy. Since the olive groves of Canaan are out of the question, let us sit down once more by the flesh-pots of Egypt. It does not pay to seek the land of rest."

There were, doubtless, in the Jewish Church in the wilderness, discouraged and despairing members annoyed by any witnesses favorable to Canaan exhibiting the clusters of Eshcol. Such persons were finding little enjoyment in their mixed and wilderness experience, and were inclined to abandon a joyless, unsatisfactory, and irksome service and return to hopeless eternal bondage. Because a Canaan of perfect soul-rest is not pointed out to Christians — or if pointed out is regarded as unattainable — they turn back to a life of sin. Love unmixed, and therefore perfect, enjoyed or earnestly sought is the divine safeguard against backsliding. When filled with the Holy Spirit we may jubilantly sing : —

> " Creatures no more divide my choice;
> I bid them all depart:
> His name, his love, his gracious voice,
> Have fixed my roving heart."

The tribe of Asher now puts forward its prince, Sethur, one of the far-famed explorers. "Hebrew brethren, I indorse all that has been said in praise of Canaan. But it gives me great pain of heart to proclaim without reserve my honest convictions. There are invincible obstacles to the conquest of the land of promise. Others have spoken of the vast number and gigantic stature of the foe, their impregnable walls, and closely cemented alliance, our feebleness, lack of military drill and arms. But there is another drawback to which it is my painful duty to allude. Moses and Aaron are excellent men. I do not wish to utter a word which shall detract from their influence, but I suppose I shall be telling no news when I say that there is a growing distrust of their capacity for leadership. Their haste to rush instantly into deadly conflict, trusting that Jehovah himself will descend from heaven and work miracles for us on the battle-field, routing our foes, betrays so much fanaticism that a widespread distrust of their guidance has already sprung up in the camp; and the popular enthusiasm which once loudly shouted, "On to Canaan," has visibly declined. We have not heard this shout for several days. We do not regret the change, for the cry had become distasteful to us ; but it shows the waning influence of those two sons of Levi who have usurped the leadership of Israel. I recommend that we bring our minds to the idea of a rather protracted stay where we are, making ourselves as comfortable as possible, while we wait to see whether something favorable will not happen. Confidence in our leaders may be restored; the popular enthusiasm may revive. The Canaanites may die off of a pestilence without our risking our necks to kill them in battle. By no means should we advance another step. It is the height of presumption that we have come thus far."

Well would it be if the Jewish Church were the only one cursed with cowardly members distrustful, of all who urge them forward into complete victory over foes within their own hearts. The chief work that these do is to put the brakes on the chariot-wheels of King Jesus while it is laboring up the hill, and to predict that the trusty horses tugging with all their might at the traces will run away with it, and smash it all to pieces.

Nahbi, prince of Naphtali, now mounts the stand: "My beloved brethren in Israel, all twelve of us spies agree that Canaan is a splendid country. But war is horrid and barbarous. I am for peace at any sacrifice. If we advance, picture to yourselves the streaming blood, the ghastly wounds, the wailing widows, the sobbing orphans, the smoking cities, and the desolated homes if we should triumph; and the appalling disaster, if we should be worsted in the fight, with no fortifications, no walled towns, no base of supplies, to fall back upon, nothing in our rear but enraged Amalekites embittered by their former defeat. Should we advance one day's march, we should precipitate a decisive battle. It does not require great military experience to predict the result. We should certainly be disastrously beaten. I advise that we avoid the strain and struggle, the sacrifice and slaughter of hard-fought battles, by making a treaty of peace, that our policy of conquest be effected by gradually colonizing the land, and slowly proselyting its inhabitants to Judaism by exhibiting the superiority of our style of civilization. In fact, I think that the Canaanites are a very nice people, who have been grossly slandered by the traditions which have come down to us from the patriarchs, or they have made marvellous progress since our father, Jacob, sojourned among them, and even then they only annoyed the old gentleman a very little by filling up some of his wells. They are evidently a people too good to be butchered; they have a capacity for high religious culture. We spies walked in the daylight from end to end of their land in perfect safety. They offered us no violence. Then, again, I am jealous for my nation's reputation. I do not wish that we should get the name of a race of filibusters, a horde of land pirates and freebooters; a name which the whole world will fasten upon us as an indelible stigma, if we oust these peaceable Canaanites from their rightful possessions. Let us have peace."

Did you ever see the portrait of a sentimental religionist? Here it is. His outgushing sympathies are a current so strong that they bear him into positive disobedience to God. He so highly prizes his inward spiritual foes that he would not have one of them suddenly slain. His own reputation also is too good to risk in a course of unquestioning, whole-hearted, downright obedience to God. What will people say?

The last of the ten spies is quite nervous with desire to speak. Geuel, a prince of Gad, takes the stand: "How happy should I be, fellow Israelites, if my judgment could recommend an immediate movement against the enemies' works. But I must be candid, and not let my heart run away with my head. In addition to all the objections brought forward by my nine honorable colleagues, I would mention two which have made a deep impression on my mind. First, the Hittites are abundantly supplied with splendid horses and war-chariots against which we cannot cope. Secondly, I find in my studies in history that mighty Assyria in the pride of her power once conquered this very country, but failed to retain her dominion over it. Many years ago Egypt subdued these nations and took Kedesh, their capital city, and they arose after a short time and threw off the Egyptian yoke. In our explorations as spies we found monuments of both the Assyrian and Egyptian conquests. The disheartening inference is, — and I sigh as I give it utterance, — we could not retain possession even if we should conquer Canaan. Therefore, we should not waste our blood and treasure, and risk our reputation for an advantage so uncertain."

The report of this spy is a mirror in which many a Christian can see himself. Hear him think aloud: "I will not aspire to the Alpine heights of grace, because some one has fallen therefrom. If I should obtain that pearl of pearls, the love which casts out all fear, some pickpocket of an adversary may slyly rob me of my treasure. So I will remain in spiritual poverty. Burglars do not molest paupers."

Shammua, the first spy, is now ready to make his report. He has found out on which side the majority is, and he is now ready to give the policy of delay a hearty indorsement. He now regrets that he did not say so at the first, for this was his cowardly opinion all the time.

No wonder that all the congregation lifted up their voices and cried, and the people wept that night: "Would God that we had died in Egypt, or would God we had died in this wilderness! Were it not better for us to return into the land of Egypt. Let us make a captain and return." But hold! two of the spies have not reported. What are they doing? They are rending their garments in grief and righteous indignation at this cowardly report, in which the name of Jehovah, their great ally, is not even mentioned, who had conquered stubborn Pharaoh, and overwhelmed his hosts in the Red Sea, who had thundered on Sinai, and walked before Israel in pillar of cloud and pillar of fire, and who had promised to drive out their enemies in complete conquest, if Israel would obey him.

Now the two believing spies lift up their voices to stem the tide of infidelity which is surging through the camp and ingulfing all their hopes in the irretrievable ruin. "The land is an exceeding good land. If Jehovah delight in us, then will he bring us into this land, and give it us; a land which floweth with milk and honey. Only rebel not against the Lord, neither fear ye the people of the land; for they are bread for us: their defence is departed from them, and Jehovah is with us : fear them not." Here is courage. Here is insight into the real weakness of all God's foes. True faith is the best philosophy. Faith by its very existence and manifestation is a rebuke to unbelief. Courage is always a censure of cowardice. Hence, it was natural that the people bade stone them with stones. The side that has the weakest foothold in reason, right, and truth is always the first to resort to violence. But brave Caleb begs the privilege of saying one word. And he stilled the people, and said, "Let us go up at once and possess it; for we are well able to overcome it." At once, without one hour's delay, for we have Jehovah with us enthroned in the very centre of our camp; at once, despite the superior numbers, and gigantic stature, and better military preparation of our united foes; at once, despite the noise and confusion of a battle and garments rolled in blood; at once, for "Forward" is our Great Captain's order, and it is always perfectly safe to obey God. These heroic words of Caleb, worthy to be inscribed in gold on his tombstone and to be read by all nations and generations forever, received, methinks, this scornful reply from the ten; "Away with you, you have been riding this hobby ever since we left Egypt; morning, noon, and night we have heard your favorite theme till we are heartily sick of it. We tell you we are not able, just now, to go up against the people, for they are stronger than we. We object to this immediateness, this instantaneousness; it is unnatural and unreasonable. Conquest must be gradual. We must expel our foes by our growth, little by little crowding them out. This will be much better than risking a decisive battle in which we may lose all."

You know the sequel. The anger of Jehovah was kindled. He would have smitten them with a pestilence, all the people as one man, if Moses had not stood before him in the breach to turn away his wrath. Though he did not destroy them on the spot, yet he said, "As truly as I live all those men who have seen my glory, and my miracles, which I did in Egypt and in the wilderness, and have tempted me ten times, and have not hearkened to my voice, surely they shall not see the land which I swear unto their fathers. But my servant Caleb, because he had another spirit with him, and hath followed me fully, him will I bring into the land; and his seed shall possess it." Here is God's opinion of those who follow him fully, and of those who oppose an immediate, total, irreversible self-surrender to him for instantaneous and entire sanctification through the provisions of the atonement as administered by the Holy Spirit. For says St. Paul, "These things happened unto them for examples : and they are written for our admonition, upon whom the ends of the world [*R. V.*, ages] are come." In this age there is a minority who are preaching and testifying God's ability instantaneously to stay our inward foes and to bring every believer into the state of rest from inbred sin. If you believe this in your inmost soul, you are a Caleb whom God will soon bring in. But if you inwardly disrelish this doctrine, and are quite content with your mixed wilderness life, and are satisfied with a philosophy of your own in opposition to revelation, God will let you wander all your days and die in the desert at last.

Let *us* also fear lest a promise being left *us* of entering into his rest, any of you young converts, any of you veterans, any of you Christian workers, Sunday-school teachers, deacons, class-leaders, or preachers, should seem to come short. For unto them was the gospel preached as well as unto us, but it was not mixed with faith. There is a Canaan before every Christian, to be attained in the present life if he will credit the promise of Christ. I speak of perfect love, or evangelical perfection, in which Adamic depravity is destroyed root and branch through the Holy Spirit, whose sanctifying office is secured through the efficacy of the blood of Jesus Christ:—

> "Thy blood shall over all prevail,
> And sanctify the unclean;
> The grace that saves the soul from hell,
> Will save from present sin."

On the possibility of the whole church moving promptly forward and entering in and dwelling permanently in the land of holiness, there are two kinds of reports,—the majority, who see the giants and shrink back like frightened children; and the minority, who see the same terrible giants, but they see also the almighty giant-killer, with his drawn sword ready to behead them at a single blow. It is said that the Federal Army of the Potomac was for several days kept from assaulting a strong redoubt on their way to Richmond by an array of great guns looking defiantly at them. The guns were just like those which Satan uses to keep Christians from capturing the spiritual Canaan of rest; they were Quaker guns,—logs bored and blackened to imitate cannon.

Every Christian is believing one of these reports. If he believes the majority report on the impracticability of attaining perfect purity in the present world, he is settling down in a wilderness life, and has ceased to strive to enter in at the strait gate of entire sanctification. In this case, grace is attempting the impossible task of living on neighborly terms with the family of original sin, occupying another apartment of the same house. Or he is believing the minority report, and has either already been allotted his portion by his great Joshua in the spiritual land of promise, or he is urging his way thither. My only justification for my earnest advocacy of this advanced and victorious Christian experience is that the salvation of the church and her aggressive power lie in her eminent spirituality, deadness to the world, and testimony by life and lip to Christ's uttermost salvation from sin, not in her rich men, her fine churches, her high social position, her millions of members, and her hundreds of seminaries and colleges. These are good things for Christianity to have, but bad to lean upon. These are not the hidings of her all-conquering power : —

"Thanks to thy name for meaner things,
But they are not my God,"

There are several important inferences to be made.

1. The question of faith in God is the test question of every age, God's perpetual touch-stone of character, the hinge of probation, and the pivot of destiny. "What must we do, that we may work the works of God?" To this inquiry of the Jews, Jesus answered, "This is the work of God which he requires, that ye

believe on him whom he hath sent." That through faith in Christ we have forgiveness is among evangelical Christians an easily accepted truth. It is so elementary that with believers it has lost its testing-power. Beyond and above this is the truth, that the gospel contains a power to purge human nature of its vileness, to wash out even the old Adamic principle of sin, and to make the soul whiter than snow. This doctrine affords the Christian a test of faith, as the doctrine of forgivness tests the faith of the penitent seeker. Hearer, do you abide this higher test, or does your faith break down under it as did that of the ten spies?

2. The fact that we are God's people delivered out of Egyptian bondage to sin by faith in the blood of Christ, our Passover, is not an insurance policy against unbelief, rebellion, and rejection by God. The Israelites were all church-members in good and regular standing; they were ALL baptized unto Moses, they ALL passed through the sea, they were ALL regular attendants at the sacrament table, for they ALL did eat the same spiritual meat, and did ALL drink the same spiritual drink; but these ordinary means of grace were not sufficient to bring them into Canaan. For with MANY of them God was not well pleased. Now, these things are our examples, types of the faithful few and the unbelieving many in the church, who assent to the easier gospel truths, and reject those glorious doctrines which really test faith.

3. This historic scene should be earnestly contemplated by all Christian leaders, showing as it does their awful responsibility for their right influence on the

mass of Christians who look to them for guidance in the spiritual life. In the question of faith or unbelief in God's promises, the adage is still true, "Like priest, like people." Unbelief is more contagious than faith, because of the greater susceptibility of fallen humanity to distrust God's promises and threatenings. Says Dr. Daniel Curry, "Let the pulpit be silent on any doctrine a single generation, and that doctrine will be exterminated from the faith of the church." I can but think that a sad era of spiritual weakness and incoming worldliness, with no dike to keep out the devastating flood, would follow Methodism's relaxed grip upon this distinctive truth committed to her by God through John Wesley. If mere silence will exterminate a vital truth, then silence is culpable. It is easy to proclaim accepted truth. It seems to be difficult to herald distasteful and unpopular truth. But this is just the kind of truth which God wants to have published. The false prophets can all be depended on to advocate doctrines pleasing to the masses. Only the true prophets will voice unpleasant truth, with the gibbet, the stake, and the block in full view. There is about as good a chance for martyrdom in our day as in the time of Nero; that is, as good an opportunity of suffering with God's truth, his unaccepted truth, which he has a special partiality for. On the other hand, there is just as wide a scope for selfish ambition in the pulpit as in politics, especially in denominations having a graded ministry, from an exhorter up to a bishop.

If worldliness dominates the church and controls the pulpit, the temptation will increase to neglect the doctrine of sin and repentance, regeneration and retribution, and above all, the necessity of self-crucifixion and entire sanctification, in order to the attainment of the most vigorous spiritual life and the highest efficiency in service.

What became of the ten spies? No ordinary punishment was inflicted (read Num. xiv. 36, 37). They died by the plague before the Lord. A plague is a stroke. This was given immediately by Jehovah, without secondary causes. They died suddenly by a bolt which proceeded visibly from Jehovah.

4. God's estimate of religious cowardice, or the subordination of religious convictions to selfish ends through fear of loss of popular favor or worldly gain. Cowardice in military law is a capital crime. So is it in God's law. (Read Rev. xxi. 8.) Here we have the world of wicked men trooping in platoons down from the left-hand of the judge to the open gates of hell. Beginning at the rear of the column, scrutinize each platoon, and see how they increase in the enormity of their guilt, — 1st, liars; 2d, idolaters; 3d, sorcerers, pretenders to a control of spiritual agencies; 4th, whoremongers, who have blighted human happiness and ruined souls for gold; 5th, murderers red with blood; 6th, the abominable, those polluted with unnatural lusts, such as the sin of Sodom; 7th, the unbelieving, who wilfully reject sufficient proofs of the truth through stubbornness or some selfish end; 8th, the last platoon is the cowards. They are not stained with crimes, nor filthy with vices. They do not defiantly reject the word of God, but they are convinced of the truth as it is in Jesus; yet from fear of loss of reputation, property, or life, they refuse to follow where the

truth leads. Such, be they preachers or laymen, will head the procession which will march from the judgment-seat down to the lake of fire. Jesus has his eye on religious cowardice when he says, "If any man is ashamed of me or of my words." His own life-blood throbs in his words. Are you ashamed of the words "perfect," "perfection," "sanctify," and "sanctification"? and do you dodge them whenever you meet them? Beware, lest Jesus dodge you when you seek his recognition in the day of the saints' coronation.

5. The question how much God can do for a soul in probation is not left to be determined by the majority vote of the great men of any church. This question, in the words of Joseph Cook, has not been left to be decided "by a count of heads and a clack of tongues." In a question of speculative theology or of scriptural interpretation, it will do to lean on the authority of a majority of experts; but on the practical question of the extent of gospel salvation from sin, through the power of the Holy Spirit, the unlearned minority who have put the doctrine to experimental proof may be very much wiser than the learned majority of the magnates of the modern church, who have never subjected the question to the test of personal experience. Here the testimony of some Uncle Tom or Amanda Smith of the slave plantation may outweigh the opinion of a whole faculty of German theological professors. Experience outweighs theory; faith makes philosophy kick the beam.

6. As Caleb and Joshua were kept out of Canaan thirty-nine years through the unbelief of the majority of the church in the wilderness, so many in our day

are kept from perfect soul-rest in entire sanctification through the chilling apathy and palsying unbelief of the body of Christians with whom they are in fellowship. We mean to say that their own faith never mounts up and grasps the prize because so heavily weighted with the unbelief of others. Are not these, who thus obstruct the faith of earnest souls, near akin to those woe-deserving Jews, who entered not themselves, and them that were entering they hindered?

7. Let us therefore fear, lest a promise being left us of entering into his rest any of you should seem to come short of it. Fear for yourselves, and fear for the disciples kept out of full salvation through your influence. I may be addressing professors who have so little love for holiness that their most anxious inquiry is to find the lower limit of the Christian life, and their highest ambition to live as near down to that limit as will enable them to escape from hell, instead of mounting up to the upper boundary line of possible salvation this side of glory, and pitching their tents —

> "Where dwells the Lord our Righteousness,
> And keeps his own in perfect peace,
> And everlasting rest."

Let us labor to enter into this rest; labor to conquer the pernicious habit of unbelief, to tear away from our souls the deadening apathy of half-hearted Christians around us; labor to pile up promise upon promise, till we have a pyramid on whose summit we may plant our feet, and with outstretched hand of faith grasp the realization of the tallest promise in the word of God.

The future of obedient Israel — alas that it is only ideal — is fully described in Lev. xxvi. 3–13. This typifies a state of perpetual victory over sin, not repressed, but exterminated, the enjoyment of cloudless communion with the Father and the Son by the Holy Spirit, who maketh free indeed.

Each of you choose this day between Israel as he might have been, God's ideal Israel, and Israel as he was through his lack of faith, actual Israel, wandering forlorn and comfortless, under the ban of the Almighty, sowing the Sinaitic desert with his bones, with the vineclad hills of Canaan in full view. Ye choose to-day between the majority and the minority report, and ye shall be forever richer or forever poorer for your choice : —

"'Let us go up:' were we redeemed by blood,
    And by the wonders of a mighty hand,
That we should linger this side Jordan's flood,
    Heirs of a wilderness of sand?

Why did the sea open her crystal gates,
    Bidding her waves stand up like jasper walls?
'Forward!' the waters said, ' for Canaan waits,
    With palms and vines and Salem's princely halls.'

'Let us go up,' and end the desert strife,
    Claiming the land of plenty as our own;
Beyond the river is the better life,
    Of harvest, harps, with Temple and a Throne.

'Let us go up,' the Jordan's waves will part;
    Faith, like her Lord, can walk upon the sea:
God's promised lands are for the brave of heart —
    Obedience, trust, these are the only fee.

'Tis God who gives us rest, we but receive;
  'Tis he who fights, we gather up the spoil;
His strength is ours if we will but believe,
  And ours the land of corn and wine and oil.

We conquer by surrender; loss is gain
  If self and sin are lost, for Christ is won:
In Christ abiding, Satan tempts in vain,
  And having Christ, we have a heaven begun.

To those who doubt, God gives a desert grave,
  A lonely burial in the burning sands:
The Calebs pass beyond the Jordan wave,
  To find an Eshcol in the southern lands.

Who follow 'fully,' with a heart that clings
  Fast to the promise of the faithful Lord,
They find the upper and the nether springs;
  Cities of 'peace' and 'song' are their reward.

Go up, then, children of the promise, claim
  The land of rest and plenty as your own;
You have the Ark, you have the mighty NAME;
  Pass up, the kingdom waits, the palm, the Throne!"

HENRY BURTON.

XXXV.

FAITH HEALING.

OF late there has been earnest effort to restore to modern Christianity the lost charisms or extraordinary gifts of the Spirit described in 1 Cor. xii. 4-11. The Irvingites, recently organized under the name of the Catholic Apostolic Church, profess to have recovered these gifts by restoring the various orders of a complex ecclesiasticism, — apostles, prophets, evangelists, and pastors. There is good evidence that several persons, mostly women, were endowed with the gift of tongues, and some remarkable cases of instantaneous healing were attested in the early stages of the movement, between 1828 and 1848. More recently there has been a very widespread inquiry about healing by faith. It is taught by some in various evangelical churches that the atonement covers sickness as well as sin, and that any invalid may as confidently trust for healing as the penitent trusts for the pardon of sin; in other words, the grace of faith attainable by all is the only requisite to healing every disease. Hence, we infer that every sick person is, to a certain extent, an unbeliever and responsible for his own continued sickness. "The sick man is a rascal," was the vigorous Saxon in which Dr. Samuel Johnson expressed the *reductio ad absurdum* to which he brought the advocates of this doctrine in his day.

Let us now examine the texts alleged to prove that the atonement conditionally removes all sickness as well as all sin.

Isa. liii. 4, the *R. V.*, margin, "Surely he hath borne our sickness." This is one of the items of the sufferings of the coming Messiah. It is correctly translated in *Matt. viii.* 17,— and bare our sicknesses. The best scholarship rejects the idea of atonement here. "The idea is poetical," says Meyer, who adds, "When their ailments are taken away from the diseased, the marvellously compassionate One who does this stands forth as he who *bears* the *burden* lifted from the shoulders of others." This is the figurative way of saying he healed them under circumstances which awakened a painful sympathy. We are to think of a pure and sensitive soul brought into contact with forms of suffering, and beholding them as a specimen of a millionfold more misery in a groaning world. To the heart of Jesus all our woes and pains were present, and they pierced him through with many sorrows. Read carefully the account of a single day's work of Christ in *Luke iv.* 33–41, the healing of the demoniac in the synagogue, of Peter's wife's mother in Peter's house; and at eventide let your imagination individualize the vast number sick with divers diseases crowding the house and yard and street, "on every one" of whom Jesus laid his healing hands. With patient love the Good Physician *takes up* each new case, and *bears away* the burden of manifold diseases by his mighty power. Yet as a man he must have felt the nervous strain of such a draft upon his sympathies. This explains why Isaiah enumerated healing among the sufferings of the Man of Sorrows, and in close relation to his being bruised for our iniquities, prefiguring the atonement, while healing is not included therein, but is rather an evidence of his Messianic character and of his sonship to God.

The difficulties besetting the subject of healing by faith disappear when the distinction between the grace of faith and the gift of faith is clearly understood and acknowledged. All Christians believe in praying for the sick, and in praying with faith in humble submission to the divine will. This is the only petition which the true child of God can present, unless he is supernaturally endowed with the assurance that the healing in answer to prayer is his will, or, in other words, unless the Holy Spirit inspires in him the gift of mountain-removing faith, defined by Wesley as the inwrought assurance that God in answer to prayer will grant this or that petition.

The following are some points of difference between these two kinds of faith.

This faith is something very different from the grace of faith. We note the following points : —

1. The grace of faith is morally obligatory upon every soul having a knowledge of Christ, and the absence of such faith is the ground of condemnation. 2 Thess. ii. 12.

2. The gift of faith is not required of any one, but is sovereignly bestowed by the Holy Spirit, "severally as he will." 1 Cor. xii. 11. This is called by the theologians *fides miraculosa* (Matt. xvii. 20), or miracle-work-

ing faith, in distinction from saving faith. Meyer styles it " a heroism of faith."

3. There is no more culpability for the absence of the gift of faith than there is for that of the gift of tongues or of miracles.

4. The grace of faith is grounded on the Bible, while the gift of faith does not rest on the written word of God, but upon the revelation of the Holy Spirit made immediately to the human spirit.

5. This testimony may relate to future events, when it is called prophecy : " Let us prophesy according to the measure of faith ; " or it may be an inwrought conviction that in answer to prayer a certain sick person will be healed. "Faith" and "the gifts of healing" are in juxtaposition in St. Paul's catalogue of charisms. (1 *Cor. xii.* 9.) Wesley's note is very judicious, showing entire freedom from fanaticism. We call the attention of all who abjure physicians and medicines. " Faith may here mean an extraordinary trust in God under the most difficult or dangerous circumstances. *The gift of healing* need not be wholly confined to healing with a word or a touch. It may exert itself also, though in a lower degree, where natural remedies are applied. And it may often be this, not superior skill, which makes some physicians more successful than others." " The prayer of [charismatic] faith shall save the sick," says St. James.

James v. 15. We deny that this is the grace of faith, (1) because it is illustrated by an instance of Elijah's faith (in verse 17), in which he prayed for distress to come upon the land through the divine judgment. The grace of faith is exercised for blessings only. "Vengeance is mine," saith the Lord. (2) The 16th verse literally translated shows that it is a prayer specially inspired by the Holy Spirit, "The inwrought prayer of a righteous man availeth much." Thus MICHAELIS, HUTHER, and ŒCUMENIUS.

Of course no healing follows the prayer not prompted by this extraordinary faith. The grace of faith is not sufficient.

6. The grace of faith, when exercised in prayer, is always accompanied by the condition, "if it be thy will." The gift of faith is the *assurance* beforehand that it is God's will to bestow the thing desired. Hence, those who have experience in the charism of faith for healing — the speaker has no such experience — say that there is no *if* in this kind of prayer. It is an unconditional grasping, not of the written promise, but of God himself.

7. The grace of faith is a permanent habit, as indispensable to spiritual, as breathing is to natural life. Faith as a charism is occasional, and not permanent. St. Paul sometimes had it, and could heal (Acts xxviii. 8), and sometimes he had it not, and could not heal, as we infer from 2 Tim. iv. 20. The charism of faith is not requisite to the highest spiritual life, nor to even the lowest stage, any more than speaking with tongues or miracles.

8. The grace of faith is saving; the charism is not saving. Says Wesley, "Even the working of miracles is no proof that a man has saving faith" (Matt. vii. 22). Again, "Though I have the highest degree of miracle-working faith, and have not love, I am nothing." Judas Iscariot once wrought miracles (Matt. x. 1–4), but is now in hell (John xvii. 12). The grace of faith works

by love and purifies the heart. The gift of faith may exist without effecting any moral transfiguration of character. In support of this startling assertion, we quote 1 Cor. xiii. 2, to the Greek scholar, calling his special attention to the fact that the form of this conditional sentence (*ean* with the subjunctive) assumes the condition (charismatic faith without love) as *possible*, with some *present expectation* that it may be realized. (See the Greek grammars.) Jesus Christ strongly hints at the same possibility in Matt. vii. 22, 23. Balaam (Numb. xxiv. 4-13) and Saul (1 Sam. x. 10-12) may be quoted as instances of unregenerate men receiving the divine afflatus of prophecy without moral transformation.

When Paul was on the island called Melita, and the serpent fastened itself upon his hand, no harm came to him. "And in the same quarters were possessions of the chief man of the island, whose name was Publius," who received them and lodged them three days. And the father of Publius was sick of a fever. Paul entered in and prayed, and laid his hands upon him, and healed him. "So when this was done, others also, which had diseases in the island, came, and were healed." — Acts xxviii. 5, 9.

So Paul healed the sick.

That sometimes he could not heal those who were sick, we infer from another passage in the epistles, which reads as follows: "Erastus abode at Corinth: but Trophimus have I left at Miletum sick." — 2 Tim. iv. 20. Why didn't he heal him and bring him along? Because he was not conscious of the inwrought conviction that it was God's will to heal him. It was withheld by the Holy Spirit. The gift of faith for his healing was not then bestowed. St. Paul had not any "supernumerary preachers." He needed every one in the ever-widening harvest-field of the gospel, and he certainly would have healed this disabled laborer if he had been able.

The gift of faith may sometimes be bestowed without any corresponding growth in grace, or without effecting any moral renovation of character. Jesus Christ strongly suggests the same possibility in the Sermon on the Mount (Matt. vii. 22, 23), " Many will say unto me in that day, Lord, Lord, have we not prophesied in thy name? and in thy name have cast out devils? and in thy name done many wonderful works? And then will I profess unto them, I never knew you: depart from me, ye that work iniquity."

Balaam and Saul may be quoted as instances illustrating the fact that men may receive the gift of prophecy without moral transformation. The preaching of bad men has been the instrument in the regeneration of men, because God puts honor upon his own truth. So cures were wrought by Judas, not on the ground of his moral worthiness, but because of the name of Jesus Christ, the omnipotent Son of God. See Matt. x. 1, 4.

St. Paul did not heal every sick person, as we have seen in the case of Trophimus. St. Paul speaks of " gifts of healing," " the *plural* pointing," says Meyer, " to the different kinds of sickness, for the healing of which different gifts were needful." As there are men endowed by nature with the ability to treat special diseases successfully, so there may be specialties in supernatural healing.

In conclusion, let me say that the need of a special gift of faith for healing is evident when we consider two facts: —

1. That every exercise of faith must be under the primal curse, pronounced outside the gates of a lost Eden, "Dust thou art, and unto dust thou shalt return." Hence, there must be a special revelation that the sickness is not unto death, and that it is the will of God to heal, before there can be unwavering faith in behalf of any given case.

2. Every exercise of faith for healing is for a person in probation, in whom it may be the divine purpose to bring forth for the beautifying of the moral character, the grace of submission to the divine will. No one but God knows how hot or how long the furnace is to be heated. None but He knows the hour of deliverance. When the sufferer, or any other person, has a divinely inspired intimation that that hour has come, he can exercise unwavering faith for his cure.

We can but regard the modern eager desire for the gifts of the Spirit instead of the graces of the Spirit comprised in that charity (1 Cor. xiii.), which has been aptly styled, "the greatest thing in the world," as a sign not of real spiritual progress, but rather of decline in the divine life. St. Paul, after a full description of these extraordinary gifts in 1 Cor. xii., gives this command, "But desire earnestly the greater gifts. And a still more excellent way I show unto you." He then proceeds to give a panegyric of charity, or love, as that eternal principle without which all gifts are worthless; a principle superior in quality and dignity to all other cardinal Christian graces, and therefore infinitely superior to those miraculous gifts which may exist in the absence of love (Matt. vii. 22, 23).

Says John Wesley, "Many have had the gift of faith who thereby cast out devils, and yet will at last have their portion with them."

To prefer gifts to that fulness of love which St. Paul eulogizes is to recede from the highest spirituality, if not to fall from grace. These gifts were attended by various extravagances, excesses, and fanaticisms, which gave St. Paul much solicitude. I have been pastor of fifteen churches, and I thank God that none of them was so disorderly and so trying to my patience as the church of Corinth, where the extraordinary gifts of the Spirit were fully bestowed, must have been to St. Paul — "Wrangling over Paul, Apollos, and Cephas, running after false teachers, full of envying, strife, and divisions, carnal, walking as men, harboring an incestuous person, without discipline, degrading the Lord's Supper into a feast of appetite and drunkenness, giving to pastor Paul constant sorrow and anxiety — the Corinthians needed miracles to give them a respectable name ; and they so abused miraculous gifts by jealousy and contention that they turned their Sabbath assemblies into cabals of men and women singing, praying, shouting, prophesying, pell-mell, without order or decency."

Hence I have never offered a prayer for the restoration of the charisms, or extraordinary gifts. Following the apostle to the Gentiles as a guide, I have found the more excellent way, the way of love, and I am supremely blest.

Though the apostle to the Gentiles, on rare occasions, exercised the gift of healing, he never gave it any prominence in his practice, and never mentioned it in his recorded sermons. His only mention of it in his epistles is to relegate it to rear of the beautiful procession of the Christian graces, the fruit of the Spirit. As for himself, he had a physician as his travelling companion, who doubtless applied appropriate remedies to him in sickness. Why do I think so? It is an inference from the Holy Scripture, "Ye know that because of an infirmity of the flesh I preached the gospel unto you the first time (Gal. iv. 13, *R. V.*). Some physical disability, it may be lameness, hindered his journey through Galatia toward Europe, but did not prevent his preaching while unable to travel. From a study of the Acts, chap. xvi. 7-10, we ascertain from the change in the pronouns from "they" to "we," that Dr. Luke had overtaken St. Paul at Troas. We infer that in his detention in Galatia, near by, he sent for Luke because he was in need of his professional services. Our inference is confirmed by a study of Col. iv. 14, "Luke, my beloved physician, and Demas, salute you." Why do I say "my" instead of "the"? Because it is grammatical to express an unemphatic possessive pronoun by the article in Greek as it is in English, "the doctor" meaning "my doctor." See Hadley's Greek Grammar, § 527 d, and Kuhner, § 244, 4. The Greek scholar will find seven instances of this kind in this epistle to the Colossians. I quote only one found in the first verse, "Our brother" for "the brother," as in the *R. V.*, margin. See Bishop Lightfoot on Colossians.

There are grave perils attending the doctrine that the atonement conditionally covers all sicknesses as it does all sins. It is perilous to read more into the divine promises than the Spirit of inspiration intended. I heard William Miller read into prophecy the second advent in 1843; and in 1844 I heard him express his regret for his mistake, and the wish that he could "get a peep at God's clock, and set his watch by it." His misinterpretation of the Bible may not have subverted his own faith in God, but it utterly destroyed the faith of many of his weaker disciples. In like manner, many have been assured that the exercise of the grace of faith would heal their sickness, to be bitterly disappointed in the dying hour. This is, to my mind, the worst feature of the delusion of divine healing as it is taught in our day. The sick are often trusting for a cure while steadily approaching the gates of death. They are taught to insist that they are healed, and to regard all the symptoms of sickness as the devil's counterfeits to shake their faith. Thus they do till some kind friend informs them that they will die in a few hours. Then they exclaim, as did one of my neighbors, "Whom can I trust now?" That must be a dangerous delusion, which is liable to bring the supreme test of faith in the hour of supreme weakness. I never before fully appreciated the propriety of the following petition in the prayer-book committal service at the grave: "Thou most worthy Judge eternal, suffer us not, at our last hour, for any pains of death, to fall from thee!"

The only safe instruction is to teach the sick to pray with an *if* — "if it be thy will, O God, restore my health; if it be not thy will, give me grace to endure my sickness and victory over the fear of death through Jesus Christ!"

I cannot state in a better manner the whole subject of healing in answer to prayer than to relate this overheard dialogue between two little girls while President Garfield was lying mortally wounded: " I believe the President will get well, so many people are praying for him," said one of the girls. " I doubt it," said girl No. 2. " Then," replied No. 1, " you don't believe God answers prayer, do you?" No. 2, " Oh, yes, I do ; but sometimes he answers 'Yes' and sometimes 'No.'"

XXXVI.

ST. JOHN INTERPRETED AND VINDICATED.

THE Book of books is called the Holy Bible because it has a holy author, and aims at a holy purpose, the production of holiness in its readers. We should expect to find nothing in it in any way extenuating sin, or implying its necessary continuance in any believer. Hence we should do more than suspect an interpretation which favors sin. We should reject it as not in accord with the Holy Spirit, called *holy* because it is his office to extinguish sin, and create holiness in every consenting free agent. Nothing which justifies sin can proceed from God. He will never contradict in revelation the principles he has implanted in creation. He has created in me certain self-evident truths, styled by Joseph Cook "the activity of the immanent God in the human soul." Says Bishop Butler, "Either clear immoralities or contradictions would prove a supposed revelation false." I think it is Shakespeare who says something like this, "There is no sin which cannot find a parson to bless it with a text." In my treatment of such texts I am impelled, by self-evident truth or moral reason, or the immanent God within, either to pronounce them spurious, or to assert that they are grossly misinterpreted. I take the latter alternative in every case.

1 John i. 8, "If we say we have no sin, we deceive ourselves, and the truth is not in us."[1] Many so erroneously explain this verse as to make it the greatest stumbling-block to Christian holiness in this life. It is interpreted as teaching that all Christians have sin, conscious transgression of the law, all their lives, and are self-deceived and utterly destitute of truth, if they say they do not sin, or that sin as a culpable state is not in them.

Dean Alford insists that " John is writing to persons whose sins have been forgiven them, and therefore necessarily the present tense *have* refers not to any previous state of sinful life before conversion, but to their now existing state." "If we say we have not sin in the course of our walking in the light, we deceive ourselves."

Others go beyond Alford, and say that St. John purposely included himself when he said, " If we say we have no sin," because he himself was conscious of having sin, and confessed it in the use of the first person plural. For one I wish to raise my voice to vindicate the beloved disciple from so gross a libel. The truth is, the candid student of St. John's style in this letter finds that for the sake of avoiding sameness of expression, like a good rhetorician, he uses a variety of phrases such as, " If a man say (iv. 20), " He that saith (ii. 4, 9), " If we say " (i. 6, 8, 10), without any perceptible difference in meaning, even to so keen an insight as that of Bishop Westcott.

But let us apply a cardinal law of interpretation to

---

[1] This text is briefly treated on pp. 147-9. It demands a more extended exegesis.

this subject — the law of non-contradiction. We must avoid making a writer flatly self-contradictory. This interpretation contradicts the context, "The blood of Jesus Christ cleanseth [present tense] from all sin." " If we confess our sins, he is faithful and just to forgive us our sins and to cleanse us from all unrighteousness." In what sense does a forgiven man have sin, or a cleansed man have impurity? Turn now to 1 John iii. 9, " Whosoever has been born of God [perfect tense implying that the new life has continued] is not sinning, because his seed abideth in him ; and he cannot be sinning, because he has been born of God." This is John's ideal of the regenerate, which is utterly irreconcilable with the character he has in view in i. 8. Whom has he in view? This brings us to the purpose of this epistle. That purpose is strongly hinted at in the first verse, in which he appeals to three of the five special senses, to seeing, hearing, and feeling, in proof of the reality of Christ's body. But who doubted, or rather denied, that his body was real matter, and asserted that it was a phantom which walked the earth thirty-three years? The Docetae, or seemers, who taught that the incarnation was a seeming and not a reality. Why did they teach thus? Their philosophy of dualism required it for the following reason. They asserted that good and evil are eternal and uncreated, and that moral evil resides only in matter, which is incurably evil. Even God cannot expel it. An immoral inference was soon made by those pretended Christians who adopted dualism ; namely, that their souls, being immaterial, were always free from moral evil or sin, and had no need of cleansing through the atonement, nor could they be defiled by sin, which could taint the body only. Hence they could practise gluttony, drunkenness, impurity, and all other sins, while their souls were perfectly free from sin. Their favorite illustration was that of a golden jewel in a dunghill, the gold being in no way alloyed or defiled by the encompassing filth. So their souls remained untarnished amid sensual sins. At a doctrine so immoral John aimed this epistle. He directed his spear to the weak spot in their philosophy. If sin exists in all matter, it existed in the person of Jesus Christ. To avoid so shocking an assertion they openly declared that he was a sham man. At this idea John directs his batteries from the beginning to the end of this epistle, again and again asserting that the Son of God has come *in the flesh,* not in a shadowy and unsubstantial form of a man. This aim of John at the Dualists, or Docetae, commonly called Gnostics, "the knowing ones," or "the illumined," is the key to the entire epistle, unlocking its difficulties. Carry this key through the first chapter, and see how it opens the doors and lets in the sunlight. God's character is first cleared of all clouds, and made to stand forth as diffusive light, a personality in whom is no darkness, "no, not even one speck." (ALFORD.) "If we [not genuine Christians, but professors corrupted by Gnostic notions and practices] say we have fellowship with him, and walk in darkness [i.e. in sin], we lie, and do not the truth." Says Dr. Whedon, "In truth, the three instances in this chapter of 'if we say,' are quotations of the language of Nicolaitan Antinomians, who maintained that however bad their conduct, they were still sinless."

Our next point is, that "to have sin" is a phrase so strong that it totally excludes the new birth, and that St. John could not have had genuine Christians in view when he wrote the words "If we say we have no sin." Bishop Westcott calls attention to the fact that this phrase "have sin" is peculiar to St. John, and is used elsewhere in the Bible only in John ix. 41 and xv. 22, 24, that it is much stronger than the verb to sin, and always implies guilt and desert of punishment. Bengel concurs. What logically follows? Either that St. John does not include real Christians in "If we say," but spurious ones of the Gnostic type, or it follows that all Christians have guilt and deserve punishment, and if they say they are forgiven and are regenerate, they deceive themselves and the truth is not in them. Every one who says he is justified is self-deluded, for every professed disciple of Christ, after believing on the Saviour with all heart, is still burdened with guilt and beneath divine wrath. This is the dilemma of the Alford school of expositors. Their theory that all Christians have guilt negatives justification, and contradicts St. Paul's joyful exultation in Rom. viii. 1, "there is therefore now no condemnation." The steps in our argument are few and plain. Guilt and the new birth are mutually exclusive. Sinning — a course of wilful violations of the known law of God — excludes being born of God (iii. 9) because guilt is incurred. "To have sin" in the meaning of St. John is to have guilt. Therefore the words "to have sin" exclude from regeneration and the spiritual life.

The difficulty with the Alford school is in the use of the phrase "have sin" in an indefinite, vague, and loose meaning, in the sense of weakness, defect, or involuntary error; whereas St. John always uses it in the definite sense of a guilty transgression of the law. It will not do to read into the Holy Scriptures our own modern, weakened, and blurred conception of sin.

With St. John sin always entails guilt. It originated in the devil, "who has sinned from the beginning" of sin. He inspired the first fratricide. Cain, not Adam, is the great exemplar of sin; "not as Cain was of the evil one and slew his brother." Satan suggested the betrayal of Jesus. Sin always has a Satanic character. There is no such character as "a sweet sinner." — (FATHER E. T. TAYLOR.)

James traces sin to lust swaying the will; "When lust hath conceived it bringeth forth sin." Paul traces it to Adam; "Death passed upon all men, for that all have sinned." John's doctrine of sin is more clear-cut and less hazy than Paul's, because it always means one thing, lawlessness active, voluntary, and responsible. "Sin is lawlessness" in the concrete as an act, not in the abstract merely. In its essence it is an act of moral injustice, the wilful transgression of the known law of God. John contemplates sin in the light of the law, Paul in the light of his experience. John's best synonym for sin is a lie. These are a pair, as inseparable as their opposite pair, truth and holiness. Sin is hatred of the brother, and love of a world hostile to God. With John sin always entails guilt. It is never a guiltless tendency. Nor does John weaken the term sin by confounding it with that word of various, and hence vague, meaning, the flesh, which in his epistles is not used in a bad sense, but only "to express humanity under the present conditions of life." — (WESTCOTT.)

It cannot be proved that John uses sin in a softened sense without guilt, and that he applies it "to Christians who though certainly not walking in darkness, yet have sinful tendencies in themselves, sensuous impulses, non-spiritual inclinations, lack of self-knowledge, a lowered standard, principles and views borrowed partly from the world, wavering of will, and hence even graver faults." — (SINCLAIR.) All of these defects may exist without guilt, so long as the will inclines to the right. The tenth verse, where a past tense is used, "have not sinned," strongly implies that "the sins confessed" are not wilful transgressions continuously committed since the new birth, but are pre-Christian sins. It is certainly a very unreasonable assumption that all Christians knowingly commit sins, especially in view of John's strong assertion that "he that is born of God sinneth not." It is exceedingly difficult to harmonize a defence or extenuation of sin with the Holy Scriptures. Bishop Westcott has the true idea of the phrase, "to have sin." "Like corresponding phrases, to have faith, to have life, to have grief, to have fellowship, it marks the presence of something which is not isolated, but a continuous source of influence. It is distinguished from 'to sin' as the sinful principle is distinguished from the sinful act itself. 'To have sin' includes the idea of PERSONAL GUILT." Bengel says "*not to have sin* denies *guilt;* and *not to have sinned* denies *the actual commission.*"

To assume that this guilt exists in those who are walking in the light is shocking indeed. To say that the non-imputation of personal guilt to the Christian is to deceive one's self, to be void of the truth and to make God a liar, in view of the precious doctrine of "the knowledge of the forgiveness of sins," is, to say the least, strange, severe, and contradictory language. John, the loving disciple, never applied such words to his brethren in Christ. Nor does he himself in this verse, by the use of "we," confess sin, as Dr. Sinclair asserts. Says Alford, "This state of needing cleansing from all present sin is veritably that of all of us; and our recognition and confession of it is the very first essential of walking in the light." The absurdity of this note will appear by another paraphrase. "God is light, the light of holiness. If we walk in holiness as he is in holiness, faith in the blood of Jesus Christ banishes all darkness. But if we, while consciously walking in the light, say that we are not walking in darkness, we deceive ourselves, or if, while walking in holiness, we say we are not walking in sin, the truth is not in us." "The blood of Jesus Christ is the cure of sin, but if any one attests that cure, he deceives himself. Quinine is a sure cure of the African fever. But if we who have applied the remedy and proved its curative quality certify that we are healed, we are self-deceived." The truthfulness of my exegesis all turns on the existence of Gnostic heresies in Ephesus in John's lifetime.

My readers will find some excellent commentaries, such as Alford's, which unaccountably evade any acknowledgment of the existence of these philosophies in the time of St. John's old age. But not long after his death, Polycarp, a pupil of St. John, writing to the

Philippians, quotes 1 John iv. 3, to show that this doctrine of the phantom Christ had worked down to the last fibres of the root of the creed, by two negations — no resurrection of the body and no judgment. Its natural tendency is to evaporate dogmas, sacraments, duties, and redemption. If the body of Jesus was unreal, "redemption was a drama with a shadow for a hero. The phantom of a redeemer was nailed to the phantom of a cross." The trend of modern sacred scholarship is toward the existence of these heresies, in germ form at least, as the historical setting of this epistle and the occasion of its being written.

This is the view of Bishop Westcott in his exhaustive annotations on this epistle, and of Bishop Wm. Alexander in his notes in "The Expositors' Bible," who gives a comprehensive yet concise statement of the general method and purpose of Gnosticism. "It aspired at once to accept and to transform the Christian creed; to elevate its faith into a philosophy, a *Gnosis* (knowledge), and then to make this knowledge cashier and supersede faith, love, holiness, redemption itself." We note the principal theories:

1. That "sin" is inherited depravity, which is diminished by the atonement, little by little, but leaving a residue till death. This may be styled the Calvinian theory, against which we have the following objections: (1) All the exhortations to perfected holiness are in the present tense. (2) All the prayers for this grace are in the same tense. Both exhortations and prayers are out of place if the thing sought cannot be obtained till death. (3) There is a total silence in the Bible respecting sanctification in death or after death. (4)

A gradual sanctification, completed at death, leaves the whole work on the plane of natural law, with no emphasis on the Divine Sanctifier. In fact, this theory could stand complete, even if the Holy Spirit should be left out altogether.

2. The second theory is that the entirely sanctified soul has infirmities, errors, and ignorances, which daily need the blood of sprinkling. All of this may be true, but it is to be greatly doubted whether John applies so strong a term as sin to these involuntary defects. For they lack the voluntary element, and do not entail guilt. St. John knows no guiltless sin.

3. The third theory is that sin has its full meaning, "actual and original"—(BENGEL), but that the continuous cleansing has for its object not each individual believer through all his life, but the instantaneous purification of successive believers, one after another, through all the course of time. To justify our position we quote an eminent English exegete, Prof. Joseph Agar Beet: "It is worthy of notice that in the New Testament we never read expressly and unmistakably of sanctification as a gradual process, or of degrees and growth in holiness, except perhaps in Rev. xxii. 11, 'And he that is holy, let him be made holy still,' or, 'yet more,' margin *R. V.*"

"A gradual process is not necessarily implied in the present participles of Heb. ii. 11; x. 14. "The present participle in Rom. iii. 24, 'Being justified freely by his grace,' referring to those who from time to time are justified, proves that, in these two passages, the participle may denote those who from time to time are laid on the altar of consecration." Ellicott, on Heb. x. 14, says, "It literally means those who *are being sanctified*, all those from age to age who, through faith, receive as their own that which has been procured for all men." To prove that the verb cleanse in the present tense is used of a succession of lepers, we refer the reader to Matt. x. 8, where the twelve are commissioned "to cleanse the lepers." But when an individual leper is cleansed in Matt. viii. 3, "Be thou cleansed," the aorist is used to denote instantaneous and decisive action. This use of the present tense therefore denotes the continued efficacy for purifying from all sin, actual and original, by a momentary action, every successive believer who claims his full heritage in Christ; and it does not signify the constant purification of the same individual till he dies, any more than the present tense in Rom. iii. 24 proves that justification is not one decisive act, but an action prolonged through life.

4. There is a theory, universally rejected by the best scholars, that to cleanse signifies judicial clearance from sin, in the sense of forgiveness. But this makes St. John, in verse 7, an advocate of justification by works and not by faith only. For walking in the light, or maintaining a series of good works, would be the condition on which the sinner is cleansed or cleared from sin. This would contradict that vital doctrine which teaches that God forgives not the godly, but the *ungodly*, through penitent faith in Jesus Christ. But the glory of the gospel is in the fact that Christ Jesus receives *sinners* who submit to him. "In verse 9," says Alford, "'to cleanse from all unrighteousness' is plainly distinguished from 'to forgive us our sin;' distinguished as a further process; as, in a word, sanctification, distinct

from justification. This meaning must be held fast." This is to reject the judicial meaning of "cleanse."

The theory has recently been advanced that St. John, in his first epistle, makes no distinction between love and perfect love, that the adjective perfect is an expletive adding nothing to the sense. But it will be found that St. John uses these words with great discrimination and deep significance. This is seen in iv. 7, "Every one that loveth is born of God." We note that the author does not say that loving perfectly is a sign of regeneration. This would have narrowed down the number of the regenerate to a few, excluding all weak and struggling believers. For such the beloved apostle had a strong sympathy. He remembered the time in his early discipleship when he had so defective love that he asked of Jesus permission to bid fire to come down from heaven and consume the bigoted Samaritans who did not receive his Master. St. John had seen very many young converts weak and wavering because of love imperfect and intermittent, needing sympathy and encouragement while trying to lay aside their pagan habits. It would have extinguished the smoking flax to have set the standard of regeneration so high as perfect love to the exclusion of lower degrees. Instead of such a treatment of the weak in faith, this wise pastor recognized the new birth wherever divine love had been implanted, in its lowest manifestations, and he beckoned them on to the higher altitudes, the Alpine summits of grace, by presenting the possibility of entering into the experience of pure, that is perfect, love. He was not afraid of discouraging them by telling them that it is better farther on.

This good news, proclaimed in love and not with threatening, will always be welcomed by every truly regenerate person.

The same wise appreciation of any degree of love to God is seen in iv. 18. "He that feareth is not made perfect in love." He did not say, "has no love," and hence is not a Christian. St. John writes with remarkable precision and discrimination, recognizing degrees in love, from the rill slowly meandering through the meadow to the Amazon floating the navies of the world. It is quite evident that St. John discerned two quite distinct classes in the school of Christ, and he treated them in such a way as to give no offence to the lower class, those not made perfect; and that the specific difference is the presence or absence of fear. Both classes love, in the evangelical sense, the one wholly delivered from servile dread of God, of punishment, of death, and from forebodings of future ill; while the other class has a degree of fear of these objects mingling with true love toward God and men. We call the attention of a certain class of zealous public religious teachers to the fact that St. John threw no stones at those whose love was imperfect, nor did he utter any word of threatening. They were all his brethren, the fearless and the fearful, those with love perfected and those with love incomplete. Yet he plainly implies that one state of experience is preferable. This he presents as a privilege.

In 1 John iv. 12 we learn that continuous love (present tense) to one another as a brotherhood in Christ is another sign of perfect love. We believe that it is easier to love God whom we have not seen than our brethren with whom we are in daily contact, noting their defects and perhaps denying ourselves to minister to their needs. He whose affection for all the members of the family of God knows no interruption nor abatement, evinces that pure, and hence perfect, love dwells in his bosom. It is because of the decay of this love towards the brethren that so many secular brotherhoods, open and secret, have sprung up like suckers, diverting nourishment from God's vine, the visible Church of Christ.

In 1 John ii. 5 we have another sign of perfected love. "Whosoever is [constantly] keeping [present] his commandments, in him verily hath the love of God been perfected." The tense of the verb implies continuous, i.e., perfect obedience. Hence, says Alford, "The perfect observation of his commandments is the perfection of love to him." A perfect, fruit-bearing tree implies a perfect root. Love is the root of obedience. Defective obedience springs from mixed love, the self-life not having been nailed to the cross. We speak of the self that bears not the image of our adorable Lord Jesus Christ.

All English readers are perplexed with the apparently unconditional assertion of St. John in his first epistle, iii. 9, "Whosoever is born of God doth not commit sin." The reason assigned seems also to be without any conditions; "because his seed remaineth in him," the love of God shed abroad in the heart by the Holy Spirit. (Rom. v. 5.) Then both assertions are strengthened by the declaration of the impossibility of sinning; "and he cannot sin, because he is begotten of God." This seems to teach the absolute infallibility of the regenerate. This is a doctrine far beyond the final perseverance of the saints, which conceded the possibility, and even the unavoidableness, of daily sin "in thought, word, and deed." But the Greek reveals an important condition in the perfect tense, "has been born," with the emphasis on the present to which this tense extends, thus implying the continuance of the regenerate life. The assertion of St. John, therefore, resolves itself into this, that, while loving God, a person cannot be disobeying him. The declaration is also modified by the use of the present tense "is not sinning," and "cannot be sinning," as a course of life, although under stress of sudden temptation he may commit a single sin as in ii. 1. "If any man sin (aorist)" against the tenor of his character, "we have an Advocate" to whom the penitent may resort for pardon. But should there be no such penitent resort, but rather a persistent repetition of the sin, sonship to God is forfeited, and the habitual sinner is no longer included in the phrase "whosoever has been born of God." Thus St. John's "cannot sin" is harmonized with his "if any man sin."

But in v. 18 there is a statement which apparently collides with this nice theory of harmony, — "We know that whosoever is born [perfect tense] of God sinneth not, but he that is begotten [aorist tense, denoting a single, decisive event] keepeth himself, and that wicked one toucheth him not." Here we seem to have infallibility predicated of the momentary act of regeneration, a state of perpetual sinlessness beyond the reach of the tempter. It would seem, after all, that St. John is not an Arminian, but the highest style of a Calvinist.

Here the latest results of criticism on the Greek text come very opportunely to our relief. These results are seen in the *R. V.,* " But he that was begotten of God, [called only begotten in iv. 9] keepeth him." The text of Westcott and Hort has " him " instead of " himself," and the keeping is conditionally done by Christ, kept by the power of God through faith." (1 Pet. i. 5.) See Bishop Westcott's commentary on 1 John v. 18.

Verse 17. " All unrighteousness is sin " means " every unjust act is sin." — A. CLARKE, BENGEL, WHEDON, and ALEXANDER.

We will not attempt to explain the paradox of a "brother" who "sins a sin not unto death," and of the " sin unto death " for which we are under no obligation to pray. Future generations of scholars may arrive at some acceptable solution of this practical difficulty.

The best explanation I can give is that St. John speaks of the irremissible sin.

> "There is a time we know not when,
> A point we know not where,
> That marks the destiny of men
> To glory or despair.
>
> There is a line, by us unseen,
> Which crosses every path,
> The hidden boundary between
> God's mercy and his wrath."
>
> ADDISON ALEXANDER.

The inexplicable difficulty lies in the question, How may we know who are past praying for? The poet, I think, is correct in his assumption that only God knows.

XXXVII.

HOLINESS AND HUMANITY.

JAMES ARMINIUS nearly three hundred years ago announced that "it is possible for a regenerate man to live without sin." This startled the high Calvinists, who charged him with a grave heresy. It was alleged that the ability not to sin, even though it be of grace through a persevering trust in Christ, placed the man beyond the power of temptation, destroyed the motive to watchfulness, and tended to loose living. It is the purpose of this chapter to prove that there are incentives to vigilance in those regenerate souls in whom the love of God is perfected and depravity is eliminated. The grace of entire sanctification does not change men into angels. They are still human, having appetites, passions, and affections. These are innocent so long as they are normal. They are normal only when gratified within the limits of the Creator's will, made known by natural and revealed religion, conscience, and the holy Scriptures. Says Bishop Butler: "When we say men are misled by external circumstances of temptation, it cannot but be understood that there is somewhat within themselves to render those circumstances temptations, or to render them susceptible of impressions from them. Therefore temptations from within and from without coincide and mutually imply each other." The "somewhat within" is not necessarily depravity. Where immediate gratification of a normal appetite does not consist with innocence there is danger of sinning. Hence watchfulness and self-denial are necessary to holy souls so long as they are in a state of probation. If it were not so the charge of immoral tendency would be valid against the tenet of Arminius, and both wisdom and benevolence would conspire to warn the regenerate against holiness.

Here it may be well to say that some professors of this grace have fallen into the mistake of supposing that all tendencies to sin are eradicated from their hearts, and they have no longer need of circumspection amid the moral perils encircling them. The possession of appetencies tending to a vicious indulgence, but easily held in check by the sanctified will, is of itself a tendency to evil. A controlled tendency to sin is not sin. A thought of sin is not a sinful thought till it is welcomed and detained with pleasure. Concupiscence is not sin, but it carries in its bosom the fuel of sin. It is the business of the Christian to be ever on the watch, lest the spark fall into the powder magazine. Nobody in this world is out of bow-shot of the devil. No class of believers, however advanced in spirituality, can safely divest themselves of "the whole armor of God," and hang it up in some museum of antiquities as an outgrown relic of an inferior religious experience. "What I say unto you, I say unto all, watch." Jesus himself not only prayed but watched. "Tarry ye here and watch with me." (Matt. xxvi. 38.) He was perfectly human as well as perfectly divine, and had need to be on his guard against the weakness of shrinking from the awful agonies in the cup which he must drink in redeeming the sinful race. Such shrinking from pain was innocent because it was instinctive. But since the bloody cross was the appointed instrument of redemption, to avoid it and yield to a human impulse, innocent in itself, would have been to fail to do his Father's will. In the wilderness he hungered. It would have been right for him to gratify his craving for food, but not right, at the suggestion of the tempter, to use his omnipotence to relieve himself from personal discomfort. Hence, the sinless Christ had need of self-denial and watchfulness against sensibilities in themselves holy. He pleased not himself. In this respect the servant is not above his Lord. Yet, while thus walking in his footsteps on the earth, he may be in righteous character as his risen Lord is in heaven.

Thus we have given a description of those whom Dr. Pope styles the "perfectly regenerate," in whom "the entire removal of iniquity in the present life" has been effected (vol. ii. 85). This has not been accomplished in all who have been born of God, only in those in whom the new life has reached this consummation. Both alike "do not commit sin," and both have need to deny the unlawful gratification of innocent natural impulses. (1 John iii. 9.) But in one class there is a struggle to overcome an inborn repugnance to obedience still existing, but not dominant, thank God, while in the other the native resistance is absent. The expulsive power of the new affection of love divine has taken such possession of the believer that it neutralizes the sinward inclination, as the inflated balloon, overcoming gravitation, mounts upward toward the zenith. The other class is like the balloon which has cleared the earth, but does not majestically rise. The earth has still a strong grasp upon it and pulls it down. It seems to have more affinities for the world beneath than for the sky above. What is the secret of this strange downward tendency which hinders the ascent? The sand-bags have not been emptied. The earth in the basket of the aeronaut has a strong pull upon the great globe which it is trying to leave. Buoyancy only slightly overcomes gravity. Diminish the latter and increase the former, and the ascent is accomplished. Yet gravitation is still its normal attraction. It is overcome, not destroyed. To interpret our figure to the simplest reader we would say that the completest victory over the world is twofold — negative in the extinction of inherited proneness to sin, and positive in the infusion of love to God to the utmost capacity of the soul. Both of these are accomplished by the Holy Spirit simultaneously when we by faith claim the full heritage of the believer, with the will in the attitude of perfect self-surrender to Christ. But the natural desires, implanted by our Creator, are not annihilated, but held within limits prescribed by him.

Our discussion would not be complete without stating the difference between that hereditary proneness to sin called in theology — not in the Bible — original sin, and that tendency to sin which arises from our constitution itself as moral intelligences endowed with natural sensibilities.

1. Sins resulting from these natural appetencies are not sins *per se* (in themselves), but in the irregular exer-

cise of innocent affections, as gluttony is excessive eating; while the offspring of Adamic depravity, pride, envy, malice, hatred, disobedience to God, and unbelief, are not the excess of any innocent principle, but sins in themselves.

2. This difference in character argues a difference in origin. The one class spring from natural desire in the individual; the other class having their root not in nature in its rectitude, as it came from the Creator, but in nature twisted and bent by Adamic sin.

3. Hence the normal appetites, passions, and affections awaken no self-abhorrence in well-balanced and properly-instructed minds, showing that they are not products of the fall, notwithstanding Augustine's contrary view of concupiscence. But self-loathing always attends sins *per se* as not being the excess of a good thing, but the fruit of a bitter root in nature itself.

4. The safeguard against the first class of sins is not the extinction of our emotional nature, but its regulation by an enlightened intellect, and by strengthening the will in right action by the momentum of love divine "shed abroad in the heart by the Holy Spirit given unto us." (Rom. v. 5.) The safeguard against the second class is the annihilation of the inborn "bent to sinning" by the Holy Spirit, the sanctifier.

It will be naturally inferred that I do not ascribe all the sin in the world of mankind to the sin of our first parents in Eden. I do not accept the theory that the offspring of the sinless pair would have been beyond the reach of personal sin each for himself under the stress of temptation. There is a sense in which Adam and Eve stood in probation for their entire race. Its perpetuation was involved in their moral choice, but not the moral character and destiny of their descendants. No one under the just government of God will ever be punished for another's sin. Adam's transgression damaged his descendants, but it did not damn them. It did not determine their eternal destiny.

At another point my article will be criticised — my distinction between *tendency* and *proneness*. My authority for my use of *tendency* is Bishop Butler: "If particular propensions can be gratified without the allowance of moral principle, or by contradicting it, then they must be conceived to have some tendency — in how low a degree soever, yet some tendency — to induce persons to such forbidden gratification." He shows that this slight tendency may be increased "by frequency of occasions," till finally it ends in actual deviation from the right. This is his theory of the origin of sin in a holy universe. It is just as good for the origin of sin in an entirely sanctified person, in whom the so-called original sin has been extinguished. I have used *proneness* in its etymological sense as bending forward or headlong, as Milton describes the fallen angels — "Down thither *prone* in flight." It means an habitual downward bent.

The moral lesson is, "Let him that thinketh he standeth [it may be on some lofty altitude of Christian experience] take heed lest he fall." (1 Cor. x. 12.) "Mankind," says the bishop, "and perhaps all finite creatures, from the very constitution of their nature, before habits of virtue are formed, are deficient and in danger of deviating from what is right, and therefore stand in need of virtuous habits for security against this danger."

My moral lesson is not complete without another quotation for the benefit of myself and my brethren in the ministry of Christ, and all others who are brought into constant contact with Christian truth as teachers. In speaking of the formation of good habits as safeguards, the bishop says: " But going over the theory of virtues in one's thoughts, talking well, and drawing fine pictures of it, this is so far from necessarily or certainly conducing to form a habit of it in him who thus employs himself, that it may harden the mind in a contrary course and render it gradually more insensible, i.e., form a habit of insensibility to all moral considerations." This is the philosophy of downfalls in the Christian pulpit. The safeguard is the personal practice of all the precepts which the preacher preaches and the teacher teaches. Especially should he follow the example of St. Paul in the sanctification of the body: "I buffet my body, and bring it into bondage, lest by any means, after that I have preached to others, I myself should be rejected." (1 Cor. ix. 27, *R. V.*)

It is spiritually healthful for the minister of Christ often to ponder that most solemn admonition of our Lord Jesus to evangelical preachers in Matt. vii. 21–23. They are preachers because they prophesied; they are evangelical because they call Jesus Lord, thus confessing his supreme Divinity. They are revivalists and reformers because they cast out demons and wrought many miracles. Yet they meet the unexpected sentence in the final day, " Depart from me."

XXXVIII.

THE QUALITIES OF A SUCCESSFUL MINISTRY.

[*A Sermon before the Boston University School of Theology, May* 30, 1871.]

" For he was a good man, and full of the Holy Ghost and of faith: and much people was added unto the Lord." — ACTS xi. 24.

THE last clause of the text is so evidently a consequence of the qualities of Barnabas, that there is no need of the usual illative word, *therefore*. Much people, according to the Greek a vast crowd, were converted from paganism, and gathered unto the Lord Jesus, through the instrumentality of one man. It cannot be amiss, in addressing the patrons, trustees, and faculty of the Boston Theological School, to dwell for an hour upon the personal conditions of success in promoting the salvation of souls. For this is the final cause, the be-all and end-all, of the money here munificently lavished, and the time and toil here consecrated. This is the prayer of the church; this the burden of many a Christian soul bowing in secret; this the purpose of the founders, — Isaac Rich, the munificent; Lee Claflin, the bountiful; and Jacob Sleeper, the princely; and of others who have gone up on high. This the secret of the interest of holy angels, and of Jesus Christ the Lord of all. Not to magnify a sect, but to save men from sin and hell, was this institution established. St.

THE QUALITIES OF A SUCCESSFUL MINISTRY. 279

Luke asserts that Barnabas had three personal qualifications for evangelical success. He was a good man, and full of faith and of the Holy Ghost. We infer, therefore, that those characteristics which are essential to the work of the Christian ministry may all be grouped under three heads, — *Character, Creed*, and *Experience*. The discussion of these, in the order indicated, well constitutes the plan of my discourse.

I. There is no profession, no line of effort, in which character is so absolutely essential to success as the Christian ministry. Men will retain a tippling lawyer, if he have power to sway juries, running the risk of finding him tipsy on the court day. The physician, whose skill in the healing art has made him famous, may be profane and licentious, and yet retain his patronage. The rakish artist, if genius moves his brush or chisel, finds a ready and remunerative sale for his masterpieces; while the statesman, or politician rather, — alas for our times! — fears the falling off of his majorities, less because of his moral delinquencies, than for his disobedience to the mandates of his party. Not so with the gospel minister. His purity of character is an indispensable coefficient of his success. This is because Christianity is not a science only, a system of religious truth. It is this, but it is more. It is a life, a divine transforming power. It is effectually preached when its truths are exemplified in the life of the preacher, as well as inculcated by his tongue. He preaches in vain, who cannot point to his own moral rectitude, his own saintly character, as a specimen of the transfiguring power of the gospel. Even those deluded souls who risk their salvation on the efficacy of the sacraments, through successional ordinations from the apostles, find in a dissolute clergy the strongest trial of their faith — a trial which multitudes cannot endure, but go away from the altar served by debauched priests, into the arid regions of atheism, where they are relieved from the disgusting sight of a genuflecting hypocrisy. The sinless character of Jesus is the one stubborn fact, the miracle of miracles, which renders his gospel such a power among men. The existence of such a character in the world's literature is a wonder which neither Strauss nor Renan, Parker nor Emerson, can explain. The absolute rectitude of Jesus is his *pou sto* — his Archimedean foothold on which with the lever of his truth he can lift the fallen world up to God. When men read the philosophies of Hegel, Kant, or Hamilton, they are not demanding certificates of the moral integrity of these authors before they will accept the truth of their systems. But the character of Jesus Christ cannot be detached from his gospel. Christianity centres in his person. One act of sin in the author destroys our faith in a scheme whose great purpose is the destruction of the works of the devil. There is a sense in which the same is true of the preacher's relation to the truths which he preaches. Not that the truth of the Christian system depends on any or all its advocates. Christ would be true, though all his apostles had betrayed him. Yet Christ's glory among men would be obscured to the eyes of men, yea, eclipsed, by any such moral defection among his modern evangelists. The gospel would be powerless to save those who reject its claims, stumbling at the moral obliquities of its advocates. Alas, this is not all hypothetical. Church history has many a dark page demonstrating the truth of our assertion, that a vicious priesthood neutralizes the efficacy of the gospel on their lips. Wherefore, be ye clean that bear the vessels. of the Lord : —

> " Jesus, let all thy servants shine
> Illustrious as the sun,
> And bright with borrowed rays divine
> Their glorious circuit run."

But goodness is positive as well as negative. It implies the presence of benevolent affections, as well as the absence of moral obliquities. Barnabas was a man of large human sympathies. In the exigencies of the times succeeding the Pentecost, when it was desirable that the whole company of converts should be kept together at Jerusalem for their spiritual instruction, he is especially mentioned for the promptness with which he puts all his worldly goods at the disposal of the church in this extraordinary crisis, evincing thereby a perfect spirit of benevolence and of consecration the farthest removed from all selfish ends in his Christian ministry. This spirit of transparent generosity, self-abnegation, and perfect devotion to the good of the church and to the glory of Christ, was an element of power in his ministry. It is so now. The eagle-eyed world is forever prying into character, and scrutinizing motives, especially in the case of those who profess that —

> " The love of Christ doth them constrain
> To seek the wandering souls of men."

When there is found one who discards all worldly motives, and sublimely toils through life, enduring poverty as "seeing him who is invisible," the world's logic is nonplussed; it has found a practical argument which it can no more answer than it can the original witnesses of the Christian miracles, passing their lives in labors, dangers, and sufferings, voluntarily undergone in attestation of the truth. A kind heart, a large philanthropic soul, whether it comes of nature or of grace, is so kindred to the spirit of the gospel, that its possessor stands on a high vantage-ground in winning souls to Christ. A hard and unsympathetic nature is a poor medium through which the melting story of the cross is to be poured into the hearts of men. Such a man, though he had the massive intellect of Lord Bacon, would not add many souls to the Lord Jesus. He might be a Titan in polemical theology. But only one such to stand guard over our theological foundations is enough for a generation. The conversion of sinners depends more on the warm atmosphere of love, which attends the presentation of the truth, than on logical power. Few men can follow an abstruse argument, but all can *feel*. We must not forget that the Lord Jesus came to save men of low degree. These are the majority. They are more skilled in the use of the plough, the hammer, the shuttle, and the oar, than with the syllogism in Barbara. It took the greatness of John Wesley to find this out, and to adapt his preaching to the semi-barbarian peasantry and colliers, and to impress this peculiarity on all his successors to the present time. That peculiar influence which is called the *savor* of a man, the most uncultivated intuitively perceive and feel. Hence the power of a preacher who carries with him the savor of goodness,

THE QUALITIES OF A SUCCESSFUL MINISTRY. 283

evincing itself in his zeal for the suppression of the causes of vice and misery in this life, and thus commending his sincerity in his efforts to lead the people to life everlasting. When will Protestantism out of its wealth build, endow, and control, as evangelic agencies, hospitals and eleemosynary institutions, as Romanism builds them out of her gathered mites for the aggrandizement of herself? True Christianity is the only genuine philanthropy. The minister of Jesus Christ divests himself of a large element of influence when he lays aside philanthropy in its common acceptation; and he puts a powerful weapon into the hand of his adversary, when, through his neglect, he allows the enemy of the cross of Christ to assume the championship of any humane enterprise.

II. But the minister of Christ must be more than a philanthropist medicating human woes, heading moral reforms, and preventing social demoralization. His is the difficult task of eradicating sin from human souls. Sin is not a cutaneous disease, to be cured by perfumed lotions, to be rose-watered out of the world. It is a stubborn and radical fact, demanding thorough and drastic treatment. The only medicine for its cure is spiritual truth rendered effectual by the Holy Ghost. Since this truth is not discovered by reason, but is disclosed by revelation, it is apprehended and made real to the soul only by faith. This brings us to the second element of Barnabas's success, — the completeness of his faith, historical and fiducial. Jesus Christ gives a wonderful prominence to the truth as the instrument of human salvation. "For this cause was I born, that I might bear witness to the truth." "The Spirit will guide you into all truth." "Sanctify them through the truth." "The sword of the Spirit is the Word of God." He who most skilfully and vigorously wields this sword will have the greatest success in revealing the wicked heart to itself. Conviction of sin is nothing more than God's truth held up as a mirror till the sinner sees his own image hideously marred and scarred by sin. The successful preacher is characterized by an acquaintance with the mirror which has such marvellous revealing power. He adjusts it to the dull, purblind eye. He sets it in the strongest light, that it may have its legitimate effect. There are many in our day who affect to despise doctrines, creed-statements of gospel truth. They endeavor to magnify their own originality, liberality, and independence in theological inquiries by belittling creeds. They perpetually hint that a creed is enslaving and dwarfing to its believers. They assert that some men can do more with a jackknife than others with a whole chest of edged tools. This may be true, without impairing the credibility of the assertion that most builders would prefer the chest of tools. Rationalism, with its jackknife, may manage to rear a leaky wigwam out of the knotty poles and birch-bark of natural religion; but the true preacher of Christ needs better implements; for he is not building a wretched hut for a day, but an enduring palace, the habitation of God through the Spirit. Free religion begins its downward career by pouring contempt upon a historical faith. Its next step is the denial of a historical Christ. Its last is the apotheosis of human reason. Whereas it is no more derogatory to reason to accept some truths as primary in theology, than it is in metaphysics; in the one the revelations of the inspiring spirit, and in the other the testimony of the human consciousness. Through all the ages of Christianity the power and spirituality of the church have been in exact proportion to the faithfulness with which the truth has been preached. God's truth is the very soul of persuasion. He who has fed upon it, digested it, and incorporated it into the very texture of his soul by a living faith, has the grand secret of pulpit power. The word of God is *quick*, i.e., a living power on earth. It was St. Paul's boast that he had not only "fought the good fight," but that he had "kept the faith," the precious deposit of gospel truth committed to his hand as the sword of his triumph. "This is the victory which overcometh the world, even your faith." Hence, in this sifting and sceptical age, which levels its batteries at revealed truth with that satanic sagacity which assailed the Incarnate Truth himself, we, who know the secret of our strength, will "contend for the faith once delivered to the saints."

But even the truth is not ultimate. It is a means to an end. It is to be conserved for its uses. It has not an absolute, but a relative, value. It is the instrument of our sanctification.

III. Faith worketh experience. This introduces the third qualification, on which we shall amplify more extendedly.

1. Barnabas was filled with the Holy Ghost. Here is an experience deep, broad, and full, which gave an irresistible momentum to the activities and utterances of this man of God, and crowned his labors with abundant fruits. Brethren, there is a Holy Ghost. Will you

pronounce it fanaticism if your preacher should say that he has gone beyond the Apostles' Creed, and that he knows the Holy Ghost? The Master justifies this declaration. "But ye know him, for he dwelleth with you, and shall be in you." Does not even Philosophy herself teach that faith is to eventuate in knowledge? Have not all the discoveries in the experimental sciences proceeded thus on the maxim of Anselm, *Credo ut intelligam*, "I believe, in order that I may know?" Does not the faith of the Christian in a future heaven lead him to a future knowledge of that heaven, and shall his faith in the present Holy Spirit not lead into a present knowledge of the Comforter? Faith begets knowledge, and knowledge in turn begets faith in the still higher manifestations of God. Hence the maxim of Abélard is also true, *Intelligo ut credam*, "I know, in order that I may believe." Thus believing in order to know, and knowing in order to believe, my winged soul mounts up this Jacob's ladder from earth to heaven. How beautifully does St. Paul set forth this ladder of faith and knowledge, combining the maxims of Anselm and Abélard, "I know whom I have believed [here is faith a stepping-stone to knowledge], and am persuaded that he is able to keep what I have committed to him unto that day"— here is knowledge a stepping-stone to a new and higher act of faith. Therefore, it ought not to be incredible that the soul, climbing this divine ladder let down from heaven, should at length arrive at a knowledge, not only of the Holy Spirit, but of the fulness of his indwelling as the Answerer and Sanctifier. This is the doctrine of the Holy Scriptures, as interpreted by the Wesleyan fathers, and confirmed by their experience and apostolic lives. It was the key-note of Methodism when she sounded her bugles for her march round the world; and throughout her march of a century her columns have faltered when they have failed to hear this peculiar note, and have dashed on in triumph when it has been distinctly heard again.

American Methodism has come near losing the doctrine of the fulness of the Holy Spirit as a blessing distinct from regeneration. The causes are various. The growing popularity of this church, and its advance in social status, have attached to its communion many to whom a deep spirituality is distasteful. An unfortunate spirit of philosophizing on this subject, the unscriptural presentation of it with threatenings, and the many imperfect, and some counterfeit exemplifications of this blessed experience, together with the fear of Palmerism in the East, and of Nazariteism in the West, have, in the language of Charles Wesley, —

> "Staggered thus the most sincere,
> Till from the gospel hope they move;
> Holiness as error fear,
> And start at perfect love."

Yet despite all these causes, most of which troubled the Wesleys as they do us, we may, with the great poet of Methodism, join in the prayer, —

> "Lord, thy real work revive,
> The counterfeit to end."

Thank God, the eclipse of this doctrine, which once threatened to become total, is rapidly passing away, and this light of the glory of God in the face of Jesus Christ is shining forth again, betokening an era of spiritual prosperity and power.

Our Unitarian friends have recently considered and discussed the lessons which Methodism is teaching to Unitarianism. One of those lessons they find to be the entire consecration of the soul to the will of God, inspiring to a zealous and self-sacrificing life for the salvation of the world. We do not deny that they have found the secret of our success. But when they come to practise this lesson, they will certainly fail unless they begin at the Methodist alphabet, — a living and omnipotent Jesus, and an indwelling, personal, divine Comforter, sealing this consecration by his sanctifying power, and making it a divine reality, and not a mere human sentiment. We have not copyrighted this alphabet, for it is not our invention. It is as old as the New Testament, yea, as the Psalms of David — "Restore thou unto me the joy of thy salvation, and uphold me by thy free Spirit; then will I teach transgressors thy ways, and sinners shall be converted unto thee." If feeble and waning churches wish to become aggressive and prosperous, let them get down on their knees with David, and wrestle with God for the joys of his salvation, and for the mighty guidings of the Holy Ghost. If a hesitating and powerless ministry, weakened by doubts, palsied by fear, would suddenly become bold, mighty, aggressive, and conquering, let them pray to be strengthened with might by his Spirit in the inner man. This is like steam to the motionless engine. If a complaining minister, fretting and chafing on hard appointments, would be lifted into a state of perfect and cheerful acquiescence with the divine will, where none of his powers will be wasted by friction, but all subsidized for Christ, let him seek the Spirit's anointing with the oil of gladness. For the Holy Spirit in the soul is both impulse and lubrication, both steam and oil to the locomotive.

2. We are taught by many that after justification the progress of the soul is by a steady and gradual development of spiritual power, without crises, sharp transitions, and sudden emergencies from lower to higher states. It is said that this uniform and gradual unfolding of the spiritual life commends itself to reason as the natural and normal method, that only fickle, impulsive, and unstable souls, incapable of this uninterrupted and constant advance, are pushed ahead by the apparently irregular method of special spiritual impulses. It is asserted that even in the case of these, it is commonly, if not always, a sudden restoration from a backslidden state. It is asserted that a truly regenerate soul, remaining victorious over sin, needs no subsequent sudden and sharply defined outpouring unction, and baptism of the Spirit. But when we open the Word of God, we find that, both under the Mosaic and the Christian dispensations, spiritual development has been both by steady growth and spiritual crises. Thus the seventy elders were suddenly baptized with the Spirit when assembled at the tabernacle, and Eldad and Medad in the camp. But the most remarkable instance of a sudden spiritual anointing, notwithstanding an uninterrupted gradual spiritual growth, is that of the great exemplar, Jesus Christ. As he was a perfect man, soul and body, he had a normal physical and intellectual unfolding. We read, also, that his spiritual nature expanded gradually. As a man, he grew in favor with God. Yet before he entered upon

his life-mission, he received a special impulse from on high to make him the centre whence spiritual power should go forth to bless all with whom he came in contact. That impulse was given to him by the Holy Ghost at his baptism by John, and in the power of the Spirit he returned to Galilee.

We can no more fathom this mystery of the divine Son baptized by the divine Spirit, than we can that of the omnipotent Son praying to the Almighty Father in Gethsemane, and forsaken by him on the cross. Yet we must accept the historical fact of Jesus' baptism by the Holy Ghost as a preparation for his ministry, and that not till then do the evangelists speak of him as "full of the Holy Ghost," "led by the Spirit," and "in the power of the Spirit." He left us an example that we should walk in his steps in everything not peculiar to his person and mission. The blessing of the fulness of the Spirit cannot be peculiar to Christ, because it is promised to all who fully believe. Hence, it is instantaneous, as it was with Jesus at the Jordan, notwithstanding a previous uniform growth in favor with God.

Can any Christian believer, preacher or layman, addressing himself to his lifework, say that because he has a clear evidence of his conversion, he needs no anointing from on high to unify and intensify all the powers of his nature for the service of Christ? Can he assert that because he is not conscious of backsliding, or even of one act of sin, therefore he needs no unction from the Holy One? If you say that this was peculiar to Christ, and in no way an example for every believer, what mean those oft-repeated promises of the Comforter to the apostles who had been declared to be already clean, and to every one who will ask the Father in his name? If you say that this was miraculous and limited to the apostolic age, what does Christ mean when he assures his disciples that the Comforter would abide with them forever? How happens it that the common interrogatory to young converts by the apostles was, " Have ye received the Holy Ghost since ye believed?" and that believers were found, in Ephesus a few, and in Samaria a city full, on whom the Holy Ghost had not fallen till they were instructed respecting their privilege by the apostles? St. Paul teaches that " after justification through the death of Christ, much more shall we be saved by his life."

Again, this gift of the divine fulness must be instantaneous, because it is conditioned on a definite act of faith. If a soul, with all its progress, never reaches a time when it distinctly apprehends, by a definite act of faith, " the exceeding greatness of Christ's power to usward who believe," it will never obtain this heavenly baptism.

We have not time to show that in all ages of the church the experience of the holiest men and women attests this doctrine of the fulness of the Holy Ghost as a work distinct from regeneration.

If we had time to construct an argument from church history, digging down through its successive strata, after the manner of the geologist, we should find abundant proofs of the distinction between the regenerate state and the experience of the fulness of the Holy Spirit. But we have only time to direct your attention to the fossil remains of this distinction as seen to-day in the Roman, the Greek, the Lutheran, and the English Churches in the rite of confirmation, for the purpose of communicating the Holy Spirit by laying hands upon the heads of those who are supposed to have already received the grace of regeneration through water baptism. Having demonstrated the possibility of the experience of the fulness of the Holy Ghost, we proceed to argue the necessity of this deep spiritual experience in the preacher as ground of confidence in the truth, the instrument which he wields for human salvation.

3. The ground of confidence is twofold. First, logical certainties. Christian apologetics addresses the reason. The argument from prophecy, miracles, the morals of the gospel scheme, and the resplendent purity and majesty of Christ, and the propagation of the system, is designed to satisfy the intellect, and to produce the highest certainty attainable by probable, in distinction from demonstrative, proof. Hence, we cannot too thoroughly educate our young Christians, especially our candidates for the ministry, in the Christian evidences. They cannot too well know the certainty of those things wherein they have been instructed. They must be led about our spiritual Zion, and tell the towers thereof, and mark well her bulwarks, that they may intelligently defend their faith against the assaults of a rationalistic age, and be able to give a reason for the hope that is in them.

But the highest degree of certitude lies not in the logical faculty. There is still room for doubt. Error may lurk in the premises; a fallacy may exist in the process. The most that Christian apologetics can do is to leave us with an inference. What if the inference be incorrectly concluded? I find myself every day making unwarrantable inferences. Is the advocate of Christian truth in his best estate left a victim to doubt? Romanism says so. Her priests stoutly assert that no man can be absolutely certain of the forgiveness of his sins, and that the priestly absolution is conditional on the sincerity of the repentance and the completeness of the confession, of which none can be sure; and that nearly all the saints of the canon died in doubt of their acceptance with God. Thus, in her eagerness to monopolize all teaching, Rome denies the illumination of the Holy Ghost. Even after the crowning miracle, the resurrection of their Lord, the disciples were not furnished with all needful certainty respecting the divinity of the gospel. Hence, they were not commanded to go forth after the first interview with the risen Saviour, and proclaim to all the world the divine origin of the gospel. That Jesus has power to save to the uttermost is still an inference. Will these men toil, suffer the loss of all — yes, *die*, to maintain the correctness of their logic? Will they boldly meet all opposers, and conquer them with syllogisms? Jesus did not put them to this test. There is a higher ground of certainty than the logical faculty. It is the intuitions. On this loftiest summit of possible knowledge, Christ invites all his disciples to stand, "Tarry ye in Jerusalem, until ye be endued with power from on high." Not many days hence I will baptize you with the Holy Ghost and with fire. Your inmost souls shall be brought into conscious contact with God.

The soul shall with open vision gaze upon the verities of gospel truth. The Spirit of God, more pervasive than the atmosphere, more subtle than ether, shall seal upon your hearts in characters unmistakable the certainty of my doctrine. Ye shall be assured of the truth on grounds as firm as the self-evident axioms of mathematics, as firm as the intuition of your personal existence. Absolute assurance shall be yours. Doubt shall fly before this demonstration of the divinity of the gospels, and joy shall rush in to fill the soul. Hitherto each disciple might say, in view of his perplexities and harassing doubts, —

> "Like Noah's dove, I flit between
> Rough seas and stormy skies."

After the baptism of the Spirit, he can exultingly sing, —

> "But now the clouds depart,
> The winds and waters cease,
> And sweetly o'er my gladdened heart
> Expands the bow of peace."

The promise was more than fulfilled on the Day of Pentecost, and is now fulfilled to every Spirit-baptized soul. Brethren, I know whereof I affirm. I am, by the grace of God, one of a vast number of witnesses who can attest that Jesus Christ as the pardoning Saviour, and the Holy Ghost as the indwelling Sanctifier, are realities more veritable to the soul than Emmanuel Kant's two highest sources of sublimity, — the starry heavens above, and the moral law within. This certitude would not be increased by Jesus walking forth in human form before me, healing the sick and raising the dead — yea, rising from the tomb, and mounting the skies in full view of my unclouded vision. Said Jesus, It is expedient for you, for your assurance, that I, the miracle-worker, should go away. For I will send one who will give you better proofs than miracles. It is expedient for you that I, your personal friend, should depart, for I will send one who will form a closer friendship with you, even inhabiting your bodies, and abiding in your souls, who will make your fellowship with me and my Father more intimate than my human presence. Let the fulness of the Holy Spirit, the Comforter, be the experience of the preacher, and he will no longer feebly enunciate gospel truth ; he will no longer hesitate to proclaim a living Jesus. Our pulpits will no longer be afflicted with impotency, but be girded with strength : —

> "What we have felt and seen,
> With confidence we tell;
> And publish to the sons of men
> The signs infallible."

What are these signs infallible but the testimony of consciousness to marvellous changes wrought within our souls?

When the seventy returned from the trial mission, they came in exultation to Christ, because even the devils were subject to them in his name. He then told them there was a greater and more joyful miracle. "Rejoice rather that your names are written in heaven." It is the office of the Holy Ghost to attest this marvellous fact : —

> "The Spirit answers to the blood,
> And tells me I am born of God."

This assurance is so utterly indubitable, that its possessor becomes bold in the assertion of gospel truth. "And they were all filled with the Holy Ghost, and they spake the word of God with boldness." The chain of Christian evidences was complete when the clouds received Jesus from the tearful eyes of his disciples. But this did not make them bold even unto death. "But ye shall receive power from the Holy Ghost." This power is attainable by every Christian. Every preacher has an especial promise, "Lo, I am with you always." Christianity is not waning in spiritual privileges; it is not tapering off to a point as centuries roll by. It is an emanation from an unchanging power, Jesus Christ, yesterday, to-day, and forever the same. The law of progress, visible in all God's works, would demand an increase rather than a diminution of spiritual power with the lapse of time. The Spirit will abide with you forever. The promise that he will enter and abide as a Comforter is to every one who will ask the Father in the name of the Son. This fulness of the Holy Spirit is not limited, as Mr. Beecher teaches, to a few persons endowed by nature with a peculiar mental and physical organization. Such a limitation would destroy all ground of faith in the promise for any one; for each one would suppose that he was constitutionally debarred from this high experience, and so fail to apprehend it by simple faith in Jesus Christ.

4. Let me fortify the statement that we may possess an intuitive certainty that Jesus is true, beyond the certainty derived from logical proofs, and even more satisfactory than the testimony of the senses. St.

Peter constructs a splendid climax of Christian evidences when he demonstrates that "we have not followed cunningly devised fables, when we made known unto you the power and coming of our Lord Jesus Christ, but were eyewitnesses of his majesty, when there came such a voice to him from the most excellent glory." Here two senses, sight and hearing, conspire to attest Christ's supernatural person. Then Peter rises a step to a higher proof. "We have a more sure word of prophecy, unto which we do well to take heed." Here fulfilled prophecy cogently argues the truth of Christ. But we have not yet reached the summit of the mountain where the cloudless vertical sun pours down his overwhelming splendors, rendering doubt impossible. The third and crowning proof of the series is an experience, an intuitive conviction of the truth, thus poetically expressed, "unto which ye do well to take heed, until the day-star arise in your hearts." Brethren, has the day-star arisen in your hearts, chasing away your night of doubt and sadness? Study the scientific proofs of Christianity, as drawn out by the Butlers and Paleys of all the Christian ages, but continue your patient and diligent research till the day-star arises within; otherwise you will be feeble advocates for Jesus, because dimly apprehending the exceeding greatness of his power to us-ward who believe.

5. Lest any one may suppose that I bring a strange and dangerous doctrine to your ears, let me appeal to the Word of God once more. My assertion is, that the fulness of the Holy Ghost is the sunrise of spiritual illumination and the source of absolute assurance, and that this blessing is attainable by all. St. John, in his first

epistle to every Christian, says, "But ye have an unction from the Holy One, and ye know all things." Not all scientific truth, not all dogmatic truth, but the divine origin of all revealed truth, and the soul's relation to God's law and his love, a conviction clear as noonday that sin is forgiven, and King Jesus is alone enthroned over the soul. Once how dark to my unanointed eye was the following passage: "But the anointing which ye have received of him *abideth* in you, and ye need not that any man teach you: but as the same anointing teacheth you of all things." "*The anointing teacheth*" — a mystery indeed to him on whose head the oil of gladness has not been poured, but a glorious reality to him on whom the joy of this great salvation has been freely bestowed.

6. But the highest efficiency of the preacher requires that his experience be not only possessed, but professed. "The experience of one rational being is of interest to all who become cognizant of it." This is because we are so constituted as to be similarly affected by like causes. Let half a dozen persons far gone with pulmonary consumption publish to the world their complete cure by the same remedy, and the intelligence would flash over the wires, across the continent, irradiating with hope twice ten thousand sick chambers. Hence the value of testimony. The entire science of medicine has been constructed upon it. The pharmacopœia has been filled by the attestations of cures. Who can better authenticate the healing than the patient himself? Who better than the renewed and sanctified soul can attest his spiritual transfiguration, and the power by which it was accomplished? Experi-

ence avowed is one of the chief elements of the preacher's power to demonstrate the divinity of the gospel and the reality of its blessings to believing souls. Hence St. Paul, the master logician, when, on critical occasions, his liberty or even his life hanging on the balance of a Roman governor's will, he wanted something more cogent than a syllogism, told the story of his conversion from a persecutor to a preacher of the faith he once destroyed. In fact, his commission, three times renewed, was not to preach, but to testify. When the omnipresent Jesus, as Bishop Simpson graphically expresses it, " Standing on picket duty for the little church at Damascus, took Saul of Tarsus prisoner," he said to him, " For this purpose I have appeared to thee, to make thee a minister and a *witness* both of these things which thou hast seen, and of those things in which I will appear unto thee." When after three days Ananias came to him, he, by divine inspiration, repeated the declaration, " For thou shalt be a witness unto all men of what thou hast seen and heard." Years afterwards, while slumbering in the castle of Antonia, the Lord stood by him, and said, " Be of good cheer, Paul: for as thou hast testified of me in Jerusalem, so must thou bear witness also at Rome." On each of these occasions testifying is insisted on. Why? Because it is the most cogent and persuasive preaching. A herald is useful to make proclamation of the law and of the will of the court; but make way — here comes one more important. He is an unimpeachable witness, who has a testimony to give on the suit before the judge. All jurists will tell you that one word of authentic evidence is worth more than ten thousand words of sophistical, professional pleading. The witness is far more important than the advocate. The testimony can go to the jury without the argument; but it will not do to send the argument without the testimony. Yet I fear that this sad blunder the modern Christian church is committing when, through eloquent preachers, she sends to the world the argument without the evidence. It is not often that the witness and the advocate are, in our courts, combined in the same person. But all jurymen know how much more weighty are his words when the advocate is summoned from the bar to the witness-stand, and with uplifted hands attests to the facts. Here is no professional quibbling, no insincere and cunning speech. Oh, if every Christian pulpit could be for only one Sabbath converted from an advocate's stand to a witness-box, and each Spirit-baptized preacher should say, "Draw near, all ye that fear the Lord, and I will tell you what he has done for my soul," what a stir there would be among the unbelieving world! I verily believe that they would give the verdict of truth to the Man of Calvary, and falling down would acknowledge that God is with us of a very truth. Am I uncharitable when I say that Jesus Christ, on trial before the jury of an unbelieving world, has too many lawyers and too few witnesses? Am I justified in saying that the advocate who cannot in a moment, at the subpœna of his divine client, turn into a witness, has no business to plead in this court, and that Jesus has retained none such? Should this be the ruling of the court, it is possible that many would be obliged to withdraw from the tribunal. Christ wants a witnessing church. He will have a witnessing ministry. Through all the ages he has honored such with abundant fruits, while a merely scholastic ministry is a barren fig-tree, awaiting the Master's withering curse. The fears of our fathers respecting theological schools were not wholly groundless. There is constant danger of depending on mere intellectual force instead of spiritual power.

It is unfortunate that the canons of sacred rhetoric which fetter the modern preacher were the outgrowth of an age of spiritual decline, when unregenerate men sought the priest's office for a piece of bread. Such men, having no experience of the all-vitalizing power and unspeakable blessedness of the Comforter abiding within, endeavored to conceal this glaring defect by declaring it an infraction of good taste to display to public gaze the deep and sacred mysteries of the soul. But the Holy Spirit is a higher authority on points of decorum than Lord Chesterfield. He prompted David to pour forth his personal experiences in song, so that his harp has swayed a thousand-fold more souls than did his sceptre. He inspired St. Paul to utter the emotions of his inmost soul in every speech and epistle, down to his swan-song of victory over death. It is a false modesty that robs the preacher of his privilege to witness for the Lord Jesus in the pulpit, and is the Philistine Delilah who is shearing him of his locks, and betraying him to his enemies. Others deprecate the testimony for Christ in the pulpit because they fear that the precious waters of salvation, springing up within the soul unto eternal life, are in danger of evaporation by exposure to the sunlight. Not long since, in the portraiture of a recent popular divine, we are informed that he did not allow the deep and sacred experiences of his soul to evaporate in flippant speech. But the experience which Barnabas had — the fulness of the Holy Ghost — did not need to be kept dark lest it evaporate; it was in no more danger of such a calamity than the fulness of the Atlantic. God does not keep the ocean in a dark closet to preserve it from evaporation. He pours the sun's full blaze upon it, and lifts it into the sky, and diffuses it over the continents in refreshing showers. And yet the sea does not waste away. The oceanic fulness of the Holy Ghost in the preacher's soul is designed to evaporate in speech, and to come down like rain upon the mown grass. And he whose religion is in danger of evanescing, if he should speak of it often in public, has not righteousness as the waves of the sea, but as the drops of dew.

7. The fulness of the Holy Ghost is necessary to the preservation and efficient use of a great ministerial gift possessed, in an eminent degree, by Barnabas. His name was changed from Joses to the Son of Exhortation, because he was so powerful in exhortation. Exhortation is a higher gift than preaching. The preacher calmly inculcates the truth upon the intellect; the exhorter sways the sensibilities which lie nearer to the will, the executive power of the soul. It is greater to *move* than to *teach*. A candle can illumine a rock of flint, but only an anthracite blast furnace can melt it. Gospel preaching can be counterfeited. An unregenerate intellect, well read in theology, and trained in rhetoric, can preach a popular sermon; but exhortation cannot be imitated. The soul must be all aglow with

the live coal from off the divine altar. No sham is possible here. This molten stream of persuasion can flow from no galvanic phosphorescence of oratorical action and intense declamation. The pathos of a soul on fire from above, speaking through tears and sobs, prayers and entreaties, is an irresistible power which the church cannot afford to lose. This gift is not from the schools. Culture cannot bestow it. The works on homiletics and the professors of sacred rhetoric cannot impart it. God has signally demonstrated this in our day. When he would raise up a great master of the religious sensibilities, he passed by the great colleges, Yale and Harvard, the chief theological seminaries, Andover and Princeton, and fished up out of the sea an illiterate sailor-boy, sent him into Bromfield Lane, where the Holy Ghost set him all aflame with Jesus' love, and gave him a more than kingly sceptre with which to sway men for more than half a century. The Holy Ghost made Father Taylor the greatest exhorter of his generation. This is no mean gift, as many suppose. Peter did not preach, but testified and exhorted on the day of Pentecost. If this gift, which has done so much for Methodism, continues in it, it must be sought for, not in leaders' meetings, nor in Quarterly Conferences, but in the upper chamber in Jerusalem. The refined and the vulgar, the rich and the poor, can be reached and saved by this gift more than by any other. When there are no more sinners to be saved, no more believers to be stimulated to climb the mount of holiness, young men may despise the gift of exhortation. Has not this gift evidently waned away just in proportion as the baptism of power has become rare in the ministry and laity?

We have endeavored to group the qualifications of a successful evangelist under — Character, Creed, and Experience. Perhaps there is no better place on earth than Boston in which to demonstrate that an experience of the renewing Spirit of God conserves both the creed and the character. Spiritual decline always precedes doctrinal heterodoxy as a necessary antecedent. Decay in the heart is followed by decay in the head. They who will not retain the divine Spirit in their souls cannot retain the divine Christ in their theology.

> "No man can truly say
> That Jesus is the Lord,
> Unless thou take the veil away,
> And breathe the living word!
> Then, only then, we feel
> Our interest in His blood,
> And cry with joy unspeakable, —
> Thou art my Lord, my God!"

If you do not believe St. Paul, perhaps you will believe your own eyes, if you will open them and look around you in eastern Massachusetts. Here you will find churches planted by the Puritans, in which there is now no Lord Jesus, because a hundred years ago, when they closed their doors against the seraphic Whitefield, there was in them no Holy Ghost. Then how painful the evidence that, with the lapse of the doctrine of Christ's divinity, these churches, as if on an inclined plane of ice, are slipping down into Pantheism, — the negation of all foundation for ethical distinctions, and of all safeguards of moral character. I have said nothing of intellectual culture as an element in the successful preacher. My remarks have presupposed a mental development suited to this high office. Barnabas was a Levite, a member of the priestly or quasi-priestly order. The clerisy of the Jews were appointed by God, not only to conserve the sacred oracles and true worship, but to raise the people to a higher intellectual and moral life as natural educators. On the basis of this sacerdotal training, his distinctive Christian qualities were superinduced. Yet I am far from affirming that the time is past when the Spirit may send men from the plough to the pulpit : —

> "Yes, if the Lord His mind reveal
> Even to the meanest of the throng ;
> Their Father sends by whom He will,
> And teaches babes the gospel song.
> Not to the prophets' school confined,
> He gives to the unlearned His word;
> And lo, they now declare His mind,
> And husbandmen proclaim their Lord ! "

We believe in unloosing every tongue, whether male or female, and in giving to every light a candlestick corresponding to its intensity and illuminating power.

Brethren, on the subject of the fulness of the Holy Spirit as a possible and sudden attainment in modern times, I am not here to theorize, to philosophize, to dogmatize, but to testify. Let me turn my pulpit into a witness-stand for one moment. Although this school may teach that testimony in the pulpit should be of an indefinite and impersonal sort, I must speak for myself. Six months ago I made the discovery that I was living in the pre-pentecostal state of religious experience, — admiring Christ's character, obeying his law, and in a degree loving his person, but without the conscious blessing of the Comforter. I settled the question of privilege by a study of St. John's Gospel and St. Paul's Epistles, and earnestly sought for the Comforter. I prayed, consecrated, confessed my state, and believed Christ's word. Very suddenly, after about three weeks' diligent search, the Comforter came with power and great joy to my heart. He took my feet out of the realm of doubt and weakness, and planted them forever on the Rock of assurance and strength. My joy is a river of limpid waters, brimming and daily overflowing the banks, unspeakable and full of glory. God is my everlasting light, and the days of my mourning are ended. I am a freed man. Christ is my Emancipator, bringing me into the glorious liberty of the sons of God. My eyes are anointed so that I can see wonders in God's law. My efficiency in Christ's service is greatly multiplied. In the language of Dr. Payson, I daily exclaim, "Oh, that I had known this twenty years ago!" But I thank God that after a struggle of more than a score of years —

> "I have entered the valley of blessing so sweet,
>   And Jesus abides with me there;
> And His Spirit and blood make my cleansing complete,
>   And His perfect love casteth out fear.
> O come to this valley of blessing so sweet,
>   Where Jesus doth fulness bestow;
> And believe, and receive, and confess Him,
>   That all His salvation may know."

XXXIX.

THE FULL ASSURANCE OF FAITH.

[*Preached at Old Orchard in August,* 1883.]

THE preacher of the evening has been greatly edified during this faith-convention, by the Methodistic earnestness of a Quaker preaching Wesleyan doctrines with jubilant hallelujahs. The audience may be surprised this evening to hear a Methodist, in a very quiet style, enforce upon your hearts a prominent doctrine of the Friends, from a Quaker text found in Isa. xxxii. 17, "And the work of righteousness shall be peace; and the effect of righteousness, quietness and assurance forever." Also (Heb. x. 22), Let us draw near with a true heart in full assurance of faith." The soul that is perfectly saved from doubt, standing on the sunlit mountain-top of full assurance, is in the enjoyment of God's full salvation. We know an evangelical minister who secured the revision of the creed of his church in order to cut out the doctrine of assurance, because he said that "it strongly squinted toward the offensive doctrines of the higher life." There are, in fact, four roads into the experience of full salvation. As there was a river that went out of Eden, parted into four, so that Eden would be found by following up any one of these streams; so there are four streams flowing from the paradise of God's complete salvation from sin. Trace any one of these to its source, and you will find yourself in that spiritual Eden:—

> "The land of corn, and wine, and oil,
> Favored with God's peculiar smile,
>   With every blessing blest;
> There dwells the Lord, our righteousness,
> And keeps his own in perfect peace,
>   And everlasting rest."

The first of these we may call the Methodist river. They, among modern Christians, were providentially called to explore this river, and to enter the goodly land to which it leads. In other words, a sense of that "infection of nature that doth remain, yea, in them that are regenerated," — see Article IX. of the XXXIX. Articles, — and an earnest desire for its extinction, is the pathway which has led some, in all ages, into that soul-rest which follows the extinction of sin. Hence, the Methodists did not apply for a patent, as they were not the original discoverers. The second river received its name (Perfect Love) from the beloved disciple. Many a believer since John's day, distressed with a sense of partial and painfully divided love to Jesus, has sought the remedy, and has found that the Holy Spirit, who dropped from the skies the first spark of love divine in his heart, can raise it to a flame so intense as to make the whole affectional nature glow as a furnace with a sevenfold heat, in which nothing contrary to love can abide for a moment. A modern St. John (Wesley) has courageously buoyed out the channel of this river, and called it by its own name, Christian Perfection. See his "Plain Account," a tract full of the very marrow of the gospel. The third river may be called the Calvinian river, because many a disciple of the great theologian of Geneva has entered into the spiritual paradise by following up this stream to its source. A desire for the pentacostal gift, the incoming and abiding of the Comforter, the anointing or baptism of the Holy Ghost, the endowment of power for the most efficient service in the Lord's vineyard, has led many, who feared evangelical perfection or perfect love as rank fanaticism, to pray with an all-surrendering faith in Jesus, for the fulness of the Spirit; and, in answer to the prayer of faith, they have been filled with the unutterable fulness of God. Of course they were entirely cleansed, for the Holy Ghost cannot fill a soul without sanctifying it. (Read the experience of President Edwards and his wife, David Brainerd, Edward Payson, and D. L. Moody.)

The fourth river we may style the Quaker river — Full Assurance. Thousands of souls, worried by doubts and distressed by uncertainty, have sought for deliverance and have found salvation from doubt. But they have found that this is only one grape of the rich cluster of Eshcol put into their hands. Full assurance is inseparably united with entire sanctification and perfect love; and the baptism of the Holy Spirit, with the power and joy and soul-rest which flow therefrom.

By full assurance we mean a certainty, excluding all doubt, that I am now a child of God. The Spirit who imparts this wonderful knowledge of present salvation is called the spirit of adoption. "For ye received not the spirit of bondage again unto fear, but the Spirit of adoption, whereby we cry, Abba, Father." This is not mediate through the inspired Word of God, but immediate and direct to our consciousness by a contact of the divine Spirit with the human. "The Spirit HIMSELF beareth witness with our spirit [two witnesses], that we are children of God."

Many have explained the witness of the Spirit thus: the Spirit has secured in the Bible a record of the marks of the regenerate state. The believer in Jesus reads this record, and then looks into his own heart, and, if he finds these marks there, he infers that he is born of the Spirit. This is a perfectly proper thing to be done; but in order to be satisfactory, it must be preceded by an impression by the Spirit of these infallible marks. For instance, how can I be sure that love, the first fruit of the Spirit, exists in me, till I am divinely certified that I have been taken out of the class on whom God frowns,—for he is angry with the wicked every day, and I have been wicked,—and have been put into the class which God loves? I cannot love God till I am sure that he loves me and has pardoned my sins. This must be certified to me by the blessed carrier-dove of the skies,—the Holy Spirit. Without this telegram from the throne of God to my personal consciousness, I can have no valid basis for my inference that I am a son of God by adoption. The Bible does not contain this important fact. The convict in the State prison cannot ascertain his pardon by studying the general statutes. He must have a document direct from the governor authenticating his pardon.

This corresponds to the direct witness of the Spirit, sent forth, not into the Holy Scriptures, but "into our hearts, crying, Abba, Father." (Gal. iv. 6.) This is thus defined by Wesley: "It is an inward impression of the soul whereby the Spirit of God directly witnesses to my spirit that I am a child of God; that Jesus Christ hath loved me and given himself for me, and that all my sins are blotted out, and I, even I, am reconciled to God." This affords a firm ground for the process of inference, called the indirect witness of the Spirit, because it is reasoning from the fruits of the Spirit to the regenerating work of the Spirit; from effect to cause. This distinction and this precedence of the direct witness are strictly philosophical. All reasoning must proceed from admitted truths. These, in the last analysis, are truths intuitively grasped by the mind. The soul has a set of spiritual intuitions which become active under the illumination of the Holy Spirit. These intuitions are the bases of all real spiritual knowledge. The truths of the Bible are not real to the soul till they have been made real by the spirit of truth, or the spirit of reality, as it might have been translated. Before this, the Bible contains hearsay knowledge to which the reader is incompetent to give testimony. But when the Spirit gives the believer real knowledge of God and of his Son, he is qualified to be a witness for Christ. The reason for the small number of witnesses in many of our churches is, because there are only a few who have an experimental knowledge of God. They have not found out that he is real. There is much second-hand spiritual knowledge and little first-hand.

The direct witness of the Spirit is usually intermittent in the early stages of Christian experience.

Whether this is through variations in faith, or because of some hidden law of our spiritual nature, or of our bodily organism, is unknown. Young Christians are needlessly alarmed by these fluctuations. If, after careful self-examination, there is found no condemnation for any act of wilful sin, the person should go forward, walking by faith, till the cloud withdraws and the sun pours his rays again directly into the soul. This is the time, not only for heart-searching, but for Bible-searching; to get a new fulcrum for the lever of faith. It has been thought by some Christian philosophers that these intervals in the direct and joyful assurance of salvation are needful for the most rapid and healthful spiritual growth. Then the soul searches out the promises and piles them up as a pyramid on which to stand and stretch out the hands and grasp the realization of still higher spiritual blessings.

In that advanced experience called full assurance, there are fluctuations in degrees of ecstatic joy, but never a descent into the region of doubt. The witness to adoption is not intermittent, but abiding in the heart of every one who claims his full heritage in Jesus Christ in the Pentecostal dispensation. Hence the strength of such a Christian. Doubt always weakens. The inefficiency of multitudes of Christians may be traced to their doubts. Until doubt is permanently allayed, no one can have

"A heart at leisure from itself,
To soothe and sympathize"

with awakened sinners, or to enter vigorously and successfully upon the work of rescuing the perishing. Thus doubt prevents the highest usefulness. It also saddens the soul. Fog promotes melancholy; sunshine sows joy. The happiest company of people with whom I have ever mingled thus far in my earthly pilgrimage, I have found in this faith convention. I have thought that possibly the by-standers might falsely accuse us as they did the first Christian faith convention in the upper room — "these men are filled with new wine." We plead guilty of the charge. We are filled with the new wine of the kingdom, the joy of the Holy Ghost.

We urge all Christians to seek full assurance, because doubt is full of peril. It tends to indecision in the presence of temptation. Doubt leans toward unholiness; for he who doubts his sonship to a king will not act with the dignity and purity of one who knows that he is a prince of the blood royal. There is philosophy in the reply of a negro boy when told by a neighbor that he had experienced a change of heart because of his amended outward life. The young African replied: "I do not know that I have been born again! That is not the kind of religion I want; a religion that I may get and not know, I might lose and not miss." It is a great gain to have a clear, definite, and sharply defined beginning of the Christian course. This was one of the secrets of the power of early Methodism, and of early Quakerism as well. Wesley testifies that ninety-nine per cent of those converted under the preaching of the early Wesleyans had the direct witness to their pardon, and could tell the exact time of their translation out of darkness into the marvellous light of salvation. Says he: "The general rule is, they who are in the favor of God know they are so." Hence he urged the scriptural injunction as to testimony: "Let the redeemed of the

Lord say so." To the question, "Will not this discourage mourners?" he answers: "Yes, it will discourage them from stopping where they are; from resting before they have Christ revealed in them. But it will encourage to seek in the gospel way; to ask till they receive pardon and peace. And we are to encourage them, not by telling them they are in the favor of God, though they do not know it (such a word as this we would never utter in a congregation, at the peril of our souls); but by assuring them, every one that seeketh findeth."

Yet he did not teach that every doubter is lost. There is a difference between unbelief and doubt. Unbelief paralyzes the soul so that there is no movement Godward; doubts distract so that such movement is difficult and painful, yet possible. Unbelief damns, doubt damages, but does not destroy if we live on the right side of it. What is living on the right side of doubts? Live as if you had them not. Christian and Pliable fell into the Slough of Despond. Christian wallowed till he got out on the right side, toward the Celestial City. Pliable got out on the wrong side, toward the City of Destruction. The one lived on the right and the other on the wrong side of doubt; the one was saved, the other lost. The serpent-bitten Israelite, though doubting the efficacy of the brazen serpent, had faith enough to turn his glazed and dying eyes toward it, and was healed. Naaman was brimful of doubts when he turned the head of his Syrian cavalcade toward the despised Jordan; but he had faith sufficient to reach the river and bathe seven times and wash away his leprosy. So a soul may be worried by doubts all through life, and enter heaven at last, because he has had faith enough to keep his feet moving toward its open gates. A ship may sail across the Atlantic in a dense fog, and enter Boston harbor in safety. Yet it is much more comfortable and safe sailing under a clear sky, taking the requisite daily observations. For this ugly fact cannot be kept out of the sailor's mind, that many a ship sailing in the fog has been wrecked by dashing against a rock or an iceberg.

Let us now proceed to answer the inquiry, why so many Christians are destitute of that secret of the Lord which Enoch had in Old Testament times, and which is promised in far larger measure under the dispensations of the Holy Spirit.

1. Superficial conversion: I felt badly, went to an altar or inquiry-room, felt better, and was told that this was regeneration. So I joined the church; but I walk in darkness almost as dense as before. I was told to trust the written word of Christ, who says: "Him that cometh unto me I will in no wise cast out." Precious words these, but often misapplied. All the promises are designed to awaken faith in the pentitent soul by showing that God is able and willing to save now; but no one of them contains the record of your personal pardon. You are to trust the written word of God till you have the spoken word of the Spirit in your heart. The only advice we dare give to a seeking soul is this: "Trust God for Jesus' sake to do the work, till the Spirit certifies that it is done." Saving faith is a new exercise to the seeking soul, springing out of real repentance of sin. I cannot in my advice to him, assume the infallibility of his mental judgment of his own in-

ward states and spiritual exercises, and urge him to jump to the conclusion that he really does fulfil the conditions of salvation, and that Jesus does now save him. This is the prerogative of the Spirit of adoption. The Divine efficiency comes in at this point, assuring the soul that he has truly abandoned sin and accepted Christ, and may now grasp the assurance of pardon. Without the Spirit's testimony no one has in the written Word any ground for believing that God has saved or does now save the soul. Saving faith is not a leap in the dark, as some teach, but a firm stepping upon God's recorded willingness and ability to grant present deliverance from the guilt of sin, till we step upon the last stone which is the Spirit's testimony — "He doeth it."

Many have been advised to assume that their repentance and faith are evangelical, and to reckon that Jesus now pardons, when this was not the fact. They have reckoned without their host, and have been put into an exceedingly embarrassing attitude toward Christ before the world. Some of these, under the Spirit's guidance, despite the bad human advice, stumble into salvation. But many others, after groping in darkness a long time, give up the struggle, and drop back into sin. But another large class cling to their Christian profession and make up a mass of inert and lifeless members found in all our churches, who have stopped short of a satisfactory assurance of sins forgiven, and vainly imagine that they are saved.

2. Others are destitute of assurance because they have insensibly lost the evangelical spirit and slipped back into legalism, — a trust in the merit of good works

instead of a constant trust in Jesus Christ. He who trusts in his works is always afraid that he has not done enough to merit salvation. Hence, he never quite reaches the point of an absolute assurance. This is the sad condition of those trained in Romanism — that stupendous system of legalism. But many Protestants have unconsciously sunken down into the same error. Christianity is viewed as a series of duties to be done. But as no one can do them perfectly, no one can be joyfully confident that he is saved. On the other hand, if salvation is a free gift to the believer in Jesus, there is a definite point of time when this gift is consciously received. Hence, the evangelical spirit is promotive of assurance, and the legal spirit fosters interminable doubt.

3. Many are now destitute of assurance who once enjoyed its blessedness. The cares of this world have choked the spiritual life. "While thy servant was busy here and there, he [the Holy Spirit] was gone." Distant following of Jesus stifles the voice of the Comforter. "I am the light of the world: he that followeth me shall not walk in darkness." Here our adorable Saviour compares himself to the glorious orb of day. The planet Mercury, which keeps close to him, is always moving in the most intense light; while Neptune, on the outermost verge of the solar system, gropes along his chilly orbit in almost rayless night. Cloudless assurance is the heritage of complete consecration and the most intimate communion with Christ, accompanied by a careful and close following in his footsteps. Thus Enoch walked with God, and he had this testimony, that his ways pleased him. This pre-

cious testimony is more easily lost than regained. It has been said that "spiritual darkness comes on horseback and goes away on foot."

4. Since assurance is the work of the Holy Spirit, this blessing is rarely enjoyed where the personality and offices of the third person of the Trinity are not magnified. There is darkness in the pews because there is no lamp shining in the pulpit. The lamp is not lighted in many a pulpit because the scanty supply of oil has already been consumed. The oil has failed in the "candlestick all of gold," because the two olive-trees — a clear justification from past sins, and entire sanctification from inbred sin — are not growing, one "on the right side of the bowl, and the other on the left thereof." — Zech. iv. 3.

5. Others, who are favored with the light of full Christian instruction, fail of the precious grace of full assurance because of a lack of appropriating faith. This has been aptly defined as an underscoring of the "me" and "my" in the divine promises. St. Paul exercised this kind of faith. "I have been crucified with Christ; alive no longer am I, but alive is Christ in me; and that life which I now live in the flesh, I live in faith on the Son of God, who loved ME and gave himself up for ME. — Gal. ii. 20, literally translated. Mary Magdalene exercised appropriating faith, when, at the open tomb of Jesus, she said, "They have taken away MY Lord." "Tell me where thou hast laid him, and I will take him away." She talks as if she was the sole owner of Jesus Christ; and she was, for her grateful heart had appropriated him entirely to herself. He has the ability to give himself undivided to every

fully believing soul which claims its complete heritage in him.

6. Not a few Christians walk amid shadows when they might walk in the noontide of assurance, because they have seen the narrow gate of entire sanctification open before them and heard a voice saying, " Enter in at the strait gate," and, seeing the sacrifices to be made, and the idols to be unclasped, they have refused to obey. An eclipse of faith has ensued. The sun of assurance shines not upon the path of conscious disobedience. The converse is true also. " Light is sown for the righteous." Joseph Cook challenges sceptics to apply the scientific method of experiment to Christianity. "On the condition that you make an affectionate, immediate, total, and irreversible self-surrender to Christ as both Saviour and Lord, the light of God will stream through and through your soul." Try it, ye who desire full assurance.

If you would know the strength of the scriptural proofs of this doctrine, take your Concordance and see how often the words "know" and "knowledge" occur after the day of Pentecost. Study St. John's frequently occurring "we know," in his first epistle. Study Dean Alford's version of the Greek term, *epignosis*, — full knowledge, — " that the God of our Lord Jesus Christ, the Father of glory, would give unto you the spirit of wisdom and revelation in full knowledge of him. — Eph. i. 17, "Until we all attain unto the unity of the faith, and of the perfect knowledge of the Son of God." — Eph. iv. 13. Here faith is declared to be the path to " perfect knowledge ; " for there are not two unities, but one, — faith mounting up till it is merged in perfect knowledge. In all spiritual realizations we are to believe before we can know. "That ye may be filled with the thorough knowledge of his will." — Col. i. 9. ALFORD's Notes. "Unto all the riches of the full assurance of the understanding, unto the thorough knowledge of the mystery of God, even Christ." — Col. ii. 2. "Being renewed into perfect knowledge after the image of him that created him." — Col. iii. 10. "Who willeth all men to be saved, and to come to the certain knowledge of the truth." — 1 Tim. ii. 4. "And never yet able to come to the full knowledge of the truth." — 2 Tim. iii. 7.

The revision has uncovered to English readers a wonderful text, which has been obscured for nearly three centuries by a faulty translation. "I am the good shepherd, and I know mine own, and mine own know me; even as the Father knoweth me, and I know the Father." — John x. 14. Our knowledge of Christ may be as certain and exclusive of doubt as the Son's intuition of the Father. This certitude is the glorious privilege of every persevering believer in Jesus Christ. This is that spiritual manifestation of himself which he promised to every believer whose love to him is evinced by keeping his commandments. (John xiv. 21.) This manifestation of Christ is no vision or phantom addressed to the natural eye, but an awakening of the soul's spiritual perception to an undoubted and joyful realization that Jesus lives and loves even me. The heart of your preacher is a witness to this manifestation almost uninterruptedly during the past thirteen years. It is blessed indeed. Language fails to describe it.

Before bringing this sermon to a close we will state, but not fully discuss, another view of full assurance. Some define this to include not only the certainty of present sonship, but the certainty of eternal salvation. Some excellent people, whose testimony it would be difficult to impeach, have witnessed to the possession of such an assurance, covering not only the present but the endless future, and hence called the full assurance of hope. This testimony your preacher cordially receives; but he hesitates to preach it as the privilege of all God's children. It is possible that we are not all to be trusted with so rich a treasure. It might turn our heads; it might be greatly abused and perverted into a motive to a loose and unwatchful life in the case of many believers. Hence the possibility of losing the treasure of assurance of present salvation is a healthful safeguard. The Arminian training of your preacher probably has much to do with his difficulty in preaching assurance of eternal salvation as the privilege of all believers. This doctrine, it seems to him, must stand or fall with that of personal unconditional election. Hence our Calvinistic brethren have less difficulty in receiving this doctrine; though some of them, if we read them aright, limit this kind of assurance to the "*electi electorum*, — the elect of the elect," — and thus agree with your preacher in limiting it to a few favored souls. We cannot better state our views than to adopt those of that great reformer and Christian philosopher, John Wesley : —

1. "I believe a few, but very few, Christians have an assurance from God of everlasting salvation; and that is the thing which the apostle terms *full assurance of hope*.

2. "I believe more have such an assurance of being now in the favor of God, as excludes all doubt and fear; and this, if I do not mistake, the apostle means by *the full assurance of faith*.

3. "I believe a consciousness of being in the favor of God (which I do not term *full assurance*, since it is frequently weakened, nay, perhaps interrupted, by returns of doubt or fear) is the common privilege of Christians fearing God and working righteousness. Yet I do not affirm there are not exceptions to this general rule; but, I believe, this is usually owing either to disorder of body or to ignorance of the gospel promises. Therefore, I have not, for many years, thought a consciousness of acceptance to be essential to justifying faith."

(Fletcher indorses No. 1. See his "Checks" II. 659.)

In indorsing these words of Wesley, we greatly prefer to say, in No. 3, *ordinary state*, instead of "common privilege;" for Christians are generally living far below their privilege. Hence all in the third class might, by a proper exercise of faith, move up into the second, with the exception, perhaps, of those incapacitated by some "disorder of body."

A broader discussion of this topic, from which we were shut out by lack of time, would have included the deeper question of the truth of Christianity itself. For all religious doubts resolve themselves into two fundamental questions:—

1. Is the Christian system true?
2. Am I savingly included in the system?

This may be illustrated by two similar questions respecting a bank-note:—

1. Is this bank sound?
2. Is this note a genuine issue therefrom?

The first question, purposely omitted in our discussion, can be successfully answered, as well as the second, on one's knees in self-surrendering faith in Jesus Christ. Obedient faith is the short road out of all doubt. "If any man willeth to do his will, he shall know of the teaching, whether it be of God, or whether I speak from myself."

INDEX OF TEXTS.

Chap.	Verse.	Page.	Chap.	Verse.	Page.	Chap.	Verse.	Page.
GENESIS. —			PSALMS. —			MATTHEW — Continued.		
I.	14-19	202	II.	2	118	VII.	20	245
XVII.	1	166	XIV.	1-3	154		21-23	277
EXODUS. —			XXXVII.	23, 24	154		22	247
IV.	25	163	XLIV.	22	67		22, 23	248,
XXIII.	31	221	LI.	12	288			249, 251,
XXXIV.	29-35	176	XCV.	7-11	210	VIII.	3	265
LEVITICUS. —			CXIX.	32	156		17	244
XVI.	32	118		96	155	X.	1-4	247
XXVI.	3-13	241	ECCLESIASTES. —				1, 4	249
NUMBERS. —			VII.	20	152		8	265
XIV.	23	210	CANTICLES. —			XIV.	17	200
	36, 37	238	V.	10	198	XXIII.	37	34
XXIV.	4-13	248	ISAIAH. —			XXVI.	38	272
DEUTERONOMY. —			XXXII.	17	307	XXVII.	46	196
I.	21, 22	214	XL.	6-8	155	XXVIII.	19, 20	123
VI.	4, 5	160, 188		31	200	MARK. —		
XIII.	16	90	L.	10	194	VIII.	24	203
XXX.	6	46, 161, 189	LIII.	4	244	XVI.	14	205
JOSHUA. —			LVIII.	1-4	75	LUKE. —		
IV.	10	211	JEREMIAH. —			I.	20	159
1 SAMUEL. —			IX.	25	164	IV.	18	118
IX.	16	118	DANIEL. —				33-41	244
X.	10-12	248	IX.	25, 26	118	XIII.	11	91
1 KINGS. —			HOSEA. —				32	64
VIII.	46	151	XI.	1	194	JOHN (Gospel). —		
XIX.	16	118	ZECHARIAH. —			I.	32, 33	118
2 CHRONICLES. —			IV.	3	318	III.	6	146
XVI.	9	85	MATTHEW. —			V.	44	218
JOB. —			V.	43-48	46, 215	VII.	23	163
IX.	20	153		48	3, 22	VIII.	12	192, 317
						IX.	41	259
						X.	14	320

325

INDEX OF TEXTS.

Chap.	Verse.	Page.
JOHN (*Gospel*) *Continued.*		
XIV.	16	205, 207
	21	320
XV.	22, 24	259
XVI.	14	204
	22	195
	33	207
XVII.	6	171
	12	247
ACTS.—		
IV.	27	118
IX.	11	14
X.	38	118
XI.	24	278
XV.	9	204
XVI.	7–10	252
	23	42
XX.	19, 20	4
	33	61
XXI.	13	60
XXII.	10	13
	15	299
XXIII.	11	299
XXIV.	16	102
XXVI.	16	299
XXVIII.	5, 9	248
	8	247
ROMANS.—		
I.	9–12	51
	28	133
II.	29	164
III.	10	154
	20	134
	24	264, 265
V.	5	108, 268, 275
	18	269
	20	96, 158
VI.	2	6
	6	10, 42, 69, 72, 163, 168
	19	106
VII.	7–25	72, 73, 92
VIII.	1	259
	2	10
	3	71
	7	161
	15, 16	310
	17	116
	29	115
	36	67

Chap.	Verse.	Page.
ROMANS—*Continued.*		
VIII.	37	96, 158
IX.	1–3	47
X.	2	134
XIV.	7, 8	59
XV.	13	14
	29	179
	30–32	37
1 CORINTHIANS.—		
I.	21	119
II.	13	78
	14	77
	22	49
III.	1	208
	1–3	73
	3	79
IV.	16	43
VI.	15–20	91
IX.	27	66, 277
X.	6	233
	12	276
	32	102
	33	49, 61
XI.	1	43, 73
XII.	3	120
	4–11	243
	9	246
	11	245
	31	98
XIII.	1–13	84
	2	248
	12	145
XV.	31	67
	58	104
2 CORINTHIANS.—		
I.	11	37
	12	109
II.	4	48
	14	95
III.	7–18	177, 71
	10	98
IV.	2	44
	6	209
	7, 17	98
V.	17	209
VI.	6	109
	11	156
VII.	1	91, 161
	4	97, 158

Chap.	Verse.	Page.
2 CORINTHIANS — *Continued.*		
IX.	8	158
	14	98
X.	1	125
XI.	3	109
	23	67
	24	47
XII.	15	48
XIII.	7, 9	15
	9	115
GALATIANS.—		
I.	10	62
	16	115, 179
II.	18	4
	20	9, 318, 42, 52, 72
III.	3	18
	22	30
	24	199
IV.	3	252
	6	311
	15–19	51
	21–31	209
V.	17	68, 74
	22	30, 83
	24	69
VI.	14	10, 42, 72
EPHESIANS.—		
I.	4	84, 103
	16–19	31
	17	140, 319
	18	33
	19	98
II.	6	64
	7	98
III.	10	24
	14–21	18
	19	98, 206
	20	158
IV.	11–14	58
	18, 19	37
	12	115
	13	108, 141, 319
	32	123
V.	9	130
	27	103
VI.	5	33

Chap.	Verse.	Page.	Chap.	Verse.	Page.	Chap.	Verse.	Page.
PHILIPPIANS. —			2 THESSALONIANS — Continued.			JAMES. —		
I.	3, 4	26	III.	1	38	I.	4	90
	8	50					27	101
	9	38, 135	1 TIMOTHY. —			III.	17	126
	10	102	I.	5	84	IV.	5	149
	19	38		14	97, 158	V.	15	246
	25	14		15	67		16	247
II.	15	103	II.	1	48		17	246
	20	81		4	143, 320	1 PETER. —		
III.	3–11	44		15	109	I.	2	106
	4–8	59	III.	2	103		5	270
	8	21	IV.	12	110		13	114
	12	63	V.	7	103		19	100
	14	41	VI.	4	103		24, 25	155
	15, 17	42		14	101	III.	8	123
	20	33	2 TIMOTHY. —			IV.	12	195
	21	115	I.	12	58	V.	10	150
IV.	1	82	II.	18	64	2 PETER. —		
	5	125		24	125	I.	1–3	137
	9	43		25	137		8	144
	13	57	III.	7	144, 320		16–20	297
COLOSSIANS. —				17	117		19	172
I.	9, 10	135	IV.	5, 17	128	II.	20	137
	9	320		8	65	III.	14	100–103
	22	103		18	58	1 JOHN. —		
	24	49		20	247, 248	I.	6, 8, 10	256
II.	2,	129, 142	TITUS. —				7	265
		320	I.	1	139		8	147, 256
	11	88, 162	III.	4	125		9	265
	15	93, 163	PHILEMON. —			II.	1	148
III.	1	64		22	38		4, 9	256
	9	163	HEBREWS. —				5	268
	10	142	II.	11	264		20	119
	12	124	IV.	1–11	210		27	121, 298
	14	111	V.	13	113	III.	9	148, 257
IV.	3	38		14	28			268, 273
	14	252	VI.	1	113	IV.	3	263
1 THESSALONIANS. —				11	129		7	266
I.	5	130	VII.	19, 25	71		12	267
II.	4	62		25	91		18	5, 267
	7	125	IX.	9, 14	71		17, 18	180, 198
	7, 8, 11	49	X.	2	71		20	256
	10	44, 67, 72		14	264	V.	17	270
III.	12, 13	84		22	128, 307		18	270
IV.	3, 4	109		26	135	JUDE. —		
V.	23	23, 85, 89	XII.	10	109		19	73
2 THESSALONIANS. —				14	107, 108		24	29, 99, 103
II.	12	245		18, 19	38	REVELATION. —		
	13	106	XIII.	5	196	I.	6	21
				8	205			

Chap.	Verse.	Page.	Chap.	Verse.	Page.	Chap.	Verse.	Page.
REVELATION — *Continued.*			REVELATION — *Continued.*			REVELATION — *Continued.*		
II.	7	1	III.	18	119, 204	XXI.	8	238
	11	70		21	173		22	173
	17	171	VII.	14	170	XXII.	1	179
	26	171	XII.	11	94, 174		11	264
III.	5	173	XX.	14	170		14	169
	12	173	XXI.	7	174		16	172

www.ingramcontent.com/pod-product-compliance
Lightning Source LLC
Chambersburg PA
CBHW031855220426
43663CB00006B/641